Improving Student Achievement Through Mastery Learning Programs

Daniel U. Levine
and Associates

Improving Student Achievement Through Mastery Learning Programs

 Jossey-Bass Publishers

San Francisco • Washington • London • 1985

IMPROVING STUDENT ACHIEVEMENT THROUGH MASTERY LEARNING
PROGRAMS
by Daniel U. Levine and Associates

Copyright © 1985 by: Jossey-Bass Inc., Publishers
433 California Street
San Francisco, California 94104

&

Jossey-Bass Limited
28 Banner Street
London EC1Y 8QE

Library of Congress Cataloging in Publication Data

Levine, Daniel U. (date)
Improving student achievement through mastery
learning program.

(The Jossey-Bass higher education series)
Includes bibliographies and index.
1. Competency based education—United States—
Addresses, essays, lectures.   2. Competency based
education—United States—Case studies.   I. Title.
II. Series.   III. Series: Jossey-Bass higher education
series.
LC1032.L48   1985   371.1 '02   84-43029
ISBN 0-87589-645-6 (alk. paper)

Manufactured in the United States of America

The paper in this book meets the guidelines for
permanence and durability of the Committee on
Production Guidelines for Book Longevity of the
Council on Library Resources.

JACKET DESIGN BY WILLI BAUM

FIRST EDITION

Code 8515

The Jossey-Bass
Higher Education Series

Consulting Editor
Testing and Measurement

Jayjia Hsia
Educational Testing Service

Preface

Mastery learning can be generally defined as instruction organized to emphasize student mastery of specific learning objectives and to deliver corrective instruction as necessary in order to achieve that goal. Mastery learning that includes formative testing of initial skill acquisition followed by corrective instruction for nonmasters has become increasingly popular during the past ten years. Thousands of school systems around the world now are utilizing mastery learning, as defined here, to improve student achievement.

Despite this rapid movement toward the use of mastery learning to improve instruction and achievement, relatively little up-to-date, easily accessible information about its implementation and impact has been available. Several influential books were written in the early and mid 1970s, but since that time most of the relevant literature has consisted of articles in journals, papers presented at professional meetings, and school-district evaluations and internal reports. Thus most reports of recent developments with respect to mastery learning are only available in what may be termed hard-to-obtain "fugitive" literature.

Improving Student Achievement Through Mastery Learning Programs is intended to help correct this situation. Major advances have been made in the past few years in understanding how to conceptualize and implement mastery learning and in documenting the massive achievement gains that can be derived through proper implementation. Provided that mastery learning is placed productively within its larger instructional setting, and provided that serious attention is paid to predictable problems in implementation, mastery learning will result in impressive improvements in the quality and effectiveness of instruction. This book seeks to provide usable perspectives on both the implementation and impact of mastery learning as well as on the larger instructional context that determines how well it can be utilized.

In so doing, the volume should be of particular use and interest for practitioners, for college-level personnel concerned with the improvement of instruction, and for lay persons interested in overcoming the widely documented achievement problems in U.S. schools. Emphasis in much of the book is on providing analysis with illustrations of practice in the field. Although most of the analysis and illustrative material deal explicitly with elementary and secondary schools, much of the book also is adaptable and relevant for readers concerned with improvement of postsecondary education.

Special features of this book include:
- unusually detailed and practical discussion of problems and issues encountered in implementing mastery learning;
- relatively detailed description of the characteristics and components of successful programs;
- wide-ranging discussion of the larger context that must be addressed in successful implementation;
- a variety of charts and diagrams that portray successful grouping approaches, major supervisory responsibilities, step-by-step management tasks, and guidelines for instructional design;
- consideration of issues and problems at various educational levels including classroom, school, and school district;
- a final chapter summarizing analysis and conclusions regarding key implementation issues;
- a carefully selected mix of material from practitioners in the field and from scholars concerned with the implementation and impact of mastery learning.

Overview of the Contents

In the introductory chapter, Herbert J. Walberg reviews the general results of thousands of studies on the correlates of learning outcomes and concludes that mastery learning approaches and their components (for example, emphasis on reinforcement) are strongly associated with a wide range of positive effects.

In briefly describing several central issues regarding mastery learning theory and practice, Walberg also points out that before mastery learning techniques can be implemented effectively, problems need to be addressed involving the balance between instructional quality and time and possible trade-offs between enhancing achievement of slow learners by providing more time for mastery and retarding achievement of fast learners by having them wait while slower students attain mastery.

In Chapter Two, Beau Fly Jones and William G. Spady conclude that mastery learning, together with high-quality instruction, can bring about achievement gains approaching the two standard deviations associated with individual tutoring. After citing recent research by Benjamin S. Bloom and his colleagues regarding the benefits of mastery learning for individual classes using criterion-referenced testing, Jones and Spady describe school- and district-level mastery learning programs that have produced high student achievement on standardized tests. They conclude that whole-group mastery learning may be more feasible than individualized or small-group mastery approaches for bringing about substantial gains in large, complex districts.

The next six chapters deal with central themes in planning and implementing a mastery learning program.

In Chapter Three, Doris W. Ryan discusses preactive and proactive supervision of mastery learning. Ryan believes that successful implementation of mastery learning requires fundamental changes in the nature of teacher supervision and in the roles of school administrators as instructional managers. In particular, supervisors must give much more attention than they generally do to ecological considerations, such as grouping formats, and to instructional support and development tasks, such as selection of content and objectives and decisions regarding testing.

Chapter Four, by James H. Block, describes ways of making school learning activities more playlike. Block argues that mastery learning can help make school more interesting and enjoyable for students and thus counteract current trends to make learning overly "worklike" and alienating. Citing a large amount of recent research on the value of "flow" in learning (that is, the experience of participation in learning activities that are competence-motivating and involving), Block shows that the basic concepts of mastery learning are inherently useful in ensuring that students experience success in challenging tasks. The chapter as a whole constitutes a refined plea that teachers and administrators should not view mastery learning as a mere procedural change aimed only at improving the efficiency of instruction.

Chapter Five, by Beau Fly Jones, Lawrence B. Friedman, Margaret Tinzmann, and Beverly E. Cox, views mastery learning as the scaffolding for improving achievement, and then carefully details ways in which instruction should be organized and delivered in order to improve students' comprehension skills within a mastery learning context. This chapter reviews and synthesizes several large research literatures that are relevant and important in designing and implementing a mastery learning program.

Phyllis R. Pringle, in Chapter Six, provides examples of considerations and activities that need to be addressed in a management plan for implementing mastery learning as part of an outcomes-based approach to education. Pringle gives particular emphasis to the importance of establishing or reconfirming educational goals and of decision making based on appropriate data collection as part of the implementation process.

In Chapter Seven, Mary M. Kennedy discusses problems likely to be encountered in mastery learning or other approaches that place significant emphasis on learning by objectives and on determining instructional content by the use of tests. After pointing out that these approaches frequently involve (or produce) zealous advocacy on the part of administrators and fear on the part of teachers, Kennedy describes the counterproductive reactions that may result unless implementers recognize malfunction in the classroom and respond to it.

Some of the most important techniques for assessing mastery of basic skills through summative testing are reviewed by Huynh Huynh in Chapter Eight. Huynh gives particular attention to defensible identification of passing scores in determining whether students have attained sufficient mastery to proceed to the next major instructional level.

The next four chapters describe and discuss successful implementation of mastery learning in elementary and secondary schools. Thus all these chapters deal, in one way or another, directly or indirectly, with key implementation issues involving instructional quality and time, treatment of fast and slow learners, and related issues regarding grouping of students, initiation and conduct of the change process, and coordination of instructional components. The case study material and related discussion in these chapters can help practitioners identify and overcome impediments to successful implementation of mastery learning.

In the first of this group, Chapter Nine, Albert Mamary and Lawrence A. Rowe describe student grouping arrangements that have resulted in very large achievement gains among students in the public schools of Johnson City, New York. This chapter focuses on flexible instructional arrangements that utilize small-group mastery learning to avoid the problem of traditional, nonmastery instruction for homogeneous groups.

In Chapter Ten, Marsha Menahem and Leon Weisman describe the mixture of top-down and bottom-up activities that has been effective in raising reading scores in a school district in New York City. Menahem and Weisman conclude that appropriate central-office initiative combined with building-level adaptation can overcome the difficult teaching–learning problems that exist in inner city schools.

Some of the mastery learning procedures and practices that have been used to bring about achievement gains at a junior high school in Bayport, New York, are described in Chapter Eleven, by William J. Smith. Smith particularly stresses ways in which testing in a mastery framework can be made more productive in the "real world" setting of the average teacher. He also emphasizes the importance of motivational considerations (involving both teachers and students) in the mastery learning process.

In Chapter Twelve, Donald W. Robb offers three case studies of elementary schools that have used Chicago Mastery Learning Reading materials to improve reading achievement. Robb reports that mastery learning in these schools has reduced the gap between low- and high-achieving students without detracting from the achievement of the latter. Regarding implementation, he concludes that in all three schools success was related to voluntary and meaningful participation on the part of teachers, emphasis on staff development, effective grouping of students for fast-paced instruction, variation in time for mastery learning in accordance with student needs, and outstanding leadership by the school principal.

In the final chapter, I have summarized some of the implications of research and experience dealing with effective implementation of mastery learning and other instructional innovations. Educators who are trying to install mastery learning must make sure that their programs are manageable for the average teacher and that they avoid specific pitfalls that frequently result in the failure of mastery learning and other instructional innovations. I also discuss several central issues involving time allocated to mastery learning and grouping of students.

I wish to express gratitude for their contributions to the authors who contributed to this volume. I also wish to note that a shorter early version of the chapter by James Block appeared in *Elementary School Journal.* The chapters by Phyllis Pringle, Doris Ryan, and William Smith were developed from short articles that first appeared in *Outcomes,* the journal of the Network for Outcome-Based Schools. Many readers of this book may be interested in this journal. Subscription information is available from Far West Regional Educational Laboratory, 1855 Folsom, San Francisco, California 94103. I also want to thank Jayjia Hsia and Michael Kean, of Eduational Testing Service, who made helpful suggestions for preparing and organizing this volume.

Kansas City, Missouri   Daniel U. Levine
February 1985

Contents

Preface   ix

The Authors   xvii

1. Examining the Theory, Practice, and Outcomes of   1
    Mastery Learning
        Herbert J. Walberg

2. Enhanced Mastery Learning and Quality of Instruction   11
        Beau Fly Jones, William G. Spady

3. Preactive and Proactive Supervision of Mastery   45
    Learning Programs
        Doris W. Ryan

4. Making School Learning Activities More Playlike   69
        James H. Block

5. Guidelines for Instruction-Enriched Mastery Learning   91
    to Improve Comprehension
        *Beau Fly Jones, Lawrence B. Friedman,
        Margaret Tinzmann, Beverly E. Cox*

6. Establishing a Management Plan for Implementing   155
    Mastery Learning
        Phyllis R. Pringle

7. Teacher Reactions to Use of Tests for Accountability   173
        Mary M. Kennedy

8. Assessing Mastery of Basic Skills Through   185
    Summative Testing
        Huynh Huynh

9. Flexible and Heterogeneous Instructional Arrangements   203
    to Facilitate Mastery Learning
        Albert Mamary, Lawrence A. Rowe

10. Improving Reading Ability Through a Mastery   223
    Learning Program: A Case Study
        Marsha Menahem, Leon Weisman

11. Incorporating Testing and Retesting into the   241
    Teaching Plan
        William J. Smith

12. Strategies for Implementing Successful Mastery   255
    Learning Programs: Case Studies
        Donald W. Robb

13. Key Considerations for Achieving Success in Mastery   273
    Learning Programs
        Daniel U. Levine

    Index   295

The Authors

Daniel U. Levine is professor of education at the University of Missouri at Kansas City. He received his B.A. degree (1954) and M.A. degree in social science (1958), and his Ph.D. degree (1963) in educational administration, all from the University of Chicago.

Since 1969 Levine has been director of a metropolitan-education research center at the University of Missouri at Kansas City and has been particularly interested in research on desegregation and compensatory education. Much of his own research has focused on assessment and analysis of efforts to improve the quality and effectiveness of instruction in urban schools. In recent years, Levine's research has involved aspects of the effective schools movement, particularly organizational and instructional arrangements that may improve the effectiveness of elementary and secondary schools.

With Robert J. Havighurst, Levine is coauthor of recent editions of *Society and Education,* a textbook in educational sociology, and he is coauthor, with Allan C. Ornstein, of the second and third editions of *An Introduction to the Foundations of Education* (1981 and 1985, respectively). He has also contributed chapters to many books and has published numerous articles and papers in professional journals and periodicals.

James H. Block is associate professor of education, Department of Education, University of California at Santa Barbara.

Beverly E. Cox is a consultant in curriculum, Chicago Public Schools.

Lawrence B. Friedman is a consultant in curriculum, Chicago Public Schools.

Huynh Huynh is professor of statistics, Department of Educational Studies and Services, University of South Carolina.

Beau Fly Jones is project director, Improvement of Instruction Program, North Central Regional Educational Laboratory.

Mary M. Kennedy is conducting research on compensatory education for the National Institute of Education and is former director of planning, research, evaluation, and dissemination in the Pennsylvania State Department of Education.

Albert Mamary is superintendent of schools, Johnson City Central School District, Johnson City, New York.

Marsha Menahem is director of research and evaluation, School District 19, Brooklyn, New York.

Phyllis R. Pringle is director of research and program development, Educational Services Institute, Cincinnati, Ohio.

Donald W. Robb, is vice-president of Mastery Education Corporation, Watertown, Massachusetts.

Lawrence A. Rowe is assistant superintendent for instruction, Johnson City Central School District, Johnson City, New York.

Doris W. Ryan is professor and assistant director, Office of Field Services and Research, Ontario Institute for Studies in Education, Toronto.

William J. Smith is principal, James Wilson Young Junior High School, Bayport-Blue Point Union Free School District, Long Island, New York.

William G. Spady is director of Far West Regional Educational Laboratory, San Francisco.

Margaret Tinzmann is a consultant in curriculum to the Chicago Public Schools.

Herbert J. Walberg is research professor, College of Education, University of Illinois, Chicago.

Leon Weisman is director of reading and language arts, School District 19, Brooklyn, New York.

Improving
Student Achievement
Through
Mastery Learning Programs

1

Examining the Theory, Practice, and Outcomes of Mastery Learning

Herbert J. Walberg

Mastery learning programs prove to be one of the most effective procedures for promoting academic attainment. This chapter first reviews briefly the history and current theoretical context of mastery learning. Second, it summarizes extensive syntheses of classroom research showing large effects of its components. Third, it analyzes several issues and controversies regarding mastery learning.

Theory

What is *mastery learning?* Its antecedents may be traced back to Aristotle and through a long line of Anglo-American philosophers and psychologists, including Locke, Bacon, Thorndike, Dollard, Miller, and Skinner. In psychology's ancient triumvirate, it is aligned more closely with behaviorism than with cognitive and affective theories, and it takes as given the external representation of the subject matter to be impressed upon the student. The subject matter is divided into atomistic parts such as exercises, larger logical collections of which are termed *units*. Students, alone or in groups, work through units in an organized fashion at their own pace and must *master* a given amount of one unit, typically 80 percent on end-of-unit or formative tests, before going on to subsequent units in the sequence. Each student is given sufficient time and appropriate instruction to complete each unit.

Benjamin S. Bloom (1976) is widely viewed as the major theoretician and promulgator of mastery learning. He and his students have conducted many empirical studies that demonstrate the effectiveness of mastery programs in a wide variety of circumstances. As he acknowledges, however, he drew on prior psychological research in formulating his theory—upon the work of Dollard and Miller (1950) and of Carroll (1963; see Lysakowski and Walberg, 1982; and Haertel, Walberg, and Weinstein, 1983, for more extended historical and comparative accounts).

Dollard and Miller (1950) helped to advance scientific applied psychology by stressing the interactive or dyadic nature of human activities in social settings (in contrast to the then pervasive individualistic behavioral psychology). For them, the essential social-psychological processes were cues, participation, and reinforcement or reward. Bloom recognized the usefulness of such a theory since the teacher or materials of instruction provide cues to which the learner actively reacts. To the traditional concept of reinforcement of desired responses, Bloom added the fourth component of corrective feedback in the case of undesirable responses. Thus, four components make up the quality of instruction.

From Carroll (1963), Bloom derived the other critical and quantitative ingredient of instruction—time. Carroll defined aptitude as the amount of learning time necessary for a student to master an objective under optimal conditions. Perseverance, in the Carroll model, refers to the amount of time the student is willing to spend mastering an objective, and opportunity to learn is the amount of time allocated to particular content.

Effects

One of Bloom's contributions was to unify the qualitative and quantitative conceptions of instruction and to show their joint and powerful effects on the amount learned. Another was to show the importance of early learning. Research he carried out before his book on mastery learning had shown the stability of intelligence and other traits from early childhood through adolescence and the large effects of home environments on academic learning. The theory of mastery learning is founded on the notion that early lack of mastery of elementary aspects of subjects greatly impedes later learning.

Matthew Effects. Though scattered across a number of disparate investigations, considerable evidence suggests that early advantages can lead to subsequent advantages and rates of gains. This rich-getting-richer effect (from the New Testament, Matthew 25:29) is also termed a cumulative advantage. Perhaps the most notable evidence for it was the Equality of Educational Opportunity survey (see Walberg and Tsai, 1983, for a review of this and related studies). The survey showed that social and ethnic groups that started school with small deficits in test performance had large deficits in the later grades. Other studies showed that enriched early environments had greater effects on more advantaged, typically middle-class children; thus the television program "Sesame Street," even though it benefited most children, actually widened the gap between children of different social classes. Subsequent research showed that advantaged home and school conditions continue to produce more efficient learning into the years of young adulthood.

Mastery learning is an attempt to avoid such Matthew effects. Since early mistakes in conception or fact can continue to interfere with more complex learning, it is assumed that careful and fairly complete mastery will be worth the extra time investment. Not only may cognitive deficits be reduced, but the learner may become more confident.

Mastery and Time. The amounts of time required by different learners may vary considerably—perhaps by ratios as high as ten to one. Thus, equality of learning outcomes may require highly unequal resources of time or intensity of instruction. Maximum performance (perhaps *excellence* is the right word) may demand huge investments. To make the requirements plain, Frederick and Walberg (1980) cited swim-training data that suggested 1,000 yards of practice per day produced 75 percent of maximum attainment; 2,000 yards produced 85 percent; but 10,000 yards was required to produce 95 percent.

It appears, moreover, that world-class performance or performing one's best in many fields, including school learning, may require near-exclusive time and energy commitments (Walberg, 1983b). For example, Japanese students as a group are world-class performers in science and mathematics since they score far above students in other countries (including two standard deviations above Americans in mathematics). Their outstanding performance may be attributable to as many as ninety-six hours of instruction and homework per week (compared with about thirty-four hours in the United States).

Productivity Effects. Contemporary theories of instruction, following Carroll and Bloom, posit both quality and quantity of instruction as well as ability and motivation as what might be called essential factors (see, for example, Haertel, Walberg, and Weinstein, 1983, for an analysis of eight instructional models). For a more complete account of the determinants of learning, however, four supplementary or supportive factors also deserve inclusion—the psychological morale of the classroom group, academic stimulation in the home, peer group influence outside school, and exposure to mass media, in particular, television.

Classroom learning is consistently correlated with, and may be a multiplicative, diminishing-returns function of, the eight essential and supplementary or supportive factors. Each of the essential factors appears to be necessary but insufficient by itself for classroom learning; that is, all four of these factors appear to be required at least at minimum levels for such learning to occur. It also appears that the essential factors may substitute, compensate, or trade off for one another at diminishing rates of return; for example, immense quantities of time may be required for a moderate amount of learning if motivation, ability, or instructional quality is minimal.

The roles of the other four factors are less clear. Although they are consistent correlates of classroom learning outcomes, they may supplement as well as support classroom learning. If, for example, an eighteen-year-old student attends school six hours a day for 180 days for twelve years and requires ten hours on average for sleep and meals, then only 21.2 percent of the potentially educative hours are spent in school. If the first six years of life are counted as potentially educative and if half the hours in school are subtracted because of absences, disruptions, cocurricular, extra curricular, and non-curricular activities, and inattentiveness (Frederick and Walberg, 1980), then only 7.1 percent of the potentially educative time is spent learning in academic subjects in school. If it is true, as Aristotle held, that experience teaches—not just teachers—then the less deliberate but large blocks of time devoted to potentially educative but nonschool activities must be considered as important determinants of what is learned.

Learning Effects. During the past five years, investigators have quantitatively synthesized the effects of both the essential and supportive or supplementary factors. These yield numerical estimates of the size of the effects or correlations of the factors with cognitive, affective, and behavioral outcomes. They allow comparisons of effects of mastery with other programs that can be implemented. Tables 1 through 3 show the effects or correlations of student aptitude (ability, developmental stage, and motivation); quality and quantity of instruction; the psychological environments of the classroom, home, and peer group outside school; and the amount of extramural television exposure. In several instances, separate estimates are available for science learning from syntheses funded by the National Science Foundation. In other instances, several estimates from different investigators are available. All of these allow comparisons of the robustness of the effects. Numbers in the tables are either effect sizes or correlations calculated for a one-standard-deviation increment in a given independent variable. In all, the tables are based on approximately forty-five syntheses of about 2,800 empirical studies conducted during the past half century.

Table 1 shows that IQ is a strong correlate of general academic achievement but only a moderately strong correlate of science achievement. A student's Piagetian stage of development correlates moderately with both general and science achievement. Motivation and self-concept are moderate correlates.

Table 2 shows the effects of various aspects and methods of instruction. Of the twenty-nine factors in the table, the psychological components of mastery rank first and fourth in their effects. Reinforcement or reward for correct performance has an overall average effect of 1.17 standard deviations (SD); cues, participation, and corrective feedback have effects equal to approximately one SD.

Table 1. Estimated Effects of Ability, Development, and
Motivation on General Academic Achievement and Science Achievement.

Factor Method	Effect
Ability	
IQ	0.71
IQ & Science	0.48
Development	
Piagetian Stage	0.47
Piagetian Stage & Science	0.40
Motivation	
Motivation	0.34
Self-Concept	0.18

Note: Except where specified for science achievement, estimates are
for general academic achievement.
Source: Walberg, 1984a, p. 23.

Mastery programs in science have an average effect of 0.8. In
addition, many programs that resemble mastery learning or are used
in conjunction with it have moderately strong effects ranging from
0.3 to 0.8. These include cooperative learning in small groups,
personalized and adaptive instruction, tutoring, diagnostic-
prescriptive methods, and individualized instruction.

Of the remaining methods, many can be used with mastery
as their basis. These include the post-Sputnik science and mathematics curricula, sequenced lessons, and accelerated grouping.

Instructional time, as shown at the bottom of Table 2, has
an overall correlation of about 0.4 with learning outcomes. It is
neither the chief determinant nor a weak correlate; like the other
essential factors, time appears to be a necessary ingredient but
insufficient by itself to produce learning.

For at least two reasons, time is a particularly interesting
factor: First, several national reports have called attention to the
need for lengthening the school day and year to the levels of other
countries, particularly those of Japan (Walberg, 1983a). Second,
time is the only factor that can be roughly measured on a ratio scale
with equal intervals between scale points and true zero point.
Perhaps because it can be measured on an absolute scale resembling
measures of distance and mass in the natural sciences, and of capital

Table 2. Instructional Quality and Time Effects on
General Academic Achievement.

Method	Effect
Reinforcement	1.17
Acceleration	1.00
Reading Training	0.97
Cues Feedback	0.97
Science Mastery	0.81
Cooperative Learning Programs	0.76
Experiential Reading Programs	0.60
Personalized Instruction	0.57
Adaptive Instruction	0.45
Tutoring	0.40
Individualized Science	0.35
Higher Order Questioning	0.34
Diagnostic/Prescriptive	0.33
Individualized Instruction	0.32
Individualized Math	0.32
New Science Curricula	0.31
Teacher Expectations	0.28
Computer Assisted Instruction	0.24
Sequenced Lessons	0.24
Advanced Organizers	0.23
New Math Curricula	0.18
Inquiry Biology	0.16
Homogeneous Groups	0.10
Teacher Praise	0.08
Mainstreaming	0.03
H.S. Programmed Instruction	−0.03
Class Size	−0.09
Mainstreaming	−0.12
Instructional Time	0.38

Note: The estimated effects are for general academic achievement,
except where specific subject areas are indicated.
Source: Walberg, 1984a, p. 24.

and labor inputs to production processes in economics, time shows
diminishing returns (Frederick and Walberg, 1980). Equal additions
of time, with other factors held fixed, yield ever smaller gains in
learning. It is also reasonable to think that zero time results in zero
learning no matter what the level of the other factors, and, to
generalize, that each essential factor, if well measured, would prove

necessary but insufficient by itself and would show diminishing returns and multiplicativity.

Table 3 shows the major results of syntheses of the supportive or supplementary factors. Factors that are ordinarily untreated in instructional theories and models have strong influences on academic achievement. Homework that is graded, for example, has three times the effect of socioeconomic status (SES). By comparison, homework that is merely assigned has an effect comparable to SES. Leisure-time television viewing, perhaps because it displaces more educationally constructive activities, has a weak deleterious influence on school learning.

The psychological morale or climate of learning in the classroom group strongly predicts learning. Morale refers to the cohesiveness, satisfaction, goal direction, and related social-psychological properties of the classroom group perceived by students. By comparison, the influence of the peer group outside of school is relatively weak and comparable to the student's SES.

Issues of Mastery

Several theoretical and practical issues concern mastery learning. Three of the most important deserve discussion here: measurement, the possible trade-offs of quality and time, and the possible trade-offs of means and variances.

Table 3. Home, Peer, Class Morale, and Media Effects.

Method	Effect
Graded Homework	0.79
Class Morale	0.60
Home Interventions	0.50
Home Environment	0.37
Assigned Homework	0.28
Socioeconomic Status	0.25
Peer Group	0.24
Television	−0.05

Note: Estimated effects are for general academic achievement.
Source: Walberg, 1984a, p. 24.

It might be argued that mastery can be guaranteed by administering easy tests, particularly those that simply and immediately reproduce the lesson exercises. This seems a fair criticism, but apparently it only applies to a limited number of evaluations. The most extensive quantitative synthesis of studies of mastery learning components (Lysakowski and Walberg, 1982) compared effects on locally constructed and nationally standardized outcome measures and showed no differences. In other words, mastery effects appeared to be as large on generalized outcome measures as on immediate formative outcomes. The synthesis also showed that mastery programs produced large, consistent average effects on factual, conceptual, behavioral, and affective outcomes of learning.

A second issue is the balance of instructional quality and time. Educators may take a stand in favor of one or the other, but it is somewhat defeatist to choose between the two because American school children get short shrift on both. And both the quality and quantity of instruction need upgrading (Walberg, 1983a).

A third issue is the possible trade-off between means and variances in learning outcomes and between slow and fast learners. It would seem possible that giving a great deal of time to the slow learners would decelerate the progress of the faster learners; because they are impeded, the group average would be lower than control groups. This point is counter-factual as syntheses have shown, and the trade-off apparently would only apply if the faster learners are deliberately held back to make the group homogeneous for egalitarian reasons instead of proceeding in the subject beyond the mastery level at their own pace *(acceleration)* or on to other advanced activities *(enrichment)*. In fact, the greater degree of control over the learning process afforded by mastery learning permits such a choice, which is more a matter of educational philosophy and values than of science.

Conclusion

Mastery learning is based on ancient educational wisdom: stimulate learners with effective opportunities; engage their active participation; reinforce desirable responses; correct mistakes; and keep the goals, means, and assessments of learning well aligned.

Much research that has recently been synthesized shows that when these things are done, far greater amounts of learning can be expected.

References

Bloom, B. S. *Human Characteristics and School Learning.* New York: McGraw-Hill, 1976.

Carroll, J. B. "A Model of School Learning." *Teachers College Record,* 1963, *64,* 723–733.

Dollard, J., and Miller, N. E. *Personality and Psychotherapy: An Analysis in Terms of Learning, Thinking, and Culture.* New York: McGraw-Hill, 1950.

Frederick, W., and Walberg, H. J. "Learning as a Function of Time."*Journal of Educational Research,* 1980, *73,* 183–194.

Haertel, G. D., Walberg, H. J., and Weinstein, T. "Psychological Models of Educational Performance: A Theoretical Synthesis of Constructs." *Review of Educational Research,* 1983, *53,* 75–91.

Lysakowski, R. S., and Walberg, H. J. "Instructional Effects of Cues, Participation, and Corrective Feedback: A Quantitative Synthesis." *American Educational Research Journal,* 1982, *19,* 559–578.

Walberg, H. J. "Scientific Literacy and Economic Productivity in International Perspective." *Daedalus,* 1983a, *112* (2), 1–28.

Walberg, H. J. "We Can Raise Standards." *Educational Leadership,* 1983b, *41* (2), 4–7.

Walberg, H. J. "Improving the Productivity of America's Schools." *Educational Leadership,* 1984a, *41* (8), 19–27.

Walberg, H. J. "Synthesis of Research on Teaching." In M. C. Wittrock (Ed.), *Handbook of Research on Teaching.* Washington, D.C.: American Educational Research Association, 1984b.

Walberg, H. J., and Tsai, S.-L. "Matthew Effects in Education." *American Educational Research Journal,* 1983, *20,* 359–373.

2

❧ ❧

Enhanced Mastery Learning
and Quality of Instruction

Beau Fly Jones
William G. Spady

Everyone wants to aim for what is the very best possible education
for America's children. In reading the recent reports on the state of
education today, such as *A Nation at Risk* (National Commission on
Excellence in Education, 1983), there are numerous references to the
poor quality of public education and some scattered references to the
outstanding schools and programs that can be found here and there.
While these reports are informative regarding the nation's desire for
effective schooling, they offer no consistent, core set of criteria that
clearly define what is ideal or consistently successful with regard to
curriculum and instruction (Spady and Marx, 1984). The purpose of
this chapter is three-fold: to provide a standard of excellence that can
be used to judge individual programs; to identify a set of mastery
learning programs that appear to meet these criteria; and to identify
the variables within these programs that make them both manageable and successful.

A Standard of Excellence: Two-Sigma Results

Benjamin Bloom has spent much of his time during the past
decade identifying and describing instructional models that produce excellence. Among the important elements in this program of

work is his effort to define what he believes to be the domain of home and school variables that are alterable (Bloom, 1980). Of particular importance here are the two key school variables that relate to curriculum and instruction: *cognitive entry characteristics* and *quality of instruction.*

Cognitive entry characteristics refer to the knowledge of content and skills that is relevant and necessary for effective functioning in a given course or unit of instruction. Such prerequisites correlate highly with measures of success in a subject, and they are entirely alterable. *Quality of instruction* refers mainly to the instructional cues that are provided, reinforcement activities and behaviors, the extent of student participation, and the diagnosis and correction of learning errors. According to extensive research on these variables (Bloom, 1976), quality of instruction accounts for about 25 percent of the variance in determining the success of instruction, cognitive entry characteristics account for about 50 percent, and affective variables account for the remaining 25 percent.

Mastery Learning: One Sigma. Having determined the key variables in organizing instruction, Bloom used these variables to design a system of instruction that would maximize excellence and also be successful in the classroom. This system is *mastery learning* (Bloom, 1976). Mastery learning (ML) is, first of all, a philosophy of education focusing on the premise that most students can learn what they are taught, given favorable teaching/learning conditions. These conditions include informing students of the goals and objectives they are to reach, providing cues to guide their learning, encouraging the active participation of all students, providing incentives and reinforcements, providing frequent feedback concerning learning errors and progress toward the goals and objectives, and providing supplementary instructional activities to help students overcome poor initial learning. When integrated into a teach, test, reteach/extend, retest format, they comprise the essential elements of mastery learning.

When combined in this model, continual feedback and the correction of errors for each student prevent the buildup of an accumulation of learning errors and also prepare each student for the next unit of instruction. In effect, then, this model works to equalize the cognitive entry characteristics of each student for each unit of instruction since all students are assisted in learning well what they need in order to proceed successfully. Therefore, when ML is operating well, there should be a zero, or near zero, correlation between students' cognitive entry characteristics (which will be nearly equal) and their subsequent achievement. Under these conditions, the characteristic differences between low and high achieving students should more or less disappear over time. When these favorable teaching/learning conditions exist, the learning gains of students are typically one standard deviation (or one sigma) higher than those attained through traditional instruction. Moreover, according to Bloom, this high rate of success has a marked and cumulative impact on affective variables; that is, the greater the success, the greater the self-esteem and self-confidence, which, in turn, stimulate further achievement. Therefore, mastery learning, as Bloom defined it, addresses all three of the key sets of alterable variables identified earlier: cognitive entry characteristics, quality of instruction, and affective characteristics.

The Tutorial Model: Two Sigmas. After defining and examining the mastery learning model, Bloom turned to two related questions: Does ML yield the maximum instructional results possible for students? Can any classroom instructional method used in schools approach the effectiveness of an "ideal" instructional program? To answer these questions, Bloom launched what he called Project Talent. He identified and interviewed the most talented young people in fields as widely varying as tennis, piano, art, chess, and so on (Bloom and Sosniak, 1981). His purpose was to define those instructional variables that were common to the backgrounds of these very high achievers.

Generally, he found that these talented people received what was essentially tutorial instruction with the following characteristics: a maximum amount of one-on-one instruction (or at least a high degree of interaction with the instructor); instruction tailored closely to the readiness of the individual; extensive practice, participation, and reinforcement; and immediate and constant correction of learning and performance errors.

Anania (1981), a student of Bloom's, designed an experimental model with all of these characteristics and compared it to both a traditional model and a mastery learning model. She found that the achievement of students in this tutorial model reached two standard deviations (two sigmas) above that of the traditional mode. The relationship among learning profiles obtained under the traditional model, the ML model, and the tutorial model is shown in Figure 1.

The Two-Sigma Problem Defined. Anania's study represented an educational landmark because now we are not limited to comparing instructional programs or models against the lowest possible denominator of traditional instruction, but, instead, we can also compare them to an ideal: the tutorial model. The two-sigma problem posed by Anania's results is this: How can we alter instruction in the regular classroom to approach the gains of the two-sigma tutorial model?

To answer this question, Bloom and several of his students turned yet again to his key alterable variables—cognitive entry

Figure 1. Achievement Distribution for Students Under Conventional, Mastery Learning, and Tutorial Instruction.

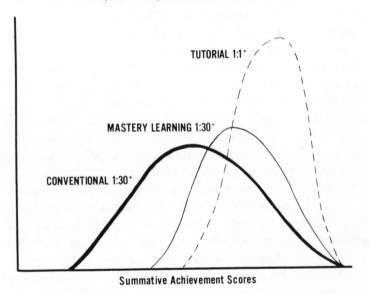

TUTORIAL 1:1*

MASTERY LEARNING 1:30*

CONVENTIONAL 1:30*

Summative Achievement Scores

*Teacher:Student Ratio

Source: Bloom, 1984, p. 5. Used with permission.

characteristics and quality of instruction—to design various models of instruction that could be successful using whole group instruction. They emphasized whole group instruction because it appeared to represent the most economical use of teacher time (compared to teaching two or more groups) and to be more manageable.

Six Solutions. In a seminal article in *Educational Leadership,* Bloom (1984) identified six solutions to the two sigma problem:

1. Improve student processing of conventional instruction.
2. Improve instructional materials and educational technology.
3. Improve the home environment to encourage good work habits, adequate stimulation and academic guidance, language development, and academic goals.
4. Control the peer group.
5. Improve the quality of teaching to provide effective learning cues, more equal participation and reinforcement, and systematic diagnosis and correction of errors.
6. Improve the teaching of higher mental processes.

For each solution, Bloom offers data from meta-analyses conducted by Walberg (1984) or the laboratory research of his students—all of whom based their work on whole group instructional configurations. Of these six solutions, two lie outside the direct influence of the school, but administrators and teachers can control the other four relatively directly. The first of these four (solution 1) involves controlling cognitive entry characteristics. The other three (solutions 2, 5, and 6) relate to quality of instruction. The remainder of this section briefly describes the research by Bloom and his colleagues on these four sets of variables.

Leyton (1983) is cited by Bloom (1984) as providing a most interesting method of improving student processing of conventional instruction. Basically, Leyton argued that learning would be most enhanced by providing prerequisite instruction and mastery learning in what he termed the *enhanced Mastery Learning condition.* Accordingly, he compared four models of instruction: (1) conventional whole group instruction, (2) conventional whole group instruction plus enhanced initial cognitive entry, (3) whole group mastery learning, and (4) enhanced initial cognitive entry plus whole group mastery learning—the maximal condition. Enhancing initial cognitive entry involved teaching all students the prerequisite concepts they needed for each of two courses, algebra and French. Students were average ninth graders in regular classrooms in an inner city school system.

In the maximal condition, students mastered 95 percent of the objectives, compared to 50 percent mastery in the unenhanced conventional group. (Note that two sigmas equal 98 percent mastery.) Students in the unenhanced ML condition mastered about 80 percent of the objectives. In addition, the correlations between the entry and exit levels in the maximal and ML conditions were typically low, which was not the case for the two conventional groups. The average correlations for French and algebra were 0.14 and 0.35 under the maximal conditions and the mastery learning conditions, respectively, whereas the correlations for the conventional plus prerequisite instruction and the conventional instruction were 0.54 and 0.80, respectively. Finally, students in the two maximal ML conditions had much more positive feelings about themselves, compared to students in the other two conditions.

Several important implications emerge from Leyton's study: when initial cognitive entry behaviors and feedback-correctives are properly applied in regular classrooms, group-based instruction can be as effective as tutorial instruction with regard to students' achievement and attitudes; mastery learning instruction facilitates instruction for all students, not just high achieving students; students can be very similar to each other in level of achievement when the learning conditions are properly designed to meet their learning needs; and student potential for learning is facilitated best by the maximal mastery model.

Regarding solution 2, improving the quality of instructional materials, Bloom refers primarily to the effects of advance organizers (Luiten, Ames, and Ackerson, 1980). Additionally, he indicates that a combination of summaries and other organizational aids may be most useful in designing materials. Bloom's reference to this variable as a major solution to the two sigma problem is critical because recent estimates suggest that over 90 percent of available instructional time is spent using commercial textbook materials

(Osborn, 1983). Moreover, extensive research shows that both basal readers and content textbooks are often so poorly written that it is difficult, if not impossible, for students to infer their meaning (Osborn, Jones, and Stein, 1984). Anderson and Armbruster (1984) refer to such books as "inconsiderate" texts.

In contrast, "considerate" texts facilitate comprehension because they have appropriate text structures, cohesive elements, and unity or clarity of purpose. Jones and others (1984) provide guidelines for developing three types of considerate text: considerate prose text, considerate graphics text, and considerate glossary text. These guidelines are based heavily on the research of Anderson and Armbruster (1984) but also integrate research on text design, readability research, and text analysis from other sources. Classroom teachers, as well as curriculum developers and instructional specialists, can use many of these guidelines to improve the quality of instructional materials.

Tenenbaum (1982) is cited by Bloom (1984) as manipulating quality of teaching variables (solution 5) by employing and testing three instructional conditions: conventional instruction, mastery learning, and a maximal condition involving an optimal amount of cues, reinforcement, participation, and correction of errors. All conditions involved about three weeks of whole group instruction dealing with subject areas selected from biology and algebra. Tenenbaum's data approximated the two sigma results in that the maximal instruction group's scores were about two standard deviations above those in the conventional group and one standard deviation above those in the mastery learning group that did not use the maximal quality of teaching practices. Thus, his work suggests that it is possible to design a maximal instruction condition for the regular classroom using whole group instruction that has exceptionally powerful results.

Solution 6, improving the teaching of higher mental processes, is based largely on the research of Mevarech and Levin, both of whom are cited by Bloom (1984). Bloom argues that a major reason for the poor performance in conventional instruction is the overwhelming emphasis on textual materials and tests that tap low order objectives. Consequently, teaching methods, instructional materials, and testing rarely rise above the lowest category of his taxonomy—knowledge. Both Levin and Mevarech combined teaching higher mental processes with mastery learning. Using this combination, Levin was able to obtain two sigma results, but, unfortunately, he did not test for the effects of teaching higher mental processes separately from those of mastery learning. Mevarech, however, did separate the two variables. In the higher mental processes condition, 73 percent of the students mastered the objectives. When he combined higher mental process instruction with mastery learning, 90 percent of the students mastered them.

Taking these different studies as a whole suggests that we have a new standard for comparing different approaches to instruction and programs, and it *is* possible to attain the maximum level of results using whole group instruction in typical content area subjects. However, even though they were replicated and involved many grade levels, all of the studies cited above employed only a handful of teachers and lasted only a few weeks. In addition, these studies did not fully address the question of how much gain is possible when students enter actual schools and classes with greatly different entry skills. The key issue for the field of education is whether it is possible to design instruction that yields maximal results under nonexperimental conditions utilizing a diversity of teachers and long-term instruction. The remainder of our chapter is focused on that issue.

Enhanced Mastery Learning
and Quality of Instruction in Schools

The obvious place to begin to look for an answer to this question is in school systems using mastery learning. Fortunately, we have access to unpublished data for a number of ML programs by virtue of their participation in the Network for Outcome-Based Schools. Analysis of these data is most revealing. First, we believe that the results in the most successful ML schools approach or approximate the gains represented in the tutorial model documented by Bloom. In this sense, they represent instruction that is beyond conventional mastery learning. Second, each of these programs represents a different adaptation of mastery learning theory and operations, suggesting that there is a diversity of models that may produce two-sigma results. Third, a close examination of these programs reveals that all of them in different ways have enhanced initial entry and high quality of instruction, even though their grouping and delivery conditions vary considerably.

   Two-Sigma Results. We could argue that at least five existing mastery learning programs approximate the results of the

Figure 2. Johnson City, N.Y., Reading Scores from the California Achievement Test, 1978–1980.

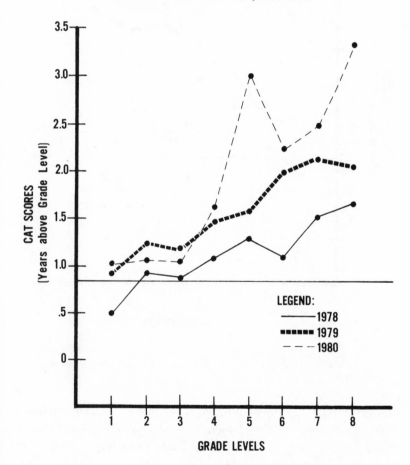

Source of data: Office of the Johnson City, N.Y., Superintendent of Schools, 1980.

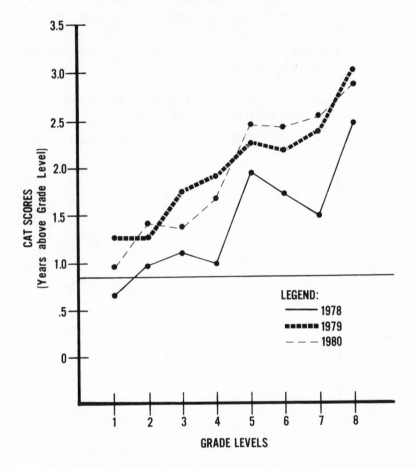

Figure 3. Johnson City, N.Y., Math Scores from the
California Achievement Test, 1978–1980.

Source of data: Office of the Johnson City, N.Y., Superintendent of Schools, 1980.

tutorial model. Figures 2 and 3 show the mean California Achievement Test scores of the elementary and junior high students in Johnson City, New York. (Also see Table 1 in Chapter Nine.) The "average" Johnson City eighth grader scored about 2.5 years above grade level on both reading and math in 1980, and Johnson City students continue to do at least as well today.

Figure 4 shows the math results for the Center School in New Canaan, Connecticut. Here, for the last seven years, about 15 percent of grade six students finished the first half of Algebra I, and some completed it (that is, quadratic equations). In addition, about 60 percent of students in grade six and 30 percent in grade five scored at the ninety-ninth percentile on the Metropolitan Achieve-

**Figure 4. New Canaan, Conn., Math Scores from the
Metropolitan Achievement Test (MAT).**

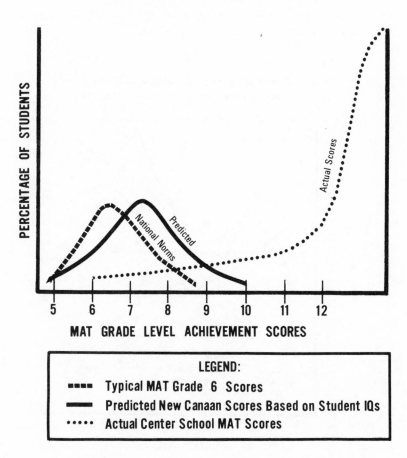

LEGEND:
- ▬▬▬ Typical MAT Grade 6 Scores
- ▬▬▬ Predicted New Canaan Scores Based on Student IQs
- ••••• Actual Center School MAT Scores

Source of data: Office of the New Canaan, Conn., Superintendent of Schools, 1981.

ment Test (MAT). Almost no students in the entire K-6 school of 200 score below grade level on the MAT, including mildly handicapped students who are mainstreamed in the regular math program.

Figures 5 and 6 show the mean MAT reading and math scores for the elementary school students in Red Bank, New Jersey. Note that the reading and math scores for 1983 are dramatically higher than in 1978 when the implementation of their mastery learning program began. Eighth graders were reading and computing close to a year and a half below grade level in 1978 and in 1983 scored a year and a half above in reading and two and a half years above in math.

Figure 5. Red Bank, N.J., Reading Scores on the Metropolitan Achievement Test (MAT), 1978-1983.

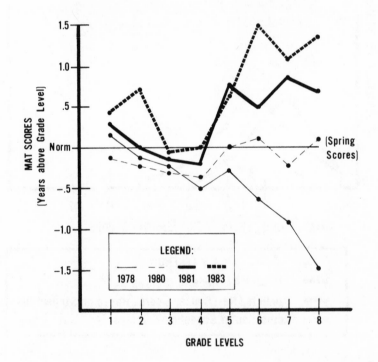

Source of data: Office of the Red Bank, N.J., Superintendent of Schools, 1981.

**Figure 6. Red Bank, N.J., Math Scores on the
Metropolitan Achievement Test (MAT), 1978-1983.**

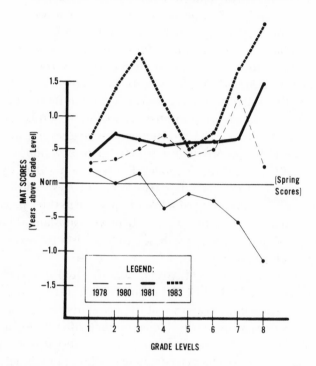

Source of data: Office of the Red Bank, N.J., Superintendent of Schools, 1983.

The achievement results for all three of these districts, reflected in various standardized tests and other measures, suggest that their levels of achievement are exceedingly high and could be equivalent to about two standard deviations or more above conventional instructional results, especially when you take into account the socioeconomic and racial composition of the Johnson City and Red Bank communities.

In addition, data from Slavin (1984) suggest that Team Assisted Individualization (TAI) might qualify as a two sigma program. As in New Canaan, Slavin reports that grade five students using TAI completed units on introduction to algebra and were able to solve simultaneous equations. Moreover, TAI students gained about twice as many grade equivalents in mathematic computations as did control students. The difference between experimental and control classes in one experiment was more than 40 percent of a grade equivalent in only twenty-four weeks, and more than half a grade equivalent for handicapped students.

Finally, there is the Lebanon Model of Mastery Learning developed by Reed (1983). He reports data showing that over 90 percent of the students in his American School in Beirut, Lebanon, passed the formative tests in English reading the first time, and over 95 percent met the mastery requirements at first testing in mathematics. Reed also reports that a 185-day math program was completed in 121 days using his model. Further, he has data showing that his model affects learning retention; that is, tests administered in math in November showed a loss of only one to three percentage points from a June test. In contrast, there were substantial losses in Arabic. The significance of these findings is discussed in the remainder of his paper.

Taken together these five programs (Johnson City, New Canaan, Red Bank, TAI, and Lebanon) share three things: high quality of instruction, assurance of high cognitive entry levels, and very high achievement results. However, they differ dramatically in the ways they group students and deliver instruction. In the following section, we characterize these five programs as belonging to one of two types of delivery systems: continuous progress models and whole group models.

Continuous Progress/Flexible Delivery Models. Johnson City is a small, blue-collar community with about 3,000 students, which utilizes various forms of team teaching, small and large group instruction, and continuous progress in all basic skills subject areas and grade levels in its schools (Brandt, 1981; also see Chapter Nine). Additionally, there is a heavy commitment to continuous staff development to improve the quality of instruction and to maximize academic learning time for students. This is the kind of time on task that targets instruction to goals and learning tasks appropriate for the student's level of achievement (Fisher and others, 1978). In fact, not only do all Johnson City teachers and principals receive continuing training in mastery learning and the components of quality instruction, Johnson City is a demonstration school for teaching reading in the content areas (Herber, 1978). Consequently, staff members have received sustained, top quality training from Harold Herber, Joan Nelson, and their colleagues at Syracuse University for many years, in addition to the regular training in mastery learning provided by their administrators. Student readiness is assessed daily by teachers who usually work in teams to plan for instruction and regroup students so that each receives instruction addressed directly to his or her specific needs.

The key to the initial delivery system in Johnson City was the willingness of teachers to share or trade students for particular assignments and lessons in order to create larger achievement groups than would exist in any given classroom. By exchanging students and responsibilities in this way, a teacher team could improve both its effectiveness and efficiency and minimize the number of times a given teacher would have to teach particular lessons to small groups. This focus on flexible time and flexible composition of targeted learning groups required planning and coordination time for teaching teams but reduced the problem of fragmented teacher focus and attention inherent in other continuous progress approaches.

Significantly, this initial delivery system has evolved considerably over the years. Now that most students are on grade level, teachers seek to teach a given unit of work within a fixed time. Thus, when the students take a formative test, mastery students typically are no longer moved forward to the next unit while nonmastery students receive correctives. Instead, mastery students receive enrichment activities while nonmastery students receive corrective instruction so that the group stays as much intact from unit to unit as possible. In fact, most of the groups in Johnson City are heterogeneous and are formed by random selection.

New Canaan is a medium-sized, middle-class city with three K-6 elementary schools. One of them, the Center School, uses a highly individualized, heavily field tested and researched continuous progress/mastery learning model of instruction that has been developed and refined by Stephen Rubin, the school's principal who also serves as assistant superintendent for instruction for the district (see Rubin and Spady, 1984). Figure 7 shows the features of this model.

Figure 7. Individualized Model of Instruction Developed by Rubin
in New Canaan, Conn.

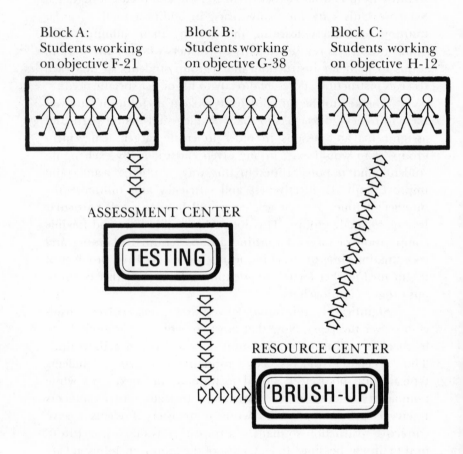

Block A:
Students working
on objective F-21

Block B:
Students working
on objective G-38

Block C:
Students working
on objective H-12

ASSESSMENT CENTER

TESTING

RESOURCE CENTER

'BRUSH-UP'

In Block A, a small group or a full class of students receive instruction on a specified objective (for example, F-21) by the teacher who has been assigned to teach that objective. When the teacher and a particular student feel that the student is ready to demonstrate mastery of F-21, she (the student) goes to the school's assessment center for testing by an aide. If she passes, she receives counseling as to what objective in the program's validated hierarchy of math skills she should seek to master next. If the objective requires skills she does not remember, she goes to the resource center for brush up instruction and testing of the necessary cognitive prerequisites, then on to another group (C) for instruction in the prescribed objective (students in Block C are working on objective H-12).

In this model, students and teachers are assigned to new units based on the progress and needs of all individual students. Any teacher theoretically could be assigned to handle any given part of the math curriculum and might teach that segment several different times a year to those students in the school who may need it at that time. A teacher's "class" would consist of any students in the school who are prepared to tackle that new lesson at that time.

Team Assisted Individualization (TAI) is an approach for elementary and junior high school students developed by Slavin and others (see Slavin, Leavey, and Madden, in press) to replace group-paced programs. Their goal was to provide individualized instruction that was manageable.

In TAI, the entire class is divided into small, heterogeneous groups of four to five students, with typically "faster" and "slower" students on each team. Students work together with their teammates in going through the instruction, checkouts (formative tests), and final tests which are scored by monitors. All other routine work is done either by partners within the teams (checking skill/sheets and checkouts) or by the students themselves (locating and filing papers). Students take tests on units outside their teams on units they completed within their teams. Team scores depend only on the number of units passed and the accuracy of the final tests. Monitorships rotate regularly so that each student in the group has opportunities to be a monitor.

The teacher works with teaching groups that are composed of students from different teams who are at the same level in the individualized curriculum. These teaching groups are re-formed every two weeks. There are no more than three teaching groups, and the teacher works with at least one group each day, so that each teaching group is seen at least once every three periods. The teacher also provides corrective instruction or explanations when students do not pass the checkout tests. Otherwise, much of the responsibility for providing instructional support to individual students resides within the team.

While these three mastery learning systems have much in common, only three commonalities are pertinent to the discussion here. First, in spite of their marked differences in handling the continuous progress approach, all three of these systems are manageable. This happens in part because each approach emphasizes staff development, uses student learning stations, and uses students as instructional resources. These systems also are manageable because they are small. Second, because students are frequently regrouped to receive instruction that meets their needs, most students have the necessary prerequisites when they begin a new unit of work. Therefore, academic learning time is maximal. Third, quality of instruction is excellent in all three systems.

Whole Group/Self-Contained Models. In contrast to the models above, in Red Bank (Abrams, 1983) and in Reed's American School in Beirut, the entire class moves through a series of instructional units together, unit by unit. We call this *whole group/self-contained* instructional delivery. Red Bank uses many commercial and teacher-made materials (as do Johnson City and New Canaan), but great care is taken to assure that the objectives, instruction, and testing are carefully aligned according to guidelines set forth in its *Reading/Language Arts Rationale and Objectives* (Abrams and Squires, 1983). Equally important, before beginning each unit of instruction, Red Bank teachers examine the records of the students so that they can provide instruction in prerequisite skills and concepts. This diagnosis is part of a formally adopted instructional sequence that includes the following eleven steps for each unit of instruction:

1. The *mental set* focuses the learners on the task ahead.
2. The *objective* of the unit is stated and displayed in the classroom to let students know exactly what they are expected to learn.
3. The *rationale* informs students why they should master the objective and why the objective is important.

4. A *model* provides students with an example of what they can do after they have mastered the objective. These four steps can take fifteen minutes or a day, depending on the unit.

5. *Input* is whole-group direct instruction to students; such instruction requires the majority of time allotted for a unit.

6. *Guided practice* allows students to practice the concept or skill with teacher supervision.

7. *Independent practice* occurs when students can perform the skill without assistance.

8. A *formative test* provides the student and the teacher with feedback on students' mastery of the objective. Two groups of students emerge, differentiated by the results of the formative test, as described in items 9 and 10.

9. One group of students comprises those who demonstrate mastery and move on to "extensions," where they apply the skills and concepts to more difficult problems or group projects.

10. The second group of students includes those who demonstrate a need for more and different instruction and who move to "correctives." In reading and math instruction, correctives are provided by supplemental teachers funded through Chapter I.

11. Last, all students are given the "mastery test." For talented and gifted students there are pull-out programs in addition to whole-group instruction.

Thus it appears that the Red Bank model embodies both enhanced initial entry and high quality of instruction.

The Lebanon Model of Mastery Learning uses a most interesting design to attain enhanced entry and quality of instruction. All students are pretested at the beginning of the year to assess learning errors and forgetfulness. As needed, some students receive systematic instruction and retesting for about four weeks to enhance their needed prerequisites, while others are given enrichment instruction. Then all students begin their mastery learning instruction in math, Arabic, and reading (English) for the remainder of the year. The reading and math curriculum involve "store-bought" materials, which include Chicago Mastery Learning Reading (CMLR) developed by Katims, Jones, and Amiran (Jones, Amiran, and Katims, 1984; Levine and Stark, 1982; also see Chapter Twelve). Reed's Lebanon model is shown in Figure 8.

Figure 8. The Lebanon Model of Mastery Learning.

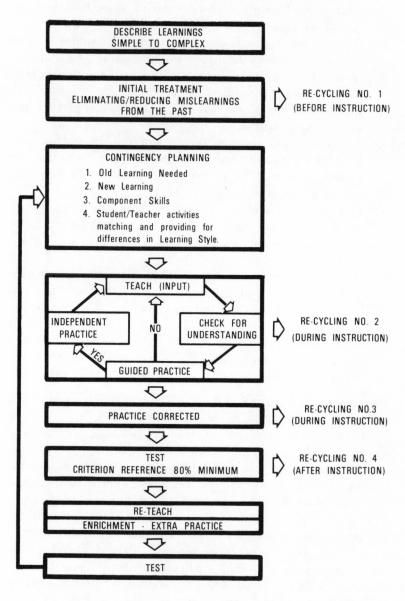

Source: Reed, 1983. Used with permission.

It is important to note that whole group models may also provide for enhanced initial entry in various ways. For example, Red Bank provides systematic prerequisite instruction for those students who need it on an objective-by-objective basis, while the Lebanon model provides systematic prerequisite instruction for students in a single period prior to entry into the program as a whole. In addition, the CMLR curriculum sequences prerequisite instruction into each instructional unit. Both Red Bank and the Lebanon model also provide sustained staff development and use high quality instructional materials that are well-aligned with the objectives and testing program and focus on higher order thinking.

Perhaps the most serious charge against whole group/self-contained instructional delivery is that it does not provide instruction that is challenging for high achieving students. Therefore, academic learning time and progress for such students are relatively low compared to a continuous progress model. We agree that this can be a serious problem. However, we have no evidence that these particular highly successful whole group programs hold back high achieving students. Moreover, we suggest numerous methods below that address this problem.

Analysis of Successful and Less-Than-Successful Models

Despite the marked diversity of successful ML models, they can be classified into two basic types according to whether they are oriented to continuous progress or to whole group instruction within the context of graded, self-contained classrooms. Historically, continuous progress models have been seen in the ML literature as having strong potential advantages over whole group graded instruction, because they aim to provide instruction to each student when he or she is most ready to receive it and because there are no limits to what the high achieving student can achieve since each student can progress at his or her own pace. These models often show substantial growth among such students.

However, because high achieving students can progress at a fast rate, there is a potential danger in continuous progress models: They may substantially increase the gap between high and low achieving students. Many ML continuous progress proponents have argued that such results are not undesirable because low achieving students are likely to have greater gains under this model than they would under other types of instruction. This is certainly true in all three of the continuous progress models described above.

However, there are also instances of less-than-successful implementations of continuous progress in which neither high nor low achieving students are achieving maximal gains. Two notable examples of serious problems with continuous progress are Chicago's continuous progress mastery learning model, which was officially rejected in 1981 after more than a decade of efforts to implement it in the classroom, and the U.S. Army's model of instruction, Instructional Systems Design (ISD), which is under increasing attack (for example, Brandon, 1984). Because of the complex management and logistical problems associated with continuous progress, we believe that less-than-successful models are likely to be at least as widespread in the public schools as are the very successful models just described.

In essence, less-than-successful implementations seem to have two types of problems. One is the pacing of low achieving students. This was a major problem in Chicago where low achieving students were often making little or no progress because it was believed that students should be allowed to progress at "their own rate." Consequently, little effort was made to pace these students or set goals for them, and when goals were set, classroom management problems made it difficult to implement them.

A second drawback associated with continuous progress models of mastery learning is essentially a management problem that affects both high and low achieving students. The larger the gap between the high and low achieving students in heterogeneous self-contained classrooms the greater the number of truly disparate groups teachers must manage and the greater the likelihood of their not being able to keep each group on task. Moreover, teachers find it difficult to provide enough instructional materials to keep all levels of students progressing. Low expectations for slow learners and high rates of student and teacher mobility compound these management problems.

Clearly, these various factors may operate to limit the gains made by high and low achieving students in individualized and small group models of mastery learning. The pattern of gains under optimal and less-than-optimal conditions is contrasted in Figures 9 and 10.

Since program success seems to be dependent on optimal conditions operating in the classroom, we are compelled to ask, *what are optimal conditions?*

Figure 9. Increased Individualized Differences as a Result of Individualized Instruction Under Optimal Conditions.

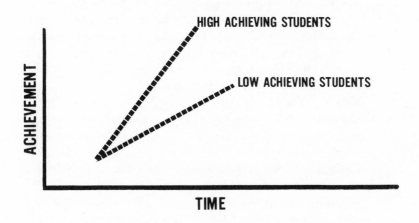

Figure 10. Increased Individualized Differences as a Result of Individualized Instruction Under Less-Than-Optimal Conditions.

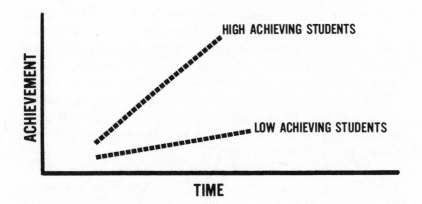

Size is certainly one of them. One could take all the school population of Johnson City and put it in two large schools in a big city like Chicago. The same can be said of New Canaan. Size is a problem in part because it frequently is associated with teacher-pupil ratio. In Johnson City, there are generally three teachers plus one or two aides per 100 students. In New Canaan, instruction takes place in classes of about twenty-five, with some small groupings of five to six students. In TAI, the teacher teaches only a few students, while other students monitor seatwork and peer instruction for the other groups. These ML approaches are manageable in part because teacher-pupil ratios are relatively low. They become less manageable in large systems, particularly those in which many more students are absent, transfer, or leave class for testing, or when there are large groupings of low achieving students.

Further, continuous progress problems are multiplied greatly when the teacher does not have the materials and management design used in these successful programs. Both academic learning time and general time on task will be relatively low when the average teacher must provide four to five different units or sets of instruction for thirty-two to thirty-six students. In addition, class size is even more critical when the students are low achievers since such students require considerable individual attention to help them understand the instruction and deal with specific learning, emotional, and social problems arising from low self-esteem and frustration. (Also see Chapter thirteen on all of these management issues.)

Ability to communicate and monitor is another optimum condition. It is rare for large school systems to provide the time for teacher planning and coordination that Johnson City and New Canaan do. In the latter cases, teachers or coordinators plan for regrouping and instruction *every day,* sometimes coming in early and staying after school. Additionally, both teaching and student progress are carefully monitored by personal visits to the classroom by various administrative staff. This is seldom done (for whatever reasons) in large systems.

Stability is another factor that affects program effectiveness. Mastery learning has been operating for twelve years in Johnson City and for fifteen years in New Canaan. John Champlin, the architect of the Johnson City model, was superintendent for eleven years. Stephen Rubin, the developer of the New Canaan model, has been there for over fifteen years. Contrast this to the average length of tenure for a superintendent in most large systems: three years or less. Moreover, teacher mobility frequently creates a problem in large cities and rural areas by undermining the impact of staff development programs. For example, in one major city thirty teachers were trained in ML over the summer. Only nineteen were still in the assigned classrooms just six months later. The resulting loss due to turnover is twofold: On the one hand, there is the loss of the trained teacher; on the other, there is the loss of training funds and the time needed for retraining replacement staff.

To summarize, while it is clearly possible to attain two-sigma results for students in the continuous progress model, this approach has serious implementation problems in many schools. Without intensive staff development, careful pacing, constant monitoring, and time for staff planning and coordination, it may increase the difference between high and low achieving students and result in less than maximal gains for both types of students. Additionally, the management problems associated with this model may make excessive demands on teachers, causing them to dislike it, especially when there are many ability groups in a self-contained situation and the entire burden of providing flexible delivery falls on each individual teacher.

Carefully designed whole group instruction can address these problems directly. It is manageable in large school systems where opportunities for staff development tend to be limited. In addition, it has the potential to attain greater time on task than does instruction of small groups in traditional classrooms. Rosenshine (1983) found, for example, that in the latter situation when the teacher teaches one group while the others do seatwork, time on task often is very low. Of course, the disadvantage of whole group instruction is that all too often it is aimed at the middle or lower middle group in the class. This is a very serious problem because it greatly limits the opportunities for growth for both high and low achieving students. Figure 11 shows this problem graphically.

At the same time, it is evident from results in Red Bank and the American School in Beirut that the needs of the low and high achieving students can be addressed in whole group instruction.

Figure 11. Traditional Whole Group Instruction Aimed at the
Average Student.

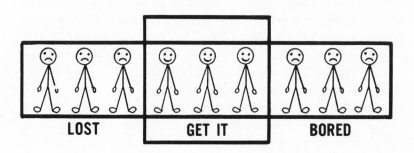

These models avoid the serious disadvantages of traditional whole group instruction because they both have enhanced initial entry and a high quality of instruction. The prerequisite instruction addresses the low achieving students by bridging the gap between old and new instruction. That is, both Red Bank and the CMLR curriculum used in Lebanon relate new content to what the student already knows. In Red Bank, this is done by providing what Madeline Hunter (1982) calls an *anticipatory set,* in which the teacher typically seeks to elicit skills and concepts the student knows and relates them to the instruction. CMLR also preteaches prerequisite skills in individual units where appropriate. Additionally, it uses a sequencing model that begins with content that is simple in structure, concrete, familiar, explicit, and short and progresses to content that is increasingly complex, abstract, unfamiliar, inexplicit, and long.

Another feature of instruction in Red Bank and the Lebanon model is the high quality of instruction. Both Abrams and Reed have provided extensive staff development for their teachers, focusing on Madeline Hunter's methods of teaching. These include: establishing the anticipatory set, a lot of modeling, comprehension monitoring, correction of errors after the instruction, guided practice (the informal correction of errors during practice), and independent practice. Recall that these are the same procedures defined as important by Johnson City and the variables that are specified as critical by Bloom: cues, reinforcement, participation, and correction of learning errors. Additionally, CMLR provides for much student participation in teacher-directed activities as well as guided practice and a strong focus on examples, explanations, explicit learning strategy instruction, and correction of errors, using a different teaching/learning strategy. The latter is also a key precept in the Johnson City model.

Finally, both Red Bank and the Lebanon model address the problem of high achieving students. Both programs have a wide range of activities to extend the capabilities of these students: optional activities, inferential reading, peer tutoring, cross-age tutoring, and extensions that really challenge the thinking skills of students. Moreover, the high achieving students appear to respond to the learning strategy instruction quite differently than low achieving students; that is, they seem to be able to learn the strategies easily and apply them to other subjects spontaneously. Figure 12 shows what we have termed the *successful whole group instruction* model that characterizes instruction in Red Bank and Lebanon. This contrasts sharply with the problems of traditional instruction shown in Figure 11.

A model that preteaches cognitive entry content and skills and provides a high quality of instruction has important advantages over traditional group instruction models and over less well designed continuous progress/small group models using mastery learning. First, the successful whole group model seems to do a good job of providing instruction for both high and low achievers without increasing the differences between high and low achieving students. Second, it avoids the management problem associated with having several distinct instructional groups in a single, self-contained classroom. Third, the two-sigma results in Red Bank and Lebanon were obtained in much less time (around four years) than the longer periods of implementation taken by Johnson City and New Canaan to develop their effective continuous progress models.

Applications for Large City Systems

Throughout this analysis, it has been apparent that a major feature of all of these successful ML systems is the small size of the districts or schools that have developed and implemented them. Can

Figure 12. Successful Whole Group Instruction
with Enhanced Mastery Learning and High Quality Instruction.

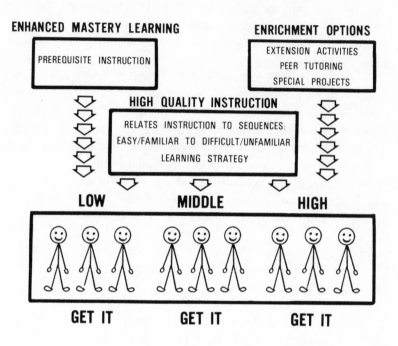

two-sigma results be obtained in large-city systems? We can answer this at two levels. On the one hand, we are confident that particular schools in a large city could obtain something like tutorial model results because small schools can provide adequate staff development and monitoring. Certainly, a few "exemplary" schools already exist in most urban districts. On the other hand, it would be risky to predict that cities the size of New York or Chicago (or even districts within such cities) would obtain two-sigma results. All large cities suffer from teacher and student mobility, high percentages of low achieving students, low teacher expectations, high teacher/pupil ratios, and limited staff development resources and capabilities. Problems such as these are hard for any program to overcome on such a massive scale.

But if two-sigma results are not likely to be attained by large districts, should large school districts use mastery learning? We unequivocally believe they should, given the constraints, realities, and problems in such districts. Specifically, we recommend the following:

• Large districts must provide a substantial citywide staff development program that focuses on the philosophy and principles of mastery learning instruction and does not ask teachers to develop instructional materials. They must recognize that it takes *years* of sustained, well-organized, and well-monitored inservice for individual teachers in the classroom to develop effective instructional materials. Large districts generally lack this capability.

• Large districts should develop high quality materials centrally in a department of curriculum or purchase high quality instructional materials (such as CMLR) that are devised expressly for mastery learning, focus on high order objectives, and have been effectively field tested.

• Large districts should use the following approaches to address the problem of teaching high and low achieving students of the same age: (1) whole group instruction because it is easy to manage and is likely to yield higher time on task for large classrooms; (2) homogeneous groupings for some or all of the instruction; (3) "walking instruction" for self-contained heterogeneous classrooms (that is, students "walk" to designated classrooms for instruction appropriate to their level of achievement for specified periods of the day, as is done in Johnson City, New Canaan, Chicago, and elsewhere); (4) acceleration programs for high and low achieving students; (5) extensions for high achieving students that are truly challenging and interesting; (6) peer tutoring; (7) extra time, instruction, and resources for low achieving students so that they can progress at a faster rate; and (8) a model of instruction that links new learnings to prior knowledge. Any or all of these suggestions work to maximize learning for both high and low achieving students. (For elaboration of these options, see Jones, 1982.)

• Large districts should do whatever it takes to implement a system of recordkeeping and supervision that involves setting goals, pacing, and monitoring student achievement. These factors are critical to the success of any ML system. Effective models of recordkeeping, pacing, and monitoring may be found in any of the successful programs discussed above. CMLR, for example, has an *Implementation Manual* (Board of Education of the City of Chicago, 1982) that discusses issues of management, classroom organization, pacing, and recordkeeping at length. It can be used as a guide for addressing these very crucial issues.

Conclusion

The key question we raised in this chapter is whether mastery learning in existing public schools can attain two-sigma results. Analysis of successful ML programs indicates that the answer is yes—provided that the model implemented addresses certain instructional conditions. First, the system must organize instruction so that the student has the prerequisite skills and concepts. Continuous progress, sequencing prerequisite instruction into learning units, and systematic testing and instruction for prerequisite entry characteristics are effective methods of addressing this problem when they are well implemented. Second, a high quality of instruction may be attained by a sustained and intensive staff development program plus the use of high-quality instructional materials. Third, sustained two-sigma results require an effective management system that addresses the needs of high and low achieving students and also provides for goal setting, pacing, and monitoring.

We also argued that the two-sigma criterion is useful in defining a standard of excellence and providing a framework for analyzing what exactly it is that is successful within a set of successful programs. In this chapter, we found enhanced initial entry and various variables related to quality of instruction to be critical. We also found that there is a variety of different ways to design programs for enhanced initial entry, a high quality of instruction, and maximal academic learning time. Finally, we hope that the two-sigma standard will stimulate similar analyses that will help educators improve their understanding of excellence in instruction.

References

Abrams, J. D. "Overcoming Racial Stereotyping in Red Bank, New Jersey." *School Administrator*, 1983, *40*, 5, 7.

Abrams, J. D., and Squires, D. A. *Reading/Language Arts Rationale and Objectives.* Red Bank, N.J.: Office of the Superintendent of Schools, 1983.

Anania, F. "The Effects of Quality of Instruction on the Cognitive and Affective Learning of Students." Unpublished doctoral dissertation. University of Chicago, 1981.

Anderson, T. H., and Armbruster, B. B. "Content Area Textbooks." In R. C. Anderson, J. Osborn, and R. J. Tierney (Eds.), *Learning to Read In American Schools: Basal Readers and Content Texts.* Hillsdale, N.J.: Erlbaum, 1984.

Bloom, B. S. *Stability and Change in Human Characteristics.* New York: Wiley, 1976.

Bloom, B. S. "The New Direction in Educational Research: Alterable Variables." *Phi Delta Kappan*, 1980, *6*, 382-385.

Bloom, B. S. "The Search for Methods of Whole Group Instruction as Effective as One-to-One Tutoring." *Educational Leadership*, 1984, *8*, 4-18.

Bloom, B. S., and Sosniak, L. A. "Talent Development vs. Schooling." *Educational Leadership*, 1981, *39*, 86-95.

Board of Education of the City of Chicago, *Chicago Mastery Learning Reading, Implementation Manual.* Watertown, Mass.: Mastery Education Corporation, 1982.

Brandon, R. K. "ISD: Is the System Out of Control?" Paper presented at the annual meeting of the American Educational Research Association, New Orleans, April 1984.

Brandt, A. "The Schools Where Everyone Gets A's." *Family Circle*, 1981, *94*, 4, 29.

DeVries, D. L., and Slavin, R. E. "Teams-Games-Tournament (TGT): Review of Ten Classroom Experiments." *Journal of Research and Development in Education*, 1978, *12*, 28-38.

Fisher, C. W., and others. *Teaching and Learning in Elementary Schools: A Summary of the Beginning Teacher Evaluation Study.* San Francisco: Far West Laboratory for Educational Research and Development, 1978.

Herber, H. L. *Reading in the Content Areas.* Englewood Cliffs, N.J.: Prentice-Hall, 1978.

Hunter, M. *Mastery Teaching.* El Segundo, Calif.: TIP Publications, 1982.

Jones, B. F. "Key Management Decisions for Implementing Mastery Learning." *School Administrator*, March 1982, 45–48.

Jones, B. F., Amiran, M. R., and Katims, M. "Teaching Cognitive Strategies and Text Structures Within Language Arts Programs." In J. Segel, S. F. Chipman, and R. Glaser (Eds.), *Thinking and Learning Skills: Relating Basic Research to Instructional Practices*. Vol. 1. Hillsdale, N.J.: Erlbaum, 1984.

Jones, B. F., and others. "Content-Driven Comprehension Instruction and Assessment: A Model for Army Training Literature." Alexandria, Va.: U.S. Army Research Institute for the Social and Behavioral Sciences, 1984.

Levine, D. U., and Stark, J. "Instructional and Organizational Arrangements That Improve Achievement in Inner City Schools." *Educational Leadership*, December 1982, pp. 41–46.

Leyton, F. S. "The Extent to Which Group Instruction Supplemented by Mastery of the Initial Cognitive Prerequisites Approximates the Learning Effectiveness of One-to-One Tutorial Methods." Unpublished doctoral dissertation. University of Chicago, 1983.

Luiten, J., Ames, W., and Ackerson, G. "A Meta-analysis of the Effects of Advance Organizers on Learning and Retention." *American Educational Research Journal*, 1980, *17*, 211–218.

Mevarech, A. R. *"The Role of Teaching Learning Strategies and Feedback-Corrective Procedures In Developing Higher Cognitive Achievement."* Unpublished doctoral dissertation. University of Chicago, 1980.

National Commission on Excellence in Education. *A Nation at Risk*. Washington, D.C.: U.S. Government Printing Office, 1983.

Osborn, J. "The Purposes, Uses, and Contents of Workbooks and Some Guidelines for Publishers." In R. C. Anderson, J. Osborn, and R. J. Tierney (Eds.), *Learning to Read in American Schools: Basal Readers and Content Texts*. Hillsdale, N.J.: Erlbaum, 1983.

Osborn, J., Jones, B. F., and Stein, M. "The Case for Improving Textbook Programs: An Issue of Quality." Paper presented at "Excellence in Our Schools: Making It Happen, A National Forum on Educational Reform," sponsored by Far West Laboratory, the College Board, the California School Boards Association, and Association of California School Administrators, San Francisco, March 14-16, 1984.

Reed, F. "The Administration of Mastery Learning: The Lebanon Model." Paper presented at the annual meeting of the American Educational Research Association, Montreal, April 1983.

Rosenshine, B. "Teaching Functions in Instructional Programs." *The Elementary School Journal*, 1983, *83*, 335-351.

Rubin, S. E., and Spady, W. G. "Achieving Excellence Through Outcome-Based Instructional Delivery." *Educational Leadership*, 1984, *8*, 37-44.

Slavin, R. E. "Team Assisted Individualization: Combining Cooperative Learning and Individualized Instruction in Mathematics." In R. E. Slavin and others (Eds.), *Learning to Cooperate: Cooperating to Learn*. New York: Plenum, 1984.

Slavin, R. E., Leavey, M., and Madden, N. A. "Combining Cooperative Learning and Individualized Instruction: Effects on Student Mathematics Achievement, Attitudes, and Behaviors." *The Elementary School Journal*, in press.

Spady, W. G., and Marx, G. *Excellence in Our Schools: Making It Happen*. San Francisco: Far West Laboratory, 1984.

Tenenbaum, G. "A Method of Group Instruction Which Is as Effective as One-to-One Tutorial Instruction." Unpublished doctoral dissertation. University of Chicago, 1982.

Walberg, H. J. "Improving the Productivity of America's Schools." *Educational Leadership*, 1984, *8*, 19-27.

3

Preactive and Proactive
Supervision of
Mastery Learning Programs

Doris W. Ryan

The North American public school has traditionally been process-based rather than outcome-based. Meyer, Scott, and Deal (1979), for example, have reasoned that schools, in order to survive, have had to conform to community-sanctioned "institutional rules" relevant to teacher categories and credentials, student selection and definition, topics for instruction, and appropriate facilities. It has not been essential in the past for schools to ensure that teaching and learning activities are efficiently coordinated. Indeed, schools have been compelled neither to ensure that any coordination that does take place is grounded in a knowledge base for the delivery of quality instruction to students nor to ensure that student achievement is documented and monitored.

However, the current public and political discontent with the educational system is changing these ground rules. Public attention has become focused more and more on the outcomes of schooling, and demands for instructional improvements can be heard everywhere. The report of the U.S. Commission on Excellence in Education (1983) is a recent case in point. The social rhetoric of this decade is not one of deschooling; rather, the public is demanding substantial improvement in the quality of education provided in publicly supported schools (Griffin, 1983).

45

National and state governments as well as local school boards and schools are responding in various ways to the pressures for reform. At policy levels some distance removed from classrooms, regulations and compliance procedures have ushered in an era of student competency assessment accompanied, in a growing number of states, by teacher evaluation systems linked to student performance (Ryan and Hickcox, 1980). Recognizing that mandated assessment programs provide insufficient means to accomplish the basic redefinition of schooling required by outcome-based premises (Spady, 1979), school district personnel have begun to develop targeted programs for curricular and instructional change. As the chapters in this volume illustrate, such programs increasingly incorporate mastery learning approaches to instructional planning and delivery.

From analyses of successful implementation efforts, educators are learning that the long-term and consistent use by teachers of a goal-based instructional delivery system such as mastery learning requires the prior commitment and ongoing leadership of district and school administrators (Levine and Stark, 1981). The focus of this chapter is on the substantial changes required in the roles of these middle managers if schools are to change from process-based to outcome-based systems. In particular, administrators whose major responsiblities revolve around teacher supervision and evaluation must gain a fundamentally different capacity to organize and manage the instructional delivery system.

An analysis of current supervisory practices, in the first section of this chapter, highlights the role/process dominated conception of management that underlies traditional administrative training and performance. The limited capacity of this conception to improve student learning is revealed both in the narrow substantive base brought to supervisory processes and in the failure to distinguish, on the basis of knowledge of probable student outcomes, between areas of teaching performance about which administrators should be directive and those about which administrators should allow teachers to make autonomous decisions.

In contrast to current practices, outcome-based approaches require a goal/substance dominated conception of management, where administrative directives are focused on areas of teaching performance about which there is clear-cut evidence to support supervisory intervention and assistance. Based upon a conceptualization of the tasks of teaching, I will argue that the primary concern of teacher supervision should shift from classroom interactive tasks to preactive and proactive instructional support and development tasks. These tasks must be accomplished if classroom processes are to reflect the premises of a mastery learning instructional system.

Finally, I will discuss the need for a team approach to management in outcome-based school districts. Central administrators and specialists must share with school principals the responsibilities to develop and marshall a mastery-based curriculum and standards structure that provides for rapid and effective student progress in school. Together, these middle managers must modify organizational arrangements in order to assist teachers in working cooperatively to accomplish the prerequisite instructional support and development tasks. Further, the shift in managerial decision-making from process events to documented student achievement is best approached from a district-wide plan for monitoring student outcomes.

The Process Orientation of Current Instructional Management

I have argued elsewhere (Ryan, 1983) that school principals and assistant superintendents are not generally prepared to adopt the new roles of instructional managers in outcome-based school systems even though they traditionally have carried the major responsibility for teacher supervision and evaluation. Specifically, the previous training and experience of school administrators have not equipped them to supervise the development and use by teachers of mastery-based instructional strategies that have been shown empirically to be effective in improving student outcomes. Further, the previous training and experience of school administrators have not provided the knowledge and skills needed to organize and manage an ongoing system of assessing student outcomes. In short, both administrative training and practice continue to reflect an overarching process orientation to instructional management.

Training programs in educational administration far too often draw upon a very narrow conceptual and substantive base.

Since it is typically persons with some training in educational administration who are given supervisory responsibilities, the processes they use in practice (those they have been taught) are also substantively narrow and even weak. Many of the substantive weaknesses of traditional administrative preparation programs are evident in the general absence of formal attention to theories and research related to teaching and learning. The result is that practicing administrators issue prescriptions to teachers on the basis of what they subjectively believe to represent "good" teaching practice. Their evaluations of teacher performance are similarly guided by subjectively defined process criteria. Accordingly, teachers often receive conflicting messages and evaluations from different supervisors.

From my review of the documentation of a case of teacher dismissal in Ontario, for example, I noted that the teacher had received a negative evaluation from the principal because she was not using a variety of materials; the ensuing evaluation by a superintendent was negative because the students, in using a variety of materials, were not studying the same topic. In another case I reviewed, the teacher was told by the principal to use more seatwork and to lecture less; the superintendent, on a subsequent visit, criticized the teacher for using too much seatwork and not teaching to the whole class. I would argue that neither the principals nor the superintendents concerned had empirical evidence to suggest that their particular directives would improve the performance of the teachers in helping students learn the intended content.

Although it is true that administrative training programs currently reflect an emphasis on newly conceived models of teacher evaluation and supervision based on systems theory, the development and use of such models continue to reflect a process-oriented conception of management. Thus, the significant resources and energies that have been devoted over the past decade to changing teacher supervision policies and practices have, in my view, been misguided.

Most school administrators today are informed about clinical supervision, preobservation setting of objectives, postobservation conferencing, evaluation cycles, and the like. They know that supervision should be ongoing and formative in nature and that evaluation, the summative process, should be preceded by efforts to help teachers improve their performance on mutually-determined objectives. However, there is little reason to expect that the movement toward systems-based models of teacher evaluation and supervision will result in more effective classroom instruction. Addressing the major problem of how to help students learn more effectively and more efficiently requires knowledge about *effective teaching* and not just about *effective supervisory processes*. Nevertheless, teacher supervision has been and continues to be notably uninformed by research on teaching or on the examined outcomes of different teaching methods.

Administrative training programs also typically fail to stress the conceptual distinction between areas of teaching performance about which supervisors can defensibly be directive and those which supervisors should best leave to teacher discretion. The work of Dornbusch and Scott (1975) is instructive in considering this important distinction. From studies, conducted over a fifteen-year period, of the evaluation of the work performance in diverse organizational settings (including engineers in a research facility, assembly line workers in a plant, doctors and nurses in a hospital, players on a football team, priests in an archdiocese, professors in a university, and teachers in public schools), they developed a general theory of evaluation and authority in organizations. Their theory assumes that work arrangements under which organizational tasks are assigned should reflect knowledge about the tasks themselves.

Applying their theory to teaching, Natriello and Dornbusch (1980-81) argued that teachers need more autonomy (a delegated work arrangement) in deciding how to reach an assigned goal where successful task performance is highly *unpredictable* (for example, teaching students with learning problems how to read), but teachers need less autonomy (a directive work arrangement) in deciding how to reach an assigned goal when successful task performance is highly *predictable* (for example, reporting student absences). Further, these researchers argue that decisions as to whether performances of assigned goals are to be subject to supervisory directive or to teacher discretion have implications for the evaluation of task performances.

When the way that tasks are to be carried out by teachers is assigned by directive, supervisors can evaluate the extent to which teachers *exert effort* in conformity with the directive. When the way that tasks are to be carried out is delegated to teachers, supervisors should be less interested in the level of conformity in teacher efforts and more concerned about the *outcomes of the performances*. For example, teachers should be able to use "bizarre" instructional methods, if method choice has been delegated, so long as these bring good results; teachers cannot, however, fail to conform to the prescribed method for turning in grades or student attendance. Thus, criteria for evaluation should differ depending upon the arrangement (directed or delegated) chosen for particular areas of task performance.

Administrators often have very limited a priori knowledge of instructional methods that have a high probability of resulting in improved student learning. Thus, they cannot readily predict successful performance of these teacher tasks regardless of the supervisory process they use in relating to teachers. One might infer, therefore, that supervisory arrangements should provide for a great deal of teacher autonomy and very few administrative prescriptions or directives. Indeed, most of the criteria on rating forms typically used in teacher evaluation seem to have little to do with the improvement of instruction and are heavily weighted toward performance tasks that are somewhat superficial to the teacher's major instructional tasks (Ryan and Hickcox, 1980). From their examination of teacher rating forms used by supervisors in a large number of U.S. school districts, for example, Wood and Pohland (1979) found that only 28 percent of the items related directly to the teacher's instructional role. Thirty percent of the items were related to personal characteristics of the teacher, and the remainder were relevant to the teacher's organizational membership role, social role, and administrative role.

Delegating to teachers decisions about *how* to achieve instructional goals may be preferable to an unjustified emphasis on supervisors' subjective beliefs about effective instructional practices, but the adoption of such work arrangements requires that supervisors at least have documented evidence of student achievement to serve as the basis of teacher evaluation. Lacking such a basis, as is typically the case, evaluators and supervisors will continue either to stress conformity in nonessential areas of job performance or conformity to subjective prescriptions for performance. Even when outcomes are documented, administrators are rarely expected to analyze achievement data systematically in order to provide an empirical base for ongoing teacher supervision.

Moreover, the implementation of outcome-based approaches to management ought not to require simply that administrators document and monitor student achievement. Rather, I believe their roles should include stronger management of the instructional system itself. That is, I believe that school principals and other administrators should become more directive in teacher/staff development and ongoing supervision. Their directives, however, must be guided by awareness of the growing body of knowledge about effective schools and effective instructional systems such as mastery learning.

What are the essential tasks of teaching that must be accomplished if targeted student learning is to occur? What knowledge do we have about successful performance of these tasks? How may we apply this knowledge to instructional management? Successful performance of the supervisor's tasks in an outcome-based school system requires proactive attention to such questions. The discussions that follow provide a starting point for such planning.

Focusing Instructional Management on
Teacher Preactive Tasks

In order to provide a substantive basis from which to move toward outcome-based instructional management, teacher supervisors and those who train supervisory officers should first analyze the job responsibilities of teachers. A conceptualization of teaching can be of assistance in drawing attention to the nature of tasks that must be performed, at different times and with regard to different structural units, in order to conduct well-organized and task-oriented classrooms. Placed in this holistic perspective, supervisors should seek knowledge about effective instructional delivery systems that incorporate and integrate work related to the various teaching tasks. Successful performance of these teacher tasks would then become more predictable and could guide supervisory assistance and directives.

Conceptualizing Teaching. In the ongoing work of the IEA (International Association for the Evaluation of Educational Achievement) Classroom Environment Study: Teaching for Learning, Robert Burns, Lorin Anderson, and I developed a conceptual framework for analyzing teaching. Our underlying assumption, congruent with that of Dreeben (1973), is that teaching is a job performed in the workplace of the school. Borrowing from the language of job analysis literature, Burns (1984) defined the teacher's job as being composed of functions which, in turn, are defined by related tasks or discrete, organized units of work.

In attempting to organize the diverse tasks of the teacher's job into broader functional domains, Burns' (1984) review of the literature on teacher planning and decision-making was especially helpful. Indeed, we found that the job responsibilities of school teachers could best be characterized in terms of decisions that vary in nature depending upon when the decisions must be made and the situational demands that are placed on teachers at different decision times during the school year. This analysis led us to a conceptualization of teaching that has three major dimensions: the timing of teacher decisions, the structural units about which teachers make decisions, and the types of teacher tasks associated with these decisions. The conceptual framework developed by Burns, Anderson, and myself is presented in Figure 1.

Timing of Decisions. The first dimension, timing of decisions, was based upon Jackson's (1962) distinction between preactive and interactive teaching decisions. *Preactive decisions* are taken while the teacher is outside the classroom (often alone), and they involve planning about what will take place in the classroom during a coming period of time. There are two kinds of preactive decisions, *long-term* and *short-term*, which vary in terms of both specificity of planning and anticipated duration of the implementation of the plans in the classroom setting. *Interactive decisions* are taken while the teacher is in the classroom and involved in the flow of instructional events and interactions with students. These decisions involve on-the-spot judgments about behaviors and activity patterns as the planned lesson progresses.

Figure 1. A Schematic for Conceptualizing Teaching in Terms of Decisions, Structural Units, and Teacher Tasks.

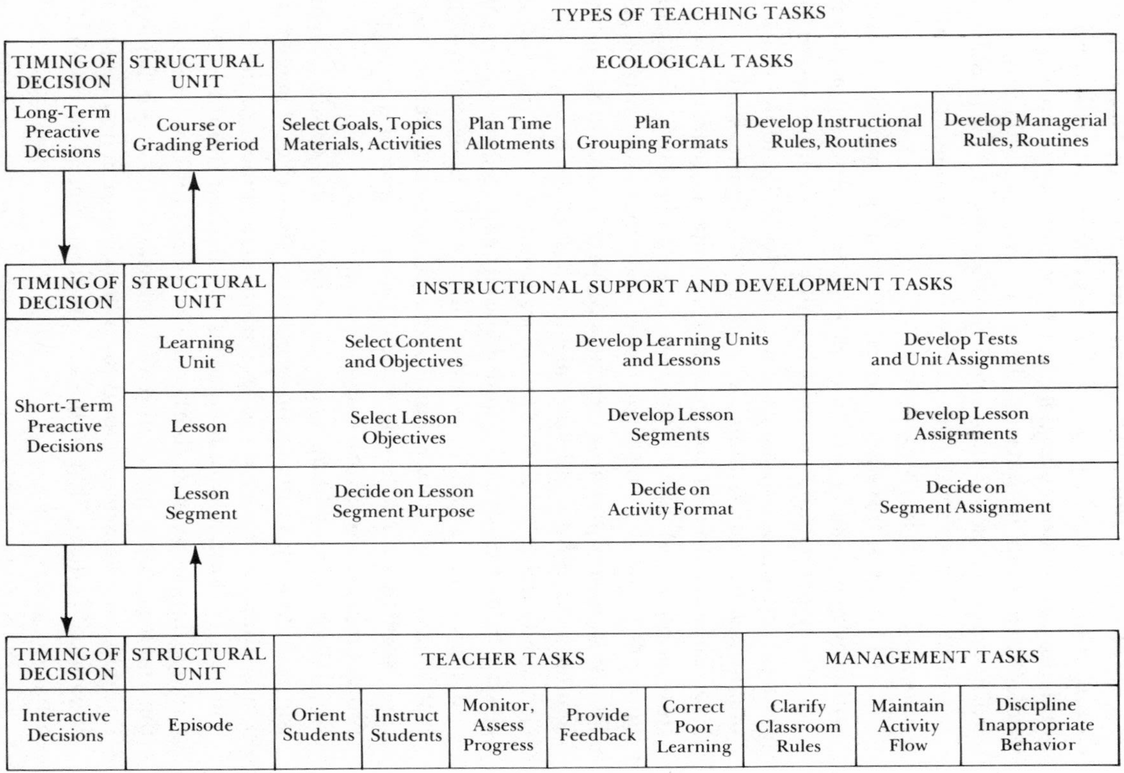

TYPES OF TEACHING TASKS

ECOLOGICAL TASKS

TIMING OF DECISION	STRUCTURAL UNIT					
Long-Term Preactive Decisions	Course or Grading Period	Select Goals, Topics Materials, Activities	Plan Time Allotments	Plan Grouping Formats	Develop Instructional Rules, Routines	Develop Managerial Rules, Routines

INSTRUCTIONAL SUPPORT AND DEVELOPMENT TASKS

TIMING OF DECISION	STRUCTURAL UNIT			
Short-Term Preactive Decisions	Learning Unit	Select Content and Objectives	Develop Learning Units and Lessons	Develop Tests and Unit Assignments
	Lesson	Select Lesson Objectives	Develop Lesson Segments	Develop Lesson Assignments
	Lesson Segment	Decide on Lesson Segment Purpose	Decide on Activity Format	Decide on Segment Assignment

TEACHER TASKS / MANAGEMENT TASKS

TIMING OF DECISION	STRUCTURAL UNIT	Orient Students	Instruct Students	Monitor, Assess Progress	Provide Feedback	Correct Poor Learning	Clarify Classroom Rules	Maintain Activity Flow	Discipline Inappropriate Behavior
Interactive Decisions	Episode								

Structural Units. The second dimension in Figure 1, structural units, are the "things" about which teachers make decisions and, thus, are closely related to the timing dimension. In descending order by temporal boundaries, there are five structural units: course, learning unit, lesson, lesson segment, and episode. Each lower unit is embedded within the next higher unit; for example, lessons are embedded within learning units.

The largest unit, *course*, is the natural temporal boundary within which school curriculum is organized, instructional activities are structured, and student learning is formally assessed. The course consists of *learning units*, the basic building block for organizing the curriculum. In making decisions about learning unit content, activities, and assessment, teachers generally plan for instruction across one or two weeks. Embedded within learning units are *lessons*, the basic planning and structural units of classrooms. In lesson planning, teachers prepare the objectives, activity sequences, and informal assessment to take place typically in one classroom period or day. *Lesson segments*, in turn, provide the activity format or structure and shape the expected roles of teacher and student for a certain number of minutes of lesson time. In mathematics classes, for example, teachers often plan a sequence of three segments for a lesson: review, development of a concept or procedure, and a seatwork assignment.

Embedded within a lesson segment are *episodes*, which consist of bounded interaction or behavior sequences. There may be a large number of such episodes within each segment of the lesson. The concept of behavioral episodes was derived from the work of ecological psychologists (Barker, 1963; Gump, 1964) as representing the smallest meaningful unit of observable classroom behavior. Episodes are characterized both by a behavior or action and by the situational context (that is, the activity structure) within which the behavior occurs.

It is important to note that the meaning of each lower structural unit is defined by the next higher unit in which it is embedded. Thus, the meaning of a behavioral episode depends upon the activity context (segment) in which it occurs. A segment derives its meaning from the nature of the lesson in which it occurs. The meaning of a lesson must be derived from the learning unit of which it is but one component in a planned sequence of instructional activities.

Types of Teacher Tasks. The third dimension shown in Figure 1, types of teacher tasks, provides the means for identifying related units of work (tasks) to be performed in fulfilling the functional responsibilities of the job of school teacher. We identified four major types of teacher tasks, each of which is nested within decisions to be taken at different times during the school year and with regard to different elements (structural units) of the intended instructional content and process.

We labeled the first set of tasks *ecological tasks* since they serve the function of establishing broad curricular, temporal, and social constraints within which classroom instruction will occur. From Burns's (1984) review of ethnographic studies of teachers, we identified five sub-tasks to be performed early in the school year: selection of course goals, topics, materials, and activities; planning of time allotments for the topics; deciding if, when, and how students will be grouped for subject matter areas; development of instructional rules and routines; and development of managerial rules and routines. Each of these sub-tasks requires long-term preactive decisions related to the single structural unit of the course.

The long-term preactive decisions taken as teachers perform ecological tasks provide general guidelines for the subsequent planning for constituent elements of the course. It is important, therefore, to recognize that national, state, and district mandates may remove or constrain the teacher's responsibility for the first two sub-tasks (choosing curriculum content and materials and planning time allotments). Similarly, district or school organizational structures and patterns (for example, class size, student placement procedures, course timetables) may limit the teacher's choice of grouping formats and compel teachers to use particular instructional and managerial rules and procedures.

Given these general guidelines, teachers must perform a number of specific sub-tasks which, together, serve the function of providing the curricular and instructional basis for actual in-class teaching. We have called these *instructional support and development tasks*. Although the performance of each of these sub-tasks requires short-term preactive decisions, there are three different structural units involved: learning units (the constituent elements of the course), lessons (the constituent elements of learning units), and lesson segments (the constituent elements of lessons).

There are three instructional support and development subtasks to be performed for each of the three structural units. Thus, each row in this task domain in Figure 1 focuses attention on a distinct structural category for teacher planning. Each column in the task domain focuses attention on one of three important task elements in teacher planning: curricular goals or content, instructional activities and formats, and student assignments and tests.

Our delineation of instructional support and development tasks reflects the work of adaptive instruction researchers and developers and is congruent with a mastery learning approach to curricular and instructional planning (Anderson and Jones, 1981; Anderson and Block, 1976; Block and Burns, 1976). Mastery learning systems require teachers to attend systematically to each of the short-term preactive tasks shown in Figure 1. For each learning unit, for example, a sequence of lessons must be developed in order to orient students as to the intended objectives, to instruct students with regard to the content, to involve students in activities applying the content, to assess student learning, to provide feedback to students, and to correct student learning errors. An entire lesson might be developed for a single purpose (for example, to correct learning errors), but the important factor is that the lesson's purpose may be understood only in the context of the plans for the unit as a whole. Furthermore, teachers may modify their timing plans for lessons in response to in-class events and student responses (for example, by providing an extra class period for the purpose of instruction or student practice), but they would still be responsible for following the lesson sequence planned for each learning unit.

Teachers' functional responsibilities for implementing their short-term preactive decisions are defined by two interrelated sets of sub-tasks, *teaching tasks* and *management tasks*. Teaching tasks serve the function of involving the students with the planned lesson activities and assignments, and management tasks serve the function of maintaining both the flow of instruction and the involvement and cooperation of students in the planned lesson activities. Both teaching and management tasks require interactive decisions by teachers in response to minute-by-minute student actions and interactions. Both types of sub-tasks are performed with reference to the structural unit of behavioral episodes.

Again, Burns's (1984) literature review served as the basis for identifying sub-tasks required for the accomplishment of in-class teaching and management tasks. In his analysis of a number of large-scale process-product and experimental field studies and of reviews of these studies, Burns found there was strong consensus about a general pattern of effective teaching. This pattern or cluster of teacher behaviors is often referred to as direct instruction, and it consists of five interrelated teaching sub-tasks: orienting students, instructing students, monitoring and assessing the progress of students, providing feedback, and correcting poor learning when it occurs. There is a very close parallel between this cluster of effective teacher in-class tasks, identified from research on teaching, and the effective preactive tasks for planning a sequence of lessons within a learning unit, identified from the work of adaptive instructional developers.

The literature on classroom management helped us identify three sub-tasks, the accomplishment of which assists in providing a classroom atmosphere conducive to effective instruction. The sub-tasks are: clarifying rules and procedures; maintaining the activity flow of lessons and, thus, student involvement; and promptly disciplining inappropriate behavior.

Although there was consensus among reviewers of research on teaching about the sub-tasks necessary for effective teaching, Burns (1984) found that there was much less empirical consistency with regard to particular teacher classroom behaviors that were more or less effective in accomplishing a sub-task. What seemed to be most important was the occurrence of *some* teacher behavior that could accomplish the goal of a sub-task, rather than the occurrence of a particular behavior. For example, teachers should perform the teaching sub-task of providing feedback to students. However, it is not clear whether it is more effective to give praise or criticism in performing this task. We suspect that the effectiveness of a particular task-relevant behavior depends upon the classroom context at that time.

The concept of *functional equivalency*, borrowed from Smith and Geoffrey (1968; cited in Burns, 1984), was useful in understanding that different teacher behaviors may accomplish the same goal, depending on the particular context. Similarly, the same behavior may serve different goals, again depending upon the instructional context in which it occurs.

In summary, then, the job of school teacher carries with it the responsibilities for performing tasks related to four major functional domains: ecological tasks, instructional support and development tasks, teaching tasks, and management tasks. In performing the various sub-tasks appropriate to the four domains, teachers must make decisions that vary in terms of timing (long-term preactive, short-term preactive, and interactive decisions) and in terms of structural referent (course, learning unit, lesson, lesson segment, and episode). Long-term preactive decisions (ecological tasks) influence the short-term preactive decisions (instructional support and development tasks) that in turn influence the performance of classroom teaching and management tasks. In implementing their plans, teachers must make interactive decisions intended to maintain both the flow of planned instructional activities and high student involvement. These classroom experiences provide feedback to teachers about their instructional support and development decisions.

Implications for Proactive Instructional Management. Not only does the conceptualization shown in Figure 1 help to differentiate the teacher tasks appropriate at various times and with regard to various structural units but the schema also helps to illustrate that in-class teacher behaviors cannot be understood or evaluated without knowledge of the broader plans for course, unit, and lesson instruction. More importantly, if teachers have not performed well the preactive tasks of selecting unit goals, developing lessons, designing evaluations, and planning for feedback and correction, there is no reason to expect that the appropriate teaching sub-tasks will be performed in the classroom. As we have seen, it is the planned provision for, and sequence of, in-class teaching tasks that predictably result in effective student learning. On substantive grounds, therefore, the managerial efforts of teacher supervisors should be shifted toward instructional support and development tasks at the unit and lesson levels and away from a concentration on interactive task performance.

Nevertheless, the prevailing model of teacher supervision continues to be based upon supervisors' observations of the performance of teachers relevant to in-class teaching and management tasks. Moreover, the directives and assistance given by supervisors to teachers as a result of their observations tend to be focused on specific *behaviors* rather than on the underlying sub-tasks. This pattern obtains even though there is very contradictory evidence about the effectiveness of competing behaviors in the interactive process of classroom teaching. Further, supervisors' ratings based on classroom observations are notably unreliable (Ryan and Hickcox, 1980). Finally, there is no reason to believe that teacher in-class behaviors should be stable and thus subject to prescription. That is, "good" teachers should adapt their behaviors to student actions and responses as the lesson proceeds.

The traditional pattern of teacher supervision, then, encourages supervisors to be directive about discrete behaviors (hows) rather than about the accomplishment by teachers of a particular sequence of tasks (whats). Teachers should be given autonomy and encouragement to try out various kinds of in-class behaviors in an effort to find preferred ways to accomplish a *prescribed* series of sub-tasks.

Teacher performance in making planning decisions appropriate to instructional support and development tasks should be stable, and there is consistent and clear-cut evidence from analyses of mastery learning implementation that successful performance of these preactive teaching tasks will result in improved student learning (Katims and Jones, 1981; Block and Burns, 1976; Ryan and Schmidt, 1979; Ryan, 1980; Levine and Stark, 1981; Anderson and Jones, 1981). Thus there are empirical as well as substantive grounds for focusing instructional management on preactive teacher tasks.

As Figure 1 shows, a major portion of the functional responsibilities of teachers requires their performance of preactive tasks that cannot be observed and, therefore, evaluated during classroom visits. Of five structural units requiring teacher task performance, only one is directly observable in classroom settings.

Stated differently, the structural units not only define the curricular and instructional boundaries for teacher tasks, but they also serve as units of observation. As such, they are useful concepts to consider, both in designing research on teaching and in planning teacher supervision and evaluation methods and criteria.

The conceptualization of teaching is also useful in proactive planning for instructional management. If the major purpose of teacher supervision is the improvement of instruction, then the supervisor must have knowledge about how teachers may effectively perform important preactive planning tasks. Figure 1 illustrates that teaching cannot continue to be conceived solely as meeting with students, a conception that underlies much of teacher education (Ryan, 1984). In reviewing research on teacher preservice preparation, for example, I found that curricular planning was usually taught with a singular focus on individual classroom lessons, with only superficial treatment given to organizing the curriculum into learning units (Romberg and Price, 1983). Prospective teachers also received little training in developing tests and student assignments relevant to course, unit, and lesson objectives (Ryan and Schmidt, 1979; Turney, 1984). Ongoing teacher supervision and inservice programs must redress these teacher training weaknesses.

Mastery learning approaches to instruction provide a means for redirecting instructional leadership and management toward goal-based preactive teacher tasks, the accomplishment of which, together with the implementation of these plans, results in improved student learning outcomes. The impact of mastery learning systems as documented in this volume, can be traced conceptually to the integrated coordination of teacher efforts relevant to what Talmage and Eash (1979) have described as the key determinants of classroom learning: curriculum (identifying what is to be taught), instructional materials (selecting the media through which curricular intents are to be experienced), and instruction (planning and using teaching-learning transactions to mediate between the materials and the curricular intents).

As noted earlier, mastery learning systems are congruent with our conceptualization of teaching tasks. Use of mastery learning prescribes an instructional delivery system requiring teacher preactive attention to unit goals, to unit-relevant development and organization of lessons, to development of student evaluation techniques appropriate to the unit and lesson goals, and to the design or selection of corrective materials and activities for use with students who have not achieved the unit's goals. Successful performances of preactive tasks have become more predictable through the analysis of proactive efforts to design and implement mastery learning approaches. The implications for supervisory directives and monitoring are obvious.

Adopting a Team Approach to Outcome-Based Instructional Management

In the introduction to this chapter, I stated that middle managers in outcome-based school systems must gain a fundamentally different capacity to organize and manage a mastery-learning instructional delivery system. In my judgment, the public demands for improvement in the quality of education in our schools cannot be met simply by changing the basis of individual teacher evaluation from process ratings to student test performance. Nor can these challenges be met by changing only the directives given to individual teachers, in supervisory processes, from prescriptions about their interactive classroom behaviors to ones about preactive planning. Individual teachers lack the time and the skills needed to accomplish the necessary instructional support and development tasks. They must have organizational assistance, and they must work cooperatively.

My review of teacher inservice programs (Ryan, 1984) revealed that, where individual teachers are seen as having the sole responsibility for improving instruction, little instructional change occurs. I agree with Howey and Vaughan (1983) that instructional managers must share this responsibility with teachers and must provide the necessary support services.

Just as educational administrators must begin to conceive of teaching as more than meeting with students, they must also begin to conceive of their supervisory roles as more than meeting with individual teachers. The introduction of a goal-based instructional management system must be predicated on proactive staff development programs targeted to preactive instructional planning appropriate to a particular school context. Individual teacher supervision should become secondary to the provision of school-wide or district-wide staff development focused on the teacher tasks embedded in a mastery learning instructional system. As the instructional support and development tasks are accomplished in these cooperative activities, teacher supervision could then serve as a complementary activity focused on teacher problems in implementing the planned instructional sequence and activities.

Several of the chapters in this volume provide documentation of the procedures used in coordinating the planning for, and implementation of, mastery-based instructional systems. There exist, in fact, numerous other examples of district-wide instructional organization and management systems informed by knowledge of probable student outcomes. A growing number of school boards in the United States, for example, have begun to assign to central office personnel the tasks of reviewing the research literature on effective schools and effective teaching and of designing instructional systems and compatible staff development programs. Largely through the Network for Outcome-Based Schools, these practitioners and several colleagues in Canada share ideas and experiences in introducing and managing systems of instruction that have a high probability of resulting in improved student learning.

In school districts in which particular instructional systems have been evaluated over time, the use by teachers of the instructional strategy has become quite directive. For example, the Chicago Board of Education now prescribes the use by teachers of mastery-based instructional materials that have been locally prepared and evaluated for the reading program in elementary schools (Katims and Jones, 1981). The Dallas, Texas, Board of Education now prescribes an outcome-based instructional approach and has implemented this new program through staff development workshops for school principals, who then provide staff training to teachers (*Outcomes*, 1983).

Levine and Stark (1981) conducted a comprehensive analysis of the organizational and instructional arrangements that underlie successful implementation of mastery learning approaches with a related emphasis on outcome-based management. Several commonalities in arrangements were found. First, it appears that "district-level initiative and monitoring represent a key element in the reform" of schools (Levine and Stark, 1981, p. 61). Often the initiatives begin with centrally developed objectives and instructional support materials congruent with a mastery-based instructional system consisting of teacher presentation, student practice, formative assessment, and corrective instruction for each curricular unit. Monitoring obviously should include student assessment, which in turn is best addressed by a district-wide management team.

The need for district-level commitment of resources in instructional reform has now been firmly documented (see, for example, Courter and Ward, 1983; Romberg and Price, 1983; Katims and Jones, 1981). The conclusions reached by those who have observed the implementation process are similar. While the greatest value of mastery learning was that it increased teachers' knowledge and skills in lesson development and instructional organization, its greatest liability is the time and effort needed in implementation (Miller and Roney, 1983). Teachers must have information, materials, time, and support, and the provision of these requires district-level cooperation and resource provision.

The training and involvement of principals also appears to be a critical factor in introducing outcome-based approaches to instruction (Cohen and Miller, 1979). In speaking to the primacy of the role of the school principal, Sarason (1971) argued that any proposal for change that is intended to alter the quality of the schooling experience depends primarily on the principal, and there is evidence to support the belief that outstanding leadership on the part of the principal is a prerequisite for unusually effective schools (Levine and Stark, 1981; Phi Delta Kappa, 1980). Nevertheless, the influence of the principal can work to resist the introduction of change or to distort or discredit innovations that are imposed by senior administrators. As Sarason wrote, "One can realign forces of power, change administrative structures, and increase budgets for materials and new personnel, but the intended effects of all these changes will be drastically diluted by principals whose past experiences and training, interacting with certain personality factors, ill prepares them for the role of educational and intellectual leader" (1971, pp. 148-9).

64 Improving Student Achievement Through Mastery Learning

I have already noted that traditional training programs have not prepared principals for the role of instructional manager. Inservice training, therefore, needs to be provided to prepare principals both to assist teachers in adopting a mastery learning instructional approach and to monitor the application and results. Grass roots involvement and inservice training of teachers is also often provided in successful districts, but there continues to be the need for structured administrative support (Levine and Stark, 1981).

In conclusion, outcome-based schools require that administrators gain the capacity to organize and manage an instructional delivery system that, on a priori substantive and empirical grounds, is likely to lead to improved student outcomes. Mastery learning provides such a system. Outcome-based schools also require a shift in managerial decision-making from process events to documented student achievement. Traditional administrative training and practice have been predicated on process conceptions of management and have not prepared administrators to fulfill the responsibilities required of them in outcome-based systems. Although the major key to effective instruction appears to be careful attention to preactive planning for the teaching of units and lessons (instructional support and development tasks), teacher supervision models continue to focus attention almost exclusively on interactive classroom behaviors.

The reforms required in the role of school administrators in outcome-based systems should affect both administrative training programs and organizational structures in school districts. With regard to the latter, a team approach to management would facilitate district and school efforts to become outcome-based through the development and use of a mastery learning system. Staff development programs and district-level initiatives in providing resources for instructional support and development tasks should replace individual teacher supervision as the primary foci of instructional leadership.

References

Anderson, L. W., and Block, J. "Mastery Learning." In D. Treffinger, J. Davis, and R. Ripple (Eds.), *Handbook on Teaching Educational Psychology*. New York: Academic Press, 1976.

Anderson, L. W., and Jones, B. F. "Designing Instructional Strategies Which Facilitate Learning for Mastery." Paper presented at the annual meeting of the American Educational Research Association, Los Angeles, April 1981.

Barker, R. G. (Ed.). *The Stream of Behavior.* New York: Appleton-Century-Crofts, 1963.

Block, J. H., and Burns, R. B. "Mastery Learning." In L. Shulman (Ed.), *Review of Research in Education, 4.* Itasca, Ill.: Peacock, 1976.

Burns, R. B. "The Process and Content of Teaching: A Conceptual Framework." In D. W. Ryan and L. W. Anderson (Eds.), *Rethinking Research on Teaching: Lessons Learned from an International Study,* a special issue of *Evaluation in Education: An International Review Series.* Oxford: Pergamon Press, 1984.

Cohen, E. G., and Miller, R. H. *Increased Accountability and the Organization of Schools.* Palo Alto: Stanford University Institute for Research on Educational Finance and Governance, 1979.

Courter, R. L., and Ward, B. A. "Staff Development for School Improvement." In G. A. Griffin (Ed.), *Staff Development.* Eighty-second yearbook of the National Society for the Study of Education, Part II. Chicago: University of Chicago Press, 1983.

Dornbusch, S. M., and Scott, W. R. *Evaluation and the Exercise of Authority.* San Francisco: Jossey-Bass, 1975.

Dreeben, R. "The School as a Workplace." In R. Travers (Ed.), *Second Handbook of Research on Teaching.* Chicago: Rand McNally, 1973.

Griffin, G. A. "Introduction: The Work of Staff Development." In G. A. Griffin (Ed.), *Staff Development.* Eighty-second yearbook of the National Society for the Study of Education, Part II. Chicago: University of Chicago Press, 1983.

Gump, P. "Environmental Guidance of the Classroom Behavioral System." In B. Biddle and W. Ellena (Eds.), *Contemporary Research on Teacher Effectiveness.* New York: Holt, Rinehart and Winston, 1964.

Howey, K. R., and Vaughan, J. C. "Current Patterns of Staff Development." In G. A. Griffin (Ed.), *Staff Development.* Eighty-second yearbook of the National Society for the Study of Education, Part II. Chicago: University of Chicago Press, 1983.

Jackson, P. W. "The Way Teaching Is." *National Education Association (NEA) Journal,* 1962, *54,* 10–13.

Katims, M., and Jones, B. F. "Chicago Mastery Learning Reading: Mastery Learning Instruction and Assessment in Inner City Schools." Paper presented at the annual meeting of the International Reading Association, New Orleans, May 1981.

Levine, D. U., and Stark, J. *Instructional and Organizational Arrangements and Processes for Improving Academic Achievement at Inner City Elementary Schools.* Kansas City, Mo.: Center for the Study of Metropolitan Problems in Education, University of Missouri, August 1981.

Meyer, J. W., Scott, W. R., and Deal, T. E. "Institutional and Technical Sources of Organizational Structure Explaining the Structure of Educational Organizations." Paper presented to a conference on Human Services Organizations at the Center for Advanced Study in the Behavioral Sciences, Stanford University, 1979.

Miller, D. P., and Roney, G. "Mastery Learning: A Statewide Initiative Implemented Through Local Effort." Paper presented at the annual meeting of the American Educational Research Association, Montreal, April 1983.

Natriello, G., and Dornbusch, S. M. "Pitfalls in the Evaluation of Teachers by Principals." *Administrator's Notebook,* 1980–81, *XXIX,* 1–4.

Outcomes. Quarterly newsletter of the Network for Outcome-Based Schools, San Carlos, Calif., Winter 1983.

Phi Delta Kappa. *Why Do Some Urban Schools Succeed?* Bloomington, Ind.: Phi Delta Kappa, 1980.

Romberg, T. A., and Price, G. G. "Curriculum Implementation and Staff Development as Cultural Change." In G. A. Griffin (Ed.), *Staff Development.* Eighty-second yearbook of the National Society for the Study of Education, Part II. Chicago: University of Chicago Press, 1983.

Ryan, D. W. "The Mastery Learning Strategy for Improving Classroom Teaching." *Teacher Education,* April 1980, pp. 14–22.

Ryan, D. W. "Improving Teaching and Learning: Is Teacher

Evaluation a Red Herring?" *Yellow Paper*, Canadian Society for the Study of Educational Administration, April 1983.

Ryan, D. W. "Improving the Content and Process of Teacher Training and Staff Development." In D. W. Ryan and L. W. Anderson (Eds.), *Rethinking Research on Teaching: Lessons Learned from an International Study*, a special issue of *Evaluation in Education: An International Review Series*. Oxford, England: Pergamon Press, 1984.

Ryan, D. W., and Hickcox, E. S. *Redefining Teacher Evaluation: An Analysis of Policies, Practices, and Teacher Attitudes*. Toronto: OISE Press, 1980.

Ryan, D. W., and Schmidt, M. *Mastery Learning: Theory, Research and Implementation*. Toronto: Ministry of Education, 1979.

Sarason, S. B. *The Culture of the School and the Problem of Change*. Boston: Allyn and Bacon, 1971.

Smith, L., and Geoffrey, W. *The Complexities of an Urban Classroom*. New York: Holt, Rinehart, and Winston, 1968.

Spady, W. G. "Competency Based Education: Maximum Confusion, Minimum Implementation." *The School Administrator*, July–August, 1979, pp. 20–21.

Talmage, H., and Eash, M. J. "Curriculum, Instruction and Materials." In P. L. Peterson and H. J. Walberg (Eds.), *Research on Teaching*. Berkeley, Calif.: McCutchan, 1979.

Turney, C. "Supervision of the Practicum in Teacher Education." In T. Husen and T. N. Postlethwaite (Eds.), *International Encyclopedia of Education*. Oxford, England: Pergamon Press, 1984.

U.S. Commission on Excellence in Education. *A Nation at Risk*. Washington, D.C.: U.S. Government Printing Office, 1983.

Wood, C. J., and Pohland, P. A. "Teacher Evaluation: Organizational Maintenance Versus Stimulation of Improved Teacher Performance." Unpublished manuscript. Department of Educational Administration, College of Education, University of New Mexico, 1979.

4

Making School
Learning Activities
More Playlike

James H. Block

Educators have been beset by a host of problems in recent years. Economic issues aside, no problem has been more persistent than the one of eliciting greater self-disciplined learning from many more students. Parents, the media, and the public alike have pressed for greater student learning and greater student involvement in learning.

Some researchers have responded to this press by encouraging educators to make their school learning activities more worklike. Drawing on what Jackson (1968) has referred to as the "economic" perspective on teaching and Grannis (1967) has called the school as "factory" or "corporation" metaphors, these researchers have encouraged the design of activities that are more tasklike, elicit more time on task, yield better learning products, or link schools closer to the workplace.

I propose, however, to take a different tack. Rather than encouraging educators to make their school learning activities more

Note: I am indebted to Lorin Anderson, Bruce Barnett, Mihaly Csikszentmihalyi, Nancy King, Mark Hartwig, Stanley Nicholson, Ellen Potter, Linda Taylor, and Deborah Stipek fo their critical feedback on this chapter.

worklike, I propose to make them more playlike instead. I realize that in the current no-nonsense and back-to-basics climate, this proposal seems heretical. The playlike school learning activities I have in mind, however, involve challenge, excellence, and responsibility in learning, not coddling, mediocrity, and license. In short, they are not inconsistent with the current educational climate at all.

This chapter consists of two basic parts. First, I shall address the question of *why* school learning activities might be made more playlike. Then I shall move to the question of *how* they can be made more playlike. Here, I shall develop a linkage between the concept of flow and the practice of mastery learning.

Why Make School Learning Activities More Playlike?

Starting with Dewey (1963), progressive educators have long advocated that school-learning activities should be made more playlike. Yet, just as often as the case has been made that play may have important potential consequences for students' learning and development (see, for example, Bettelheim, 1972), the case has been soon forgotten (Glickman, 1981). One culprit for this situation, no doubt, has been a strongly held belief that school is serious business and no place for presumably nonserious matters like play (Donmoyer, 1981). The other culprit has been the lack of supporting data that playlike activities really do promote student development and learning (see Schwartzman, 1978). Those data that do exist, in fact, have been gathered largely from preschool children or from school children engaged in forms of play that appear loosely linked, if not antithetical, to the promotion of learning and development, that is, playground fights and games (Glassner, 1976; Polgar, 1976) and interscholastic athletics (Coleman, 1971).

In the face of these two culprits, why then should I plump once again for the value of playlike school learning activities? My answer is simply, at least one of the culprits, the data, seems finally to be "going straight."

One body of research is beginning to emerge suggesting that students prefer playlike to worklike school learning activities. East Coast (King, 1981) and West Coast (Block, 1981) elementary and junior high students have been interviewed about their perceptions of school learning activities. These interviews suggest that students are quite clear about what is wrong with their assignments, tests, and homework. Such tasks are perceived as being worklike and as fundamentally undermining students' emerging self-social competence and their capacity for self-social determination as well. These activities connote that students are incapable of choosing the right substance or form for their work—it must be chosen for them; they do not know their own productive motives—they must be made to engage in work whether they want to or not; and they cannot set and enforce their own standards of learning excellence—such standards must be set for them. These interviews also indicate that students are quite clear about what can be done to rectify this situation. School learning activities could be designed so that they are perceived as being more playlike, that is, as something students want to do, even though they do not have to, because they are fun. Such playlike activities connote to students that they have some measure of control over their school learning destinies in terms of substances, form, motives, and standards.

A second body of research is also emerging suggesting that most students, not just a few, will be more self-involved with and learn more from playlike than worklike activities. In this research, Nicholls (1983a, 1983b) has distinguished between two sets of motivational conditions that affect students' achievement behavior. One set, task-involvement conditions, is very similar to what students would call playlike conditions in that most students find learning to be voluntary, desirable, and pleasurable. The other set, ego-involvement conditions, is similar to what students would call worklike conditions in that most students perceive learning to be required, resented, and potentially painful. Some of the flavor of each of these conditions, especially the playlike flavor of task-involvement conditions, is apparent to Nicholls: "In task-involvement, learning is more inherently valuable, meaningful, or satisfying, and attention is focussed on the task and the strategies needed to master it rather than on the self. In ego involvement, on the other hand, learning is a means to the end of looking smart or avoiding looking stupid, and attention is focussed on the self" (1983b, p. 214).

Nicholls (1983a) has reviewed the available theoretical and empirical data base on task- and ego-involvement. He has linked his theory of achievement motivation to other well-researched theories of achievement motivation, such as Atkinson's achievement motivation theory, Weiner's attribution theory, Seligman's learned helplessness theory, Bandura's self-efficacy theory, Covington and Berry's self-worth theory, and Maehr's continuing motivation theory. And he has detailed research indicating that task- and ego-involvement conditions may have a differential impact on students' learning and performance and, in particular, their performance attributions, choice of learning tasks, help-seeking behavior, intellectual development, and creative achievements.

On the basis of this massive review effort, Nicholls has concluded that the major classroom task educators face is to create and maintain task-involvement conditions in the classroom and to minimize ego-involvement ones: "If we can sustain task-involvement, students will be more likely to focus their attention on methods of mastering tasks and to gain a sense of competence from gains in mastery. They will find learning meaningful. They will choose tasks of suitable difficulty levels, perform on them effectively, ask for help when they need it, and have a continuing interest in learning" (1983b, pp. 224–225).

How to Make School Work Activities More Playlike

Given that students prefer playlike to worklike school learning activities and that most students are more involved with and learn more from such activities too, how might educators proceed? How can play theory, research, and practice be moved beyond the level of description and toward the level of prescription? In the remainder of this chapter, I shall suggest one avenue my students and I are pursuing.

Flow. We have been considering how to operationalize the *flow* model of Csikszentmihalyi (1975). This model was chosen for several reasons. It is one major paradigm for the study of play as an important context for human experience (see, for example, Cheska, 1981). It conceives of flow activities much as students perceive their play activities, that is, as being ". . . voluntaristic, exciting, personally meaningful" (Csikszentmihalyi in Cheska 1981, p. 22). It proposes that one can convert work-related activities into flow-promoting ones. Finally, it is just beginning to be applied in educational settings (Csikszentmihalyi, 1982; Csikszentmihalyi and Larson, 1978; Larson and Csikszentmihalyi, 1983).

What is flow? Flow is the experiential correlate of participation in activities that motivate competence (Csikszentmihalyi, 1975). Participants enjoy what they are doing and cease "to worry about whether the activity will be productive and whether it will be rewarded." They tend to "concentrate their attention on a limited stimulus field, forget personal problems, lose their sense of time and of themselves, feel competent and in control, and have a sense of harmony and union with their surroundings" (Csikszentmihalyi, 1975, p. 182).

According to the flow model, human beings experience flow only when there is a perceived match between the challenges posed by an activity and the skills that activists possess to meet these challenges. If their skills are greater than the challenges, then the activists will experience boredom. But if the challenges are greater than their skills, then they will experience worry and anxiety.

To facilitate the match between challenges and skills, the flow model contends that an activity must possess two central characteristics. First, it must provide information regarding the actor's ability to meet the activity's challenges. This implies that the activity is one with clear rules of performance whose execution can be evaluated by the actor. Second, the activity must take place in a meaningful context, that is, one where others' concern for performance will lend an element of reality to the activity's challenges.

Out of these two basic characteristics emanate four more specific characteristics of flow activities. One is that the activity must be structured so that it poses a range of challenges and different ranges of challenges. This characteristic allows actors to select and adjust each activity's challenges to match their skills. Another characteristic is that the activity have clear and unambiguous goals so that the actors can focus their attention. Still another is that the activity have clear criteria for its performance. The final one is that the activity provide periodic and concrete enroute feedback about each actor's performance.

Flow and Mastery Learning. While the flow model provides a useful conceptual analogy for making school learning activities more playlike, it is not very useful as a practical model. As noted, Csikszentmihalyi has only recently begun to draw the model's prescriptive implications, and those drawn to date have been somewhat vague. In a recent piece, for example, Csikszentmihalyi (1982) has suggested some things teachers can do to promote students' flow. To wit, he has suggested that students need more appropriate challenges and exposure to teacher role models, that is, to teachers who are doing challenging things and enjoying themselves. But no where in this piece does he indicate precisely how teachers might develop these challenges or acquire these role model characteristics. Since more than one promising idea about educational innovation has lanquished because it could not be successfully taught to teachers (Dunkin and Biddle, 1974), the practical tools necessary to design more flow-like school learning activities must be sought elsewhere.

What is needed to design more flowlike school learning activities, I would argue, seems to be a strategy that is sufficiently elaborate to be taught to classroom teachers and sufficiently comprehensive to develop and orchestrate each of the several aspects of flow. A strategy called mastery learning just may fit this bill.

First, there exists a strong conceptual linkage between the concepts of mastery learning and flow. As noted earlier, flow is the experiential correlate of participation in activities that engage competence motivation—the intrinsic rational motive for humans to interact effectively with the various environments in which they find themselves (White, 1959). These interactions cannot be successfully negotiated unless the interactant has mastered those particular intellectual, emotional, and manual skills each environment demands (Block, 1978).

Second, there are also some strong practical linkages between the notions of mastery learning and flow. In reading Csikszentmihalyi, for example, I was struck by the numerous similarities between the structure of flow activities and the structure of mastery learning activities. Indeed, the flow activity notions of personal challenges and clear goals, of performance rules and criteria, and of performance feedback are also central to mastery learning activities.

Moreover, like flow activities, mastery learning activities occur in a very meaningful context for students—the classroom achievement context.

Third, both Csikszentmihalyi and Nicholls themselves have raised the conceptual possibility that mastery learning ideas might be used to promote flow or flow-like states such as task-involvement. Csikszentmihalyi (Larson and Csikszentmihalyi, 1983) has noted that mastery learning ideas already have seemed to solve many of the long-standing motivational issues in school learning to which his flow model is addressed. But he has been concerned whether the structured nature of mastery learning activities can promote certain learning-to-learn and learning-to-think skills crucial for autonomous, self-directed learning. Research by McCombs (1983) and, particularly, Jones, Amiran, and Katims (1980) indicates that mastery learning activities can develop such skills. Nicholls (1983b) has also acknowledged the potential task-involvement value of mastery learning programs, noting that they give students more autonomy in learning, especially regarding their learning rates. But he has been concerned that mastery programs might turn into ego-involving races where students use their learning rates, not their learning levels, to place themselves relative to other students. This problem need not arise, however, if whole-class or group-based/teacher-paced mastery teaching ideas are used to prevent the need to race in the first place (Block, 1983).

Fourth, many of Csikszentmihalyi's and Nicholls' prescriptions for promoting flow and task-involvement have already been embedded within ongoing, successful mastery learning programs. Cooperative learning ideas, for example, have been used in the Philadelphia Public Schools mastery learning project. Various kinds of student self-scheduling, to take another example, have been implemented in mastery learning projects from public schools in Chicago; Denver; New Canaan, Connecticut; and Johnson City, New York. Let me review the basic concepts and techniques of mastery learning, therefore, and then turn to see precisely how the practice of mastery learning might be used to promote flow.

The Practice of Mastery Learning.* What is mastery learning? It is really two things. First, it is an optimistic theory about

*This section is adapted from Block, 1980.

teaching and learning that asserts that any teacher can help virtually all students to learn excellently, swiftly, and self-confidently (Bloom, 1976; Guskey, 1985). Second, it is an effective set of individualized instructional practices that consistently has helped many students to so learn (Burns, 1979). Some of these practices are of the group-based/teacher-paced variety where students learn cooperatively with their classmates and where teachers control the rate of the instruction (see Block and Anderson, 1975). The remainder are of the individual-based/student-paced variety where students learn independently of their classmates and control the instructional rate (see, Keller and Sherman, 1974).

Both varieties of mastery learning strategies assume that virtually all students can master a great deal of what they are taught in school if their "instruction is approached systematically, if students are helped when and where they have learning difficulties, if they are given sufficient time to achieve mastery, and if there is some clear criterion of what constitutes mastery" (Bloom in Block, 1974, p. 6). Moreover, the group-based/teacher-paced variety can be implemented without major structural changes in classroom organization. It is designed for use in the situation where teachers already possess a curriculum that must be delivered in a fixed period of calendar time, where inordinate amounts of teaching time cannot be spent in testing, and where student learning must be graded. It also relies primarily on human beings for its success rather than on machines and other technological devices.

Let me describe the genotype for most group-based/teacher-paced mastery learning strategies, namely Bloom's (1976) *Learning for Mastery* strategy. This strategy reflects several basic mastery learning concepts and techniques (see Table 1). Moreover, it has proven to be one of the easiest mastery learning strategies to implement.

At the most general level, mastery learning strategies are systematic approaches to instruction. They attempt to build a strong bridge between what the teacher desires to teach and to whom he or she wants to teach. First, the instruction is matched to the course outcomes the teacher seeks, that is, the instruction is outcome-based. Then, the instruction is matched to the learners to be taught, that is, the instruction provides multiple methods for

Table 1. Mastery Learning Concepts and Techniques.

Concepts		Techniques
General		
A. Approach instruction systematically: It should provide a bridge between whom and what you teach		
1. Match instruction to outcomes	→	Base instruction on outcomes
2. Match instruction to learners	→	Provide multiple instructional methods
Specific: Extra-Classroom		
B. Be proactive, not reactive		
1. Clarify outcomes	→	Predefine *mastery* and make it explicit
2. Provide for appropriate help in learning	→	Preplan instruction for mastery
3. Provide for appropriate learning time	→	Preplan instruction for mastery
Specific: Intra-Classroom		
C. Manage learning, not learners		
1. Provide student orientation	→	Orient students to mastery learning
2. Vary how and how long each student is taught, as necessary	→	Use preplanned instruction to teach for mastery
3. Personalize grading	→	Grade for mastery

Source: Block, 1980, p. 68.

each student to attain each of these outcomes. Typically, these methods will build on the teacher's customary pedagogical techniques.

Mastery learning strategies are also proactive approaches to instruction. Much teacher time, effort, and energy are spent outside-of-class in planning for possible inside-of-class learning contingencies. Should these contingencies occur, the teacher is then ready for them and need not manufacture solutions on the spot. Proactive teaching, from a mastery learning perspective, entails several stages. One stage is the definition of the learning outcomes the teacher is seeking. First, the curriculum developer must implicitly define what learning outcomes all students will be expected to achieve and at what levels. Second, the curriculum developer must make these implicit definitions more explicit so they communicate appropriately to the teacher what must be taught and to the students what must be learned.

Both of these steps are accomplished in the process of predefining and preexplicating mastery. The mastery-learning curriculum developer preformulates expected course learning outcomes and constructs a special final or summative, criterion-referenced examination based on these outcomes. Moreover, the practitioner presets some course mastery grading standards on the summative examination indicative either of learning excellence or of excellence in the making.

A second stage in proactive teaching is the provision of appropriate help in learning. Often, student learning problems at a particular time in the classroom instruction stem from unresolved problems from earlier times. So these earlier problems must be identified and corrected as they occur.

This identification and correction is accomplished through the preplanning of classroom instruction. Essentially, the mastery practitioner plans to teach the entire class as if each student could be provided with a tutor. First, the entire course is broken into a number of smaller learning units where each unit is long enough to convey complex information but short enough to allow the close monitoring of each student's learning progress. Second, these units are sequenced hierarchically so that the material taught in each unit is used repeatedly in subsequent units at increasing levels of complexity. Third, a preplan of mastery instruction is formulated for each unit consisting of the *original instruction,* whereby the unit's material will be first taught to the whole class in the teacher's customary style; a *feedback instrument* or formative, criterion-referenced test, whereby each student's learning progress from the original instruction can be described; a *unit mastery standard,* whereby the excellence of each student's learning progress can be judged from formative test results; *correctives,* whereby the material tested by each item on the formative test can be retaught in alternate ways from the original instruction—typically these correctives have included cooperative small-group study sessions, peer tutoring, programmed instruction, supplementary textbooks and workbooks, audio-visual materials, academic games and puzzles, and affective exercises; and *enrichments,* whereby the material tested by each item on the formative test can be studied more deeply (vertical enrichments) or more broadly (horizontal enrichments).

This preplan will allow the mastery practitioner to monitor periodically the quality of the whole-class instruction for each student. By teaching and testing on a unit-by-unit basis, the teacher can tell which students are and which are not progressing excellently from the original instruction. The former students can then engage in enrichments or serve as potential peer tutors. And the latter students can use the correctives to explore alternative ways of learning unmastered material and select those best suited to their particular learning requirements. Then, when they have finished correcting, they can engage in the enrichments too.

A third stage in proactive teaching is the provision of appropriate learning time. Clearly, if each student is to be provided with appropriate help in learning then sufficient time must be found to make use of this help. All students cannot be allowed similar amounts of learning time.

The provision of appropriate learning time for each student is also accomplished through the preplanning of the classroom instruction. In fact, it is the final piece in the preplan. Once a teaching plan has been developed for each learning unit, the mastery practitioner develops a parallel timing plan. Regular class time is set aside for the original instruction and the formative testing on each unit. Some combination of regular class, out-of-class, and out-of-school time is then set aside for correction and enrichment.

Finally, at the most specific level, the intra-classroom level, mastery strategies are *management of learning* approaches to instruction. They propose that inside the classroom "the function of the teacher is to specify what is to be learned, to motivate pupils to learn it, to provide them with instructional materials, to administer these materials at a rate suitable for each pupil, to monitor students' progress, to diagnose difficulties and provide proper remediation for them, to give praise and encouragement for good performance, and to give review and practice that will maintain pupils' learning over long periods of time" (Carroll, 1971, pp. 29–30).

Management of learning, from a mastery learning perspective, requires three basic stages. In the orientation stage, the mastery practitioner indicates in a concrete fashion how and toward what ends students will be taught. Students are first oriented by written, oral, or pictorial means to expected course learning outcomes. Then they are oriented to expected course achievement levels and, especially, course grading policy. They are told, in particular, that they will receive either a grade indicative of excellence (typically an A) or of excellence in the making (typically an I or incomplete)—which one will depend on their actual, not peer-relative, learning accomplishments. Now students are oriented to the mastery learning strategy by which they will learn. They are informed that they will learn on a unit-by-unit basis and that they should learn each unit's material excellently. They are also told they will be provided with all the help they need to master each unit. Specifically, they will be formatively tested at the close of the whole-class instruction for each unit. These tests will be self-scored and ungraded. Then they will be free to choose from a variety of alternative learning procedures, depending on their test results, either to correct their particular misunderstandings or to enrich their current understandings. They can choose to use these procedures alone or cooperatively with their classmates.

In the teaching stage, the mastery practitioner then uses the preplanned learning units to vary, as necessary, how and for how long each student is taught. Each unit is taught in sequence. First, students are oriented in written, oral, or pictorial fashion to the expected unit learning outcomes and unit mastery standards. Special attention is given to the relationship between each unit's outcomes and standards and relevant course and prior units' outcomes and standards. Next, the unit's original instruction is implemented using customary whole-class teaching techniques. When this instruction has been completed, the whole class is administered the unit's formative test. Students complete the test and score their own results. Those students who have and have not achieved the unit mastery standard are identified. The former students are then encouraged to engage in enrichment activities and to volunteer to serve as peer-tutors; the latter students are invited to use the appropriate correctives to complete their unit learning. Finally, the date for the commencement of the whole-class instruction for the next unit is announced, and both sets of students are given responsibility for making use of their chosen learning activities. Depending on the teacher's timing plan, students may discharge their responsibilities during regular class-time or during out-of-class or out-of-school time.

Finally, in the grading stage, the mastery practitioner evaluates students on a personal basis. After the cycle of original instruction, formative testing, and enrichment or correction has been completed for each unit in the sequence, the students are graded for mastery. The preconstructed and prestandardized course-summative examination is administered to the whole class. The test results are scored by the practitioner and grades indicative of excellence (typically A's) are awarded to all students whose test scores are at or above the preset course mastery achievement standard. Those students whose scores are below this standard receive grades indicative of excellence in the making (typically I's). These grades are then entered into a so-called open-record grade reporting system. And steps are taken to help "I" students complete their course learning so that their "I's" can be replaced with "A's".

Challenge, Coordination, and Feedback in Mastery Learning

Let me now elaborate the hypothesis that the practice of mastery learning can promote flow. Specifically, I shall focus on three essential characteristics of flow activities and indicate how mastery learning uses various curriculum, instruction, and evaluation techniques to build these characteristics into student learning activities. Flow activities pose clear personal challenges to potential activists, present particular means to meet these challenges coordinated to the activists' skills, and provide periodic concrete progress feedback.

Challenge. Flow activities are perceived as posing clear personal challenges for potential activists. They pose either a single challenge or a range of challenges wherein activists can test their emerging self and social skills. Activists understand both the goals to be reached in accomplishing each challenge and the goal attainment or performance criteria. And they accept individual responsibility for utilizing their skills to pursue these goals to these criteria.

Mastery learning activities, likewise, pose clear personal challenges for students. The basic challenge is learning for excellence throughout the course, as well as by its end. All students are consistently expected to master certain unit and course learning outcomes to levels of excellence traditionally expected of only the best students. For most students this means that they can no longer passively settle for mediocrity or worse in their learning; they must actively pursue excellence.

There are two basic mechanisms by which this learning for excellence challenge is made clear. First, certain curricular techniques are used to orient students early to overall course mastery learning expectations. They are told they will be expected to achieve certain course learning outcomes to a particular mastery grading standard. And they are told to achieve these outcomes to standard by mastering seriatim the material in each learning unit of the course. Second, additional curriculum and instructional techniques are used to elaborate this inital orientation as the course unfolds. In particular, students are told each unit's mastery learning expectations—both the expected unit learning outcomes and mastery standard. Then they are constantly reminded of these unit mastery expectations as each unit's material is specifically taught, tested, and retaught in alternative fashions to achieve or surpass these expectations.

One basic mechanism, namely, student evaluation, is used to personalize the learning-for-excellence challenge. Specific grading techniques are employed at the course level to alert students that they will earn a grade indicative of excellence or of excellence in the making depending solely on their actual, not peer-relative, learning accomplishments. These techniques create a competence-oriented rather than competition-oriented classroom learning environment in which students must compete against themselves and the material to be learned, not against each other (Block, 1977). Particular testing techniques are then used to reinforce this self-accomplishment theme as the course instruction unfolds. Students are repeatedly tested for self-accomplishments on each learning unit and tested so that they can become self-accomplished. The testing for accomplishments ensures that students are consistently reminded that they are being evaluated on what learning outcomes they, not their peers, have and have not mastered. They are pressed to see themselves as the primary determinant of their learning progress. And the testing to become accomplished ensures that students are constantly reminded that their accomplishments count. The formative tests will always suggest the necessary instructional alternatives students require for excellent progress; they must simply put forth the effort to use them.

Coordination. Besides being challenging, flow activities are also coordinated. They always provide activists with specific means of meeting each activity's particular challenges. Moreover, these means are always calibrated to each activist's special skills.

Mastery learning activities are likewise characterized by challenge-means coordination. Great effort is made to systematize classroom learning activities so that they provide a definite bridge between the course and unit learning outcomes to be mastered and the students who are to master them. This bridge encourages students to try to use their particular skills to learn excellently and to show them that if they try, they can learn excellently too.

Certain mastery learning curricular techniques facilitate students trying to learn for excellence. Essentially, these techniques adjust the size and difficulty of the overall course learning challenge so that students will not perceive it as being overwhelming. They parse the whole course into a number of smaller learning units so that students encounter a series of micro-learning-for-excellence challenges at the unit level enroute to tackling the macro-learning-for-excellence challenge at the course level. Likewise, they sequence these units hierarchically so that students will spiral from easier to more difficult material: they will not face greater learning challenges cold.

Specific instructional techniques also promote students trying to learn for excellence. The preplanned mastery instruction, in particular, encourages students to apply their specific learning skills to meet or surpass each unit's micro-challenges. The original instruction and correctives allow students to test their particular learning skills against teacher-selected unit learning-for-excellence challenges. Depending on their particular intellectual and motivational skills, students can choose to learn excellently from the original instruction alone or from some combination of the original instruction and self-selected correctives. The enrichments allow students to match their particular learning skills against student-selected unit learning-for-excellence challenges. And, as was the case with the correctives, they can tackle each of these challenges as they see fit.

Finally, special evaluation techniques also foster students trying to learn for excellence. Since the essence of these techniques lies in the kind of feedback they provide students about their learning progress and progress feedback is the third essential element of flow activities, let me reserve my discussion of these techniques for just a moment.

Feedback. In addition to being challenging and coordinated, flow activities are characterized by mechanisms that provide periodic concrete feedback to activists regarding their progress in meeting particular challenges. Such feedback allows them to adjust their skills to meet these challenges or these challenges to meet their skills, accordingly.

Mastery learning activities are also characterized by periodic concrete feedback mechanisms. These mechanisms provide the feedback students need to be successful in learning for excellence at either the unit or the course level.

The primary concrete feedback mechanisms in mastery learning are, of course, the unit formative tests. These tests are designed to be informational rather than judgmental in nature, a critical feature of flow-generating feedback devices (Csikszentmihalyi, 1975). Since they are self-scored and ungraded, they allow students to try to learn for excellence without fearing that they will be punished if they fail. Students know their test results will not be made public nor part of their permanent record if their initial attempts at mastery of each unit's material are substandard. Consequently, they can attack each unit's material without worrying about the social or promotional consequences of learning errors. And since the tests are criterion-referenced and prescriptive, they allow students to try to learn for excellence with the knowledge that their tries will count. Students know they will receive detailed diagnostic information regarding what learning outcomes have and have not been mastered in each unit. They also know that even if their results are submastery, their formative test will provide the necessary additional study guidance to make their subsequent learning attempts more successful. In short, students know these formative tests provide them with not only detailed knowledge of their learning progress but guidance as to what they can do to keep that progress at par.

The summative course examination also provides informational, rather than judgmental, feedback within a mastery learning context. True, this examination is typically teacher-scored and graded. But by the time it is given, students have already begun to be socialized as to how their grades are to be interpreted. Students should interpret them as only one more piece of information about their learning progress. This particular piece informs them about their progress in the course as a whole, just as the formative tests gave them information about their progress on each segment of the course. If they have learned excellently on each unit in the course, this grade should be only one more testimony, albeit a public not a private one, to the fact that they are excellent learners. They can take pride in having a mark indicative of excellence entered on their record. Or, if they have not learned excellently on each unit, it should be only one more testimony to the fact that they still have some learning to do. Since the recordkeeping system is open, they can subsequently complete this learning and earn a mark of excellence, too.

It should also be noted that to emphasize the informational meaning of summative test results, many mastery programs go beyond simply reporting a final grade to students. They also enclose a written or pictorial form, adumbrated from their pattern of summative test scores. This form indicates the precise meaning of students grades in terms of what course learning outcomes they have mastered and what ones they have not. The grade, therefore, comes to represent a series of personal accomplishments and nonaccomplishments rather than an isolated letter on a report card.

Conclusion

To summarize, I have asserted that educators currently face pressure to elicit greater self-disciplined learning from more students. While some researchers have suggested relief from this pressure by making school learning activities more worklike, I have suggested that they be made more playlike instead. Not only do students prefer playlike to worklike school learning activities, most may be more involved with and learn better from them, too.

I have also outlined one possible line of attack for making school learning activities more playlike. Specifically, I have proposed that the concept of flow and the practice of mastery learning be used respectively as the conceptual and practical models for the design of such activities. Mastery learning activities should generate flow-like school learning experiences by establishing clear personal challenges, by coordinating students' personal skills to meet these challenges, and by providing periodic concrete feedback about students' challenge progress.

Obviously, the proposed link between the concept of flow and the practice of mastery learning will require rigorous theoretical and empirical testing. As I have noted, Csikszentmihalyi, in particular, has raised questions as to whether the mastery programs he has experienced are not antithetical to flow and to autonomous, self-directed learning. And others (Nancy King, letter to the author, July 1982; Block, 1982) have raised the same question, as the number of programs, especially commercially available ones, that use the rhetoric of mastery learning without delivering its reality grows daily. Clearly, it is time for proponents and opponents to examine the motivational basis for mastery learning; flow production would seem to be a useful starting point for this examination.

Should the linkage be established, however, it will have distinct implications for practice. Since there are already many successful mastery learning programs in use, practitioners can choose to adopt existing mastery learning programs to promote flow. Or, since mastery learning programs consist of a variety of concepts and techniques that are nominally different but functionally similar to many of the concepts and techniques that underlie other instructional programs (see, for example, Gronlund, 1974; Hambleton, 1974; Rosenshine, 1983), the practitioner could use mastery learning ideas to adapt current instructional programs to produce more flow. Curricular, instructional, and evaluation techniques that are functionally similar to the specific mastery techniques that promote flow could be sieved and synthesized into flow-generating strategy. For example, if certain mastery techniques promote flow by challenging students with high expectations for learning, then any of the current techniques that foster similar expectations ought to do likewise. Or, to take another example, if specific mastery learning techniques promote flow by encouraging students to spend time on their school learning activities at high levels of success, then any of the current techniques that affect students' time on task, and especially their academic learning time, ought to promote flow too.

Whether we choose to adopt or to use mastery learning concepts and techniques, we have the starting points for the development of an instructional craft for making school learning activities more flowlike. If my experience with mastery learning is any guide, this craft will allow us to make school learning excellent and involving for many more students without neccessarily using so many of the coercive devices—more required courses and homework, longer school days and perhaps school years, and tighter discipline—that are currently being advocated by public policy makers across the country. In short, mastery learning concepts and techniques may allow us to move *forward* to make qualitative changes in current school learning activities that will yield the same results of the back-to-basics movement, and we will not necessarily have to move *backwards* at all.

Using mastery learning concepts and techniques to make school learning activities more flowlike is, of course, only one important step to making them more playlike. If school educators can make them more flowlike today, however, then perhaps we can make them even more playlike tomorrow. As Csikszentmihalyi (1981) has wisely noted, the concept of flow involves the process of one's involvement in a given reality whereas the larger concept of playfulness involves one's attitude toward reality. I look forward to the day that students, when asked by parents what they did at school today, say they played.

References

Bettelheim, B. "Play and Education." *School Review*, 1972, *81*, 1-13.

Block, J. H. (Ed.). *Schools, Society and Mastery Learning*. New York: Holt, Rinehart and Winston, 1974.

Block, J. H. "Motivation, Evaluation, and Mastery Learning." *UCLA Educator*, Winter, 1977, *19*, (2) 31-36.

Block, J. H. "The 'C' in CBE." *Educational Researcher*, May 1978, 7 (5), 13-16.

Block, J. H. "Promoting Excellence Through Mastery Learning." *Theory into Practice*, 1980, *19*, 66-74.

Block, J. H. "Some Neglected Parameters of the Student Role in Teaching: Play and the Play/Work Dialectic." Report to National Institute of Education, Washington, D.C., 1981.

Block, J. H. "Learning for Excellence." Keynote address at the 3rd annual mastery learning conference, Chicago City Colleges, Chicago, May 1982.

Block, J. H. "Learning Rates and Mastery Learning." *Outcomes*, 1983, *2* (3), 18-25.

Block, J. H., and Anderson, L. *Mastery Learning in Classroom Instruction*. New York: Macmillan, 1975.

Bloom, B. *Human Characteristics and School Learning*. New York: McGraw-Hill, 1976.

Burns, R. "Mastery Learning: Does It Work?" *Educational Leadership*, 1979, *37*, 110-113.

Carroll, J. "Problems of Measurement Related to the Concept of

Learning for Mastery." In J. Block (Ed.), *Mastery Learning: Theory and Practice.* New York: Holt, Rinehart and Winston, 1971.

Cheska, A. (Ed.). *Play as Context.* West Point, N.Y.: Leisure Press, 1981.

Coleman, J. *The Adolescent Society.* New York: Free Press, 1971.

Csikszentmihalyi, M. *Beyond Boredom and Anxiety.* San Francisco: Jossey-Bass, 1975.

Csikszentmihalyi, M. "Some Paradoxes in the Definition of Play." In A. Cheska (Ed.), *Play as Context.* West Point, N.Y.: Leisure Press, 1981.

Csikszentmihalyi, M. "Learning, 'Flow', and Happiness." In R. Gross (Ed.), *Invitation to Lifelong Learning.* Chicago: Follett, 1982.

Csikszentmihalyi, M., and Larson, R. "Intrinsic Rewards in School Crime." *Crime and Delinquency,* 1978, *24,* 322-338.

Dewey, J. *Experience and Education.* New York: Collier, 1963.

Donmoyer, R. "The Politics of Play: Ideological and Organizational Constraints on the Inclusion of Play Experiences in School Curricula." *Journal of Research and Development in Education,* 1981, *14,* 11-18.

Dunkin, M., and Biddle, B. *The Study of Teaching.* New York: Holt, Rinehart and Winston, 1974.

Glassner, B. "Kid Society." *Urban Education,* 1976, *11,* 5-22.

Glickman, C. "Play and the School Curriculum: The Historical Context." *Journal of Research and Development in Education,* 1981, *14,* 1-10.

Grannis, J. "The School as a Model of Society." *Harvard Graduate School of Education Bulletin,* 1967, *21,* 15-27.

Gronlund, N. *Individualizing Classroom Instruction.* New York: Macmillan, 1974.

Guskey, T. *Implementing Mastery Learning.* Belmont, Calif.: Wadsworth, 1985.

Hambleton, R. K. "Testing and Decision-making Procedures for Selected Individualized Instructional Programs." *Review of Educational Research,* 1974, *44,* 371-400.

Jackson, P. *Life in Classrooms.* New York: Holt, Rinehart, and Winston, 1968.

Jones, B., Amiran, M., and Katims, M. "Embedding Structural Information and Strategy Instructions in Reading and Writing Instructional Texts: Two Models of Development." Paper presented at the NIE/LRDC conference on thinking and learning skills, University of Pittsburgh, Pittsburgh, Pennsylvania, October 1980.

Keller, F., and Sherman, J. *The Keller Plan Handbook.* Menlo Park, Calif.: W. A. Benjamin, 1974.

King, N. "Play in the Workplace: Ethnographic Perspectives on the Construction of Curriculum in Classrooms." Paper presented at the annual meeting of the American Educational Research Association, Los Angeles, April 1981.

Larson, R., and Csikszentmihalyi, M. "The Praxis of Autonomous Learning." Unpublished manuscript, University of Chicago, 1983.

McCombs, B. "Motivational Skills Training: Helping Students Adapt by Taking Personal Responsibility and Positive Self-control." Paper presented at the annual meeting of the American Educational Research Association, Montreal, April 1983.

Nicholls, J. "Conceptions of Ability and Achievement Motivation." In R. Ames and C. Ames, (Eds.), *Research on Motivation in Education: Student Motivation.* New York: Academic Press, 1983a.

Nicholls, J. "Conceptions of Ability and Achievement Motivation: A Theory and Its Implications for Education." In S. Paris, G. Olson, and H. Stevenson, (Eds.), *Learning and Motivation in the Classroom.* Hillsdale, N.J.: Erlbaum, 1983b.

Polgar, S. "The Social Context of Games: Or When is Play Not Play?" *Sociology of Education,* 1976, *49,* 265–271.

Rosenshine, B. "Master Teachers and Master Developers." Unpublished manuscript, University of Illinois at Champaign-Urbana, 1983.

Schwartzman, H. *Transformations: The Anthropology of Children's Play.* New York: Plenum, 1978.

White, R. W. "Motivation Reconsidered: The Concept of Competence." *Psychological Review,* 1959, *66,* 297–333.

5

❧ ❧

Guidelines for Instruction-Enriched Mastery Learning to Improve Comprehension

Beau Fly Jones
Lawrence B. Friedman
Margaret Tinzmann
Beverly E. Cox

In this chapter it is argued that mastery learning philosophy and principles as stated by early proponents do not provide adequate guidelines for developing and implementing effective day-to-day instruction and assessment. Accordingly, it is argued that while mastery learning philosophy defines the sequence of instruction and testing, it is not in itself a full-scale model of instruction; rather it is scaffolding for instruction and assessment.

Note: An earlier version of this chapter was developed through a contract with the U.S. Army Research Institute for the Behavioral and Social Sciences, Alexandria, Virginia. It was entitled "Mastery Learning as Scaffolding for Instruction and Assessment," and appeared in a 1984 Army Research Institute technical report entitled *Content-Driven Comprehension Instruction and Assessment: A Model for Army Training Literature.* The authors are indebted to the U.S. Army Research Institute and to the

This chapter seeks to provide a model of comprehension instruction to fit within a mastery learning framework and guidelines for implementation. We aim, therefore, not to replace mastery learning but to refine it. We have termed our model *enriched mastery learning* because it combines the early philosophy and principles with recent advances in research on instruction, management, and schooling. Following is an outline of the chapter. (Readers should note that the main and subheadings in this outline (and in the chapter) correspond to sections with identical titles and numbers in the Mastery Learning Checklist at the end of this chapter. In addition, a glossary is appended.)

A.   Mastery Learning
    1.   Early Philosophy and Principles
    2.   Program Effects
    3.   Mastery Learning versus Other Types of Instruction
    4.   Problems of Development and Implementation
B.   Principle 1: Objectives
    1.   Components
    2.   Type of Content
    3.   Sequencing Objectives and Instruction
    4.   Hierarchical Sequencing
    5.   Horizontal Sequencing
    6.   Vertical Sequencing
C.   Principle 2: Learning Unit Organization and Delivery
    1.   Four-Phase Cycle
    2.   Entry Information
    3.   Teach
    4.   Test
    5.   Reteach

subcontracting agency, InterAmerica Research Associates, Inc., of Rosslyn, Virginia, for their encouragement, editorial advice, and financial support. The authors are also indebted to the Chicago Public Schools for supporting the research and development for the Chicago Mastery Learning Reading Program.

The authors wish to thank the Chicago Public Schools and the Center for the Study of Reading for their support in developing the materials described in this chapter and for permission to use graphics from the CIRCA teacher's manual for United States history, grades 7 and 8.

      6.   Retest

      7.   Extend

      8.   Answer Keys

      9.   Glossary

D. Principle 3: Testing and Curriculum Alignment

      1.   Relationship between Objectives and Tests

      2.   Number of Criterion-Referenced Tests

      3.   Parallel Structure

      4.   Summative Test

      5.   Test Validation

      6.   Program Evaluation

E. Principle 4: Recordkeeping—Unit by Unit

      1.   Classroom Progress Charts

      2.   School Progress Charts

F.   Mastery Learning Checklist

Mastery Learning

Early Philosophy and Principles

Mastery learning (ML) is both a philosophy and a set of instructional principles conceptualized largely by Carroll (1977), Bloom (1968, 1976), and Block and Anderson (1975; see also, Anderson and Block, 1976). This philosophy assumes that learning is a function of time and learning opportunities, rather than innate abilities that cannot be altered. Students fail, according to this philosophy, not because they are inherently lacking in ability but, rather, because of the way instruction and testing are organized. Especially critical are the limitations of time and learning opportunities in traditional models. ML assumes that all, or almost all, students can learn, given appropriate teaching/learning conditions. ML also posits that the instructional process can be altered to facilitate optimum learning. The principles below encapsulate what we think are the key conditions that define mastery learning.

- Principle 1   Organize the overall curriculum in terms of stated *objectives.*
- Principle 2   Organize and deliver day-to-day instruction in

terms of learning units that have a four-phase cycle of *instruction and assessment* within each unit:

Teach according to the stated objectives. Instruction should provide learning cues and explanations, student participation, guided practice and reinforcement, and independent practice.

Test to diagnose learning errors.

Reteach nonmastery students to correct learning errors; simultaneously extend the learning of mastery students within the domain of the unit objective or by entry into the next learning unit. The reteach phase provides both additional time and instruction to those who need it. Additionally, it is critical that the reteach phase involves a teaching/learning strategy that is different from the one used in the teach stage. *Retest* nonmastery students to document their progress.

- Principle 3   Align testing and curriculum. All tests should be *criterion referenced.* Criterion-referenced tests compare the students' performance to a specific criterion established by the teacher or the school system in advance of the instruction. Criterion-referenced tests should be parallel in structure to each other and closely aligned with the objectives and instruction. Altogether, there are four types of criterion-referenced tests.

Pretests may be given before a learning unit to determine if the student is ready for the unit.

Formative tests are used in the test phase to diagnose learning errors within a given unit of instruction. Students who attain mastery on the formative test typically do not need to take the retest.

Retests are used at the end of the unit to document the mastery of nonmastery students. Many people refer to these incorrectly as formative tests, or sometimes summative tests.

Summative tests are used to assess learning after a series of learning units.

- Principle 4   Keep records unit by unit. Student progress and certification should be based on mastery of specific learning units. There should not be a large gap between the level of the instruction and the level of student achievement.

Program Effects

Mastery learning philosophy generated numerous large-scale implementations involving whole schools and school systems as well as small-scale implementations involving individual classrooms throughout the 1970s. Hyman and Cohen (1979) estimated that there were over 3,000 implementations. Moreover, it is evident that ML can have a major impact on achievement in reading (Bailey and Guest, 1980; Barber, 1979; Block and Burns, 1977; Champlin and Mamary, 1982; Katims and Jones, 1981, 1983; Reed, 1982; Reid, 1978), math (Rubin and Spady, 1984), and content area subjects (Burns, 1979; Càponigri, 1981; Hyman and Cohen, 1979). ML has also been successful at all age levels from kindergarten through graduate school and for all types of learners but especially low achieving students (Abrams, 1979; Katims and Jones, 1983; Levine and Stark, 1980).

Mastery Learning versus Other Types of Instruction

Mastery learning clearly has a substantial capability to impact on achievement; however, it is evident from presentations at professional organizations and observations from literally hundreds of schools and school systems that there are major confusions about the differences between ML and other instruction. While the focus of this chapter is on development and implementation of ML, it is important to consider first how ML is different from traditional instruction and from programs that are only mastery based or objectives based. Then we will identify the various development and implementation issues this chapter seeks to address.

Mastery Learning versus Traditional Instruction. Mastery learning and traditional instruction differ in the following ways: Traditional instruction assumes that students the same age differ greatly in innate ability. Traditional instruction also assumes that ability is essentially fixed and therefore relatively unaffected by changes or differences in the way that we organize instruction and testing. Accordingly, in such models instruction is based directly on "covering" the content in textbook materials; it is not tied to specific objectives. All students are given a fixed amount of time and the same content, regardless of differences in prior knowledge.

Instruction in such models typically consists of working through the chapters of a basal or content text. Such models have only a two-phase cycle of instruction and assessment: teach and test. Tests are norm referenced; that is, they compare student performances to each other using a normal curve.

These features of traditional instruction generate failure for many reasons, according to ML proponents. Since instruction is typically not tied to specific learning objectives established by the school or a teacher, instruction may be what Spady (1982) refers to as "vague referenced." This means that teachers may not be held accountable for student progress. Equally important, because traditional instruction assumes that performance is a function of innate ability, little effort is spent to reteach students who fail. Therefore, learning errors accumulate so that students who fail become increasingly less able to compete with those who pass. Norm-referenced tests define half of the students as average or below average each time students are tested—no matter how well they performed. Such procedures generate low expectations and poor self-images, which in turn generate additional failure.

In contrast, there is much in mastery learning to generate success. Linking the instruction to stated objectives makes it clear to educators, parents, and students what is expected; therefore, no one is assessed on his or her ability to guess what is to be tested. Specifying the objectives also makes it possible to hold teachers and students accountable for what is learned. However, the heart of mastery learning is the diagnosis and correction of errors in the test and reteach phases. These procedures prevent learning errors from accumulating. Such procedures also give slow learners more time and learning opportunities. And since performance is measured against a specific criterion, there is no limit on the number of students who master the objectives. In fact, the ML teacher is obligated to teach to the objectives and to help all students attain mastery. Under these conditions, learning expectations are consistently high, and the students develop a positive self-image, which is critical to their success.

Mastery Learning versus Mastery-Based Programs. ML programs should be sharply distinguished from mastery-based programs. The latter typically require teachers to link instruction to specific objectives and to use criterion-referenced tests, which is why such programs are referred to as mastery programs. However, in contrast to mastery learning, mastery-based programs involve only two- or three-phase cycles of instruction and assessment (teach/test or pretest/teach/posttest). That is, mastery-based programs leave out the heart of ML philosophy: the correction of errors and retesting in the reteach and retest phases of ML.

Another confusion regarding mastery learning is the relationship between mastery learning and continuous progress. Mastery learning is a set of principles regarding the organization of instruction and testing. Continuous progress is essentially a management system. Continuous progress models emphasize the focus on time as a variable in learning established by Carroll. Under continuous progress, instruction is individualized or organized in terms of multiple groupings in a given classroom or area so that individuals may work at their own speed on objectives that are appropriate for their level of achievement. Thus, under continuous progress, a teacher may be teaching a broad range of objectives within a single classroom at any given time. Theoretically, continuous progress programs may be mastery based, involving only the teach and test phases. Alternatively, such programs may be combined with the four-phase cycle of mastery learning. In practice, however, most continuous progress programs are only mastery based and almost never involve whole-group instruction in which an entire class is given the same unit of instruction.

Problems of Development and Implementation

As powerful and exciting as mastery learning is, early proponents generally assumed that most of the content of instruction would have to come from existing texts. This assumption was fraught with problems, both for mastery learning and for continuous progress models. Bloom, for example, developed what he called a *Table of Specifications* for teachers to use to align the existing texts to the objectives and to sequence instruction to proceed from the factual to the conceptual. Unfortunately, many teachers found it to be a difficult and time-consuming procedure. Moreover, the table was only for content courses, not math and reading. Additionally, early works by Block and Anderson (1975; Anderson and Block, 1976) also assumed that ML day-to-day instruction would be based on existing texts. Therefore, they sought to provide rationales and guidelines for teaching to specific objectives, developing formative and summative tests, setting levels of mastery and scoring, developing corrective instruction, and managing whole-group instruction and did not address the issue of instruction within units. Thus, for various reasons early mastery learning proponents did not provide usable guidelines for developing the substance of day-to-day instruction.

Nor is there a model for day-to-day instruction in the literature on continuous progress or other mastery-based programs. Most of these programs seem to be derived from the Wisconsin Design, Individually Guided Education (IGE), developed by Klausmeier and colleagues (Klausmeier, Rossmiller, and Saily, 1977). It is clear from descriptions of this model that at best it is scaffolding for instruction and not a model for the substance or sequence of day-to-day instruction. "The Design provides both a structure for an elementary school reading program and the means for carrying out reading instruction according to the instructional programming model. The structure is provided by an outline of reading skills and associated behavioral objectives; the means for implementing the instructional programming model are provided by assessment and resource materials and by recordkeeping procedures" (Klausmeier and others, 1971, p. 53). The instructional programming model is a six-step procedure that progresses from specifying the objectives, to instruction using existing materials, to assessment, to either recycling students through the instructional materials (for those who did not attain mastery) or moving on to the next unit of instruction (for those who did master the objective). Thus, in this model, instruction consists largely of guiding the students through a progression of skills. Moreover, there is very little data that this model works in large-scale implementations, according to Jenkins and Pany (1980).

In spite of the absence of data and detailed information on the substance of instruction and management, schools across the nation implemented various ML and continuous progress programs (mostly the latter), largely in response to national thrusts toward accountability, equality of educational opportunity, and objectives-based instruction. By the late 1970s, there were many successes. (See the November 1979 issue of *Educational Leadership*, emphasizing mastery learning.)

At the same time, there have been many problems of development and implementation arising from the focus on skills instruction. First, the focus on skills as objectives fragments instruction. That is, instruction in all too many ML and continuous progress programs consists largely of processing students through a continuum of discrete skills and subskills. Frequently, the skills are defined very narrowly, and one set of skills may be defined in isolation from the others. These practices not only preclude sustained instruction but also foster an excessive emphasis on testing and recordkeeping. Second, such curricula often over-emphasize low order objectives rather than high order thinking and comprehension objectives. Third, many ML and continuous progress programs use Bloom's taxonomy (Bloom and others, 1956) to sequence skills instruction so that students proceed in a "lock-step" order through each level of the taxonomy. Thus, instruction in each skill becomes an end in itself. We believe that this is a grievous misinterpretation of Bloom. A careful reading of the taxonomy suggests that the various levels of thinking skills are means to increasingly higher comprehension of a given text. It makes no sense, for example, to progress from literal to inferential comprehension to interpretation when the text (for example, a history text) begins with information that is complex, implicit, and perhaps poorly organized. Instead, we believe that any given level of thinking and study skills should be selected on the basis of the task and text.

Other problems of instruction arise from the reliance on the use of existing texts. First, mastery learning proponents assumed that it would be possible to align the existing materials to the stated objectives and locally developed tests. Unfortunately, these materials were inherently inconsistent with objectives-based curricula. Since these materials were not objectives based, they did not have the components, sequencing, or definition needed to attain curriculum alignment. Especially critical was the lack of a second test to assess performance after reteaching, the lack of summative tests, the lack of corrective materials, the lack of alternate teaching/learning strategies, and the lack of enrichment materials.

Second, when Bloom, Klausmeier, and other mastery theorists designed their models, they assumed that the existing materials provided effective instruction and that only low order skills such as decoding and rote memory were needed for literal comprehension and recall. All of the available evidence from text analysis (Anderson, Osborn, and Tierney, 1984; Anderson and Armbruster, 1984; Bruce, 1981; Osborn, Jones, and Stein, in press) indicates that both basals and content texts are frequently poorly written. Thus, what appears to be a factual, organized text in reality requires various inferential, translation, and analytical thinking skills for comprehension and recall.

Moreover, the instructional components of basals and content texts often provide little more than what Durkin (1978-79) calls *comprehension assessment*, that is, a heavy focus on asking "5W & How" questions and numerous drill and practice exercises. In a landmark study of twenty-four classrooms, Durkin found that out of 5,000 minutes of observation, only twenty-eight minutes were devoted to *comprehension instruction*, that is, helping students to understand the meaning of what was read. In a later study, Durkin (1983) traced these practices to the structure and organization of the existing materials. Durkin argues that most texts only mention concepts and skills, rather than providing sustained instruction. Since 70 to 90 percent of classroom instruction is based on textual materials, ML and continuous progress based largely or entirely on existing texts are likely to offer a relatively low quality of instruction. The lack of systematic, direct instruction is particularly problematic for low achieving students (Jones, Amiran, and Katims, 1984; Rosenshine, 1983).

Another set of problems relates to the *management of instruction*. Outstanding is the problem of readiness. A fundamental precept of ML and continuous progress is that students should only be assigned to units of instruction for which they have the cognitive prerequisites. The problem is that Americans currently tend to value heterogeneous groupings, and there are inherent tensions between this value, efforts to deliver instruction according to the readiness of each student, and effective management of time. Both whole-group instruction and continuous progress models manifest these tensions.

In whole-group instruction models, the problem is most pronounced in elementary schools. How can we provide units of instruction that are appropriate for each individual, yet provide whole-group instruction? The problem is not so serious in high school where courses containing many levels of instruction are modularized so that students can be placed at any given level using pretests of some kind. In elementary schools, this is often not possible. Bloom and others have argued that such strategies as giving enrichment activities to high achieving students and peer tutoring are effective methods of addressing individual needs. Other options for mastery students (while nonmastery students receive remediation) are doing homework and engaging in silent reading, according to Anderson and Block (1976).

Continuous progress addresses the readiness problem by constant regrouping of students within a given classroom, so that the instruction they receive is appropriate for their level of achievement. This may create a critical management problem because a single teacher must design, deliver, and record many levels of instruction simultaneously. While computerized instruction may relieve much of the burden of management, as it did in the Wisconsin Design, all too often teachers do not have access to computers and are unable or unwilling to take on such tasks. Moreover, these demands on the teachers' time generate low time on task and real difficulty in setting goals, pacing, monitoring, and recording student progress.

Examples of problems with continuous progress can be seen with Chicago's mislabeled "continuous progress/mastery learning" program (CP/ML), now abandoned in favor of Chicago Mastery Learning Reading (CMLR), which is a mastery learning program. Under CP/ML, Chicago had 1,400 objectives for kindergarten through grade eight. The teacher was held accountable for testing 271 objectives, so that a considerable amount of time was spent testing. For example, objectives for skills such as syllabication, guide words, and alphabetization were taught and graded separately, as were objectives for character traits and techniques of characterization. Thus, instruction focused on discrete subskills, and excessive amounts of time were spent testing. Although actually there were many high order objectives for comprehension, literature, and study skills, instruction for the objectives was not sequenced or prioritized. Consequently, teachers often selected the low order objectives to teach first because they were easier to teach and master. Thus, many students were certified to pass from one level to the next on the basis of their mastery of low order objectives.

Additionally, CP/ML was not, in fact, a mastery learning program in practice. Although inservice and descriptive CP/ML materials provided a model of instruction that closely approximated the Wisconsin Design, in reality existing materials did not contain pretests, alternate strategies, retests, enrichment activities, or summative tests, not to mention the fact that the stated objectives, tests, and existing materials were not aligned. Moreover, teachers were most unwilling and probably unable to take on the task of adapting or aligning the texts. Consequently, publishers produced numerous "correlational charts." However, these were typically neither research based nor field tested, so that in practice they were not well aligned. Worse still, they were not effective. That is, when teachers used the correlated materials, students often did not pass the tests.

Finally, there were serious outcries against the management problems arising from teaching three to seven different levels of instruction within a classroom of thirty-two children. Not only was there low time on task, but teachers were unable to pace and monitor progress effectively. These problems were compounded in the many classrooms containing low achieving students, students with special educational needs, and transfer students. In effect, many students made very little progress under CP/ML, and the system was officially rejected in favor of a graded organizational structure and the use of instructional materials devised specifically to teach mastery learning, namely, Chicago Mastery Learning Reading. Table 1 shows the major differences between CP/ML and CMLR.

Chicago's problems with CP/ML are hardly unique. The Army's official program of instruction is called Instructional Systems Design (ISD). ISD is essentially a CP/ML model of management and instruction with a heavy emphasis on the use of existing materials. Recent analyses of ISD (Cavert and others, 1980; Kern and

Table 1. CP/ML and CMLR in Chicago.

	CP/ML	CMLR
Assumptions About Differences in Achievement	Differences in achievement are due largely to differences in learning rate, which are essentially innate; i.e., some students are slower and need more time than others.	Differences in achievement are due to differences in learning rate (which can and should be increased for low achieving students) and to specific teaching/learning conditions.
Assumptions About Failure	Failure is due mainly to the fixed time constraints imposed by graded organizational structures and accreditation requirements. CP/ML eliminates failure and retention by removing constraints imposed by graded systems and accreditation requirements.	Failure is due mainly to learning errors, inadequate learning time during instruction, and testing procedures. CMLR assumes that all students can master the objectives given additional time, learning opportunities, correction of learning errors, goal setting, and pacing.
School Organization	Ungraded	Graded
Typical Classroom Organization	Individualized, small groups and/or large groups within a single classroom or area	1–2 small groups and/or whole group within a single classroom
Program Focus	*Curriculum* Hierarchical sequencing of the objectives and tests within and between levels of the curriculum *Instruction* Limited focus on the development of instructional strategies	*Curriculum* Hierarchical sequencing of the objectives and tests within and between levels of the curriculum *Instruction* Hierarchical sequencing of content and skills *within each learning unit*
Cycle of Instruction and Assessment	Usually only one set of tests for a teach/test cycle of instruction May have two sets with one specified for use as a pretest	Must have two sets of tests for teach-test-reteach-retest model May have three sets of tests for pretest-teach-test-reteach/extend-retest model
Management	Objective by objective	Unit by unit

others, 1976) suggest that the curriculum and instructional materials suffer from all the same problems of instruction that characterize CP/ML in school settings. And clearly there is considerable dissatisfaction with the model (Brandon, 1984). Equally important, we hear about and observe many of the same problems as those in Chicago with other continuous progress models.

We believe that these problems occurred because ML philosophy emerged in the late 1960s when research in classroom instruction was only just beginning. Thus, while mastery learning did indeed provide a needed set of assumptions and principles about how to organize the sequence of instruction and testing, early ML proponents did not specify clearly how to provide high quality instruction and effective classroom management. Since these early statements of ML, there has been a virtual revolution about content-area teaching (Herber, 1978), comprehension instruction (Pearson and Johnson, 1978; Tierney and Pearson, 1981), learning strategies (O'Neil, 1978; Weinstein and Mayer, 1983; Wittrock, 1984), concept development (Markle and Tiemann, 1969), metacognition (Brown, Campione, and Day, 1982), and effective classroom teaching (Rosenshine, 1983). The reader is also referred to several secondary analyses, specifically, Anderson and Jones (1981), who define instructional strategies to teach three types of objectives, and Bloom (1984), who defines how the variables associated with one-to-one tutoring may be coupled with mastery learning principles and whole-group instruction to yield achievement gains that approximate those attained by one-to-one tutoring.

Since many of the management issues delineated here have been addressed by Jones and Spady in Chapter Two and by Jones (1982), the remainder of this chapter focuses on the issue of developing high quality instruction. More specifically, the chapter seeks to develop what we call *instruction-enriched mastery learning*, a model of comprehension instruction within a mastery learning framework. The model contains the basic principles of mastery learning refurbished by recent advances in research in textual materials, knowledge acquisition, learning, instructional strategies, and curriculum development. Thus, this chapter synthesizes research on comprehension instruction with research on mastery learning.

Principle 1: Objectives

Recent research has contributed greatly to our knowledge of how to write and organize objectives. Interestingly, research funded by the military constitutes a major part of this new literature. Specifically, the military is far ahead of others in its breakdown of objectives into parts and differentiation of various types of objectives in terms of their content. The military also excels in its application of task analysis to sequence objectives hierarchically and in its attention to the specification of prerequisite skills objectives. At the same time, the definition of objectives is critical, and, as indicated earlier, there are some serious problems regarding the organization and development of objectives. This section will cover both the new research and observations based on materials in use in military and school settings.

Components of Objectives

According to many school programs and the system of instruction used in the military, ISD objectives are to be stated in two parts. First, the objective should specify the *conditions:* available equipment, materials, access to textbooks or notes, and so forth. Second, in a brief general statement, the objective should specify the *standard* or goal(s) to be achieved, giving all of the criteria that will be used to judge the achievement of the goal. For example, suppose the goal is to administer emergency medical care for burns: the conditions specify the type of field location, the type of burns, available medical equipment, and the condition of the casualty. The standards state the time constraints within which the actions (goal) must be achieved and the specific outcomes expected: to determine the severity of the burns, to place a sterile dressing over each burn, and to administer a medicine. Specifying these measures clearly is important information for the learner and the teacher.

Problem. The failure to specify the level of learning or the test format for the written component of a test is a major problem in mastery learning programs. Bloom and others (1956) have specified various levels of learning and thinking. While one may disagree with the definition of each level given within each of the various taxonomies of levels of objectives, there clearly is a difference between requiring literal comprehension of a given text or demonstration and requiring inference, transfer, or reasoning. Moreover, objective tests, such as multiple choice, provide all or most of the answer and therefore involve only recognition or inference rather than free recall (recall without prompts). Consider, for example, comparing two characters in a novel or a chemistry procedure involving numerous, complicated steps. The level of learning would vary greatly depending on whether or not the text gave the answer explicitly. Yet, objectives often exclude reference to the level of the response.

Solution. State at the outset as part of the objective the level of learning as literal, inferential, or interpretive (Herber, 1978) and the test format, such as completion, multiple choice, matching (Mager, 1975). Also, Ellis, Wulfeck, and Fredericks (1979) have a most useful definition of the two levels of instruction that are used in most military settings, which have applications for school settings: *recall* and *use*. Recall objectives focus on learning information. They usually involve such verbs as *name, state,* or *list* (from memory), *recall, remember, relate, recognize, explain,* or *describe* (from memory). Use objectives require using the information in some way. Typically, use objectives involve action verbs such as *apply, classify, analyze, evaluate, solve, operate, repair, calculate, troubleshoot,* and so on. Ellis, Wulfeck, and Fredericks also distinguish sharply between objectives that are unaided and those allowing aids of some sort (for example, given the steps of a procedure, apply the procedure to . . .). These distinctions are directly relevant to developing school objectives; that is, what they call use is parallel to applications in Bloom's taxonomy.

Type of Content

Ellis, Wulfeck, and Fredericks (1979) and others (Anderson and Jones, 1981; Reigeluth and Merrill, 1982) have argued that objectives should be classified according to their content. While all three classification schemes presented by the various authors cited above have merit, the one developed by Ellis and his colleagues shows each definition most clearly and succinctly (see Table 2). The table is largely self-explanatory, and their manual provides numerous examples and practice exercises and is well worth reading for military and school staff. Anderson and Jones's material is also useful because it contains step-by-step instructional strategies for teaching information, procedures, concepts, and information objectives.

Four points about Table 2 are noteworthy. First, note that it defines five different types of content objectives: facts (information), categories (concepts), procedures, rules, and principles.

Second, Ellis, Wulfeck, and Fredericks earlier had used the term *concept* as one type of objective. They changed this term to the word *category* because, according to them, concept has too many meanings and is confusing. We must agree. Moreover, after examining Army materials, we could find very little that resembled a concept in the traditional sense. However, concept or some equivalent term is needed to teach such content terms as *charter, rebellion,* and *revolution* from social studies texts or such terms as *respiratory system* or *fungus* that appear in science texts.

Third, a close examination of Army and school materials reveals a learning outcome that is *not* specified as a type of objective by Ellis and colleagues, by Reigeluth and Merrill, or by Anderson and Jones: *comparative objectives.* That is, many objectives in school and military settings require the student to learn about two or more of something: for example, two or more procedures, (such as techniques for crossing a river or conditions before and after X). It is crucial to specify when objectives involve making comparisons because students need explicit instruction in developing compare/contrast skills. That is, the instruction should work to make students aware of the similarities and differences. Consider two techniques for creating X compound in a chemistry laboratory. The student must be able to specify how the techniques are similar and how they are different.

Finally, Ellis, Wulfeck, and Fredericks do not distinguish different types of procedures. Anderson and Jones (1981) argue that *procedural objectives* are either linear, in which case a sequence of activities is performed in a certain order regardless of the outcome, or branching, which requires making decisions at certain steps,

Table 2. Classification of Objectives.

	Fact	Category	Procedure	Rule	Principle
Remember	Recall or recognize names, parts, dates, places, vocabulary definitions, and so on.	Remember the characteristics of each category and the guidelines for classification.	Remember the steps of the procedure.	Remember the formula or the steps of the rule.	Remember the cause and effect relationships or the statement of the principle.
Use Unaided		Classify or categorize objects, events, ideas, according to their characteristics, with no memory aid.	Apply the steps of the procedure in a single situation or on a single piece of equipment, with no memory aid.	Apply the formula or rule to a variety of problems or situations, with no memory aid.	Use the principle to interpret or predict why or how things happened or will happen, with no memory aid.
Use Aided		Given category characteristics and guidelines, categorize objects, events, ideas, according to characteristics.	Given steps of the procedure, apply the procedure in a single situation, or on a single piece of equipment.	Given the formula or rule steps, apply the formula or rule to a variety of problems or situations.	Given a statement of the principle, interpret or predict why or how things happened or will happen.

Source: Ellis, Wulfeck, and Fredericks, 1979, p. 35.

depending on the outcome of the previous steps. Examples of linear procedures are dissecting a frog, putting on a protective mask, or assembling and mixing ingredients for experiment X. Examples of branching procedures are finding the main idea, developing a computer program, or loading explosive rounds in hot tubes.

Sequencing Objectives and Instruction

Once the type of objective is established, it is necessary to establish the order or sequence of the objectives and instructional strategies for each objective. Altogether, there are three types of sequencing. *Hierarchical sequencing* refers to the order of objectives and instruction for large units of instruction over a series of related courses, modules, grades, or levels. *Horizontal sequencing* refers to the order of objectives and instruction within a given instructional unit consisting of daily lessons, a formative test, correctives, enrichment activities, and a retest. *Vertical sequencing* refers to the order of objectives and instruction within a given lesson.

Hierarchical Sequencing

A major principle that is used to organize instruction over a series of related courses, modules, grades, or levels is the concept of *spiraling*. Using this concept, the designer or developer begins with the lowest (most simple, most subordinate) concepts in a complex concept hierarchy. Then, in the next level the simplest concepts are reviewed and expanded, and new concepts within the same concept hierarchy are introduced. In a strand on geography, for example, units in lower grades may teach about familiar bodies of water, such as lake and river, while units in higher grades focus on objectives involving more unfamiliar bodies of water, such as tributary or strait. This type of sequencing is widely used for organizing the objectives and sequence of instruction for content courses.

Problem. This type of instruction can become very fragmented when poorly implemented. In one school system, for example, we found elementary students in grade five who did not know what a lake was. Careful analysis of classroom practices revealed that instruction for subordinate concepts related to the superordinate concept, bodies of water, was distributed over several grade units without effective linkages to each other or to the superordinate concept. This happened in large part because the review and compare/contrast analysis that constitutes the heart of spiraling was not built into the objectives and instruction. In effect, there was no procedure to link new concepts to existing ones, nor was there systematic analysis to establish similarities and differences among related concepts. As a result, students we interviewed were confused about both the superordinate concept (bodies of water) as well as subordinate concepts.

Solutions. Both Bloom (1984) and Reigeluth and Darwazeh (1982) have developed systematic methods for spiraling content. However, both methods are quite complex and require intensive training. If this cannot be attained, we recommend simply to include a thorough review of previously learned concepts—not only as part of the content of the course but also as part of the glossaries. Also, make sure that students systematically compare/contrast related terms. Procedures for doing this have been developed in the *Vocabulary Learning Strategies* strand of *Chicago Mastery Learning Reading* for grades five, six, seven, and eight in units on Categorizing (Board of Education of the City of Chicago, 1983).

Task analysis is a second principle that is used to organize the order of instruction. Typically, task analysis is used to sequence skills courses. The Army has developed an excellent procedure (Extended Task Analysis Procedure) to analyze the prerequisite skills and levels of objectives (Reigeluth and Merrill, 1982). This procedure, referred to as ETAP, provides step-by-step guidelines for figuring out terminal and enabling objectives and their relationships. ETAP is used for sequencing whole courses and skill levels (that is, the overall curriculum). ETAP is excellent reading for anyone interested in task analysis; even though it has a military content, it has important parallels for developing objectives and instruction for school settings. ETAP may also be adapted for use in developing content curricula.

Horizontal Sequencing

As stated earlier, horizontal sequencing refers to the sequence of instruction from lesson to lesson within a single unit. Horizontal sequencing is critical because the principles that drive it determine much of the scope and sequence of the course of instruction and also the capability of the instruction to develop both knowledge and skills. The most prevalent model for sequencing across lessons assumes that skills instruction should be sequenced from easy to difficult. This model argues that content and instruction should progress from simple/concrete/familiar/explicit/short to information and instruction that is increasingly complex/abstract/unfamiliar/inexplicit/long (Stoll, 1981).

Problem 1. The primary problems in horizontal sequencing are identified in Section A of this chapter, namely, the fragmentation of instruction that occurs when instruction of each discrete skill is seen as an end in itself and the focus on low order objectives. These problems are critical because the objectives define the sequence of instruction. In fact, if the movement toward ML and mastery-based instruction fails or becomes a passing fad, poorly sequenced skills instruction may be a major cause.

Solutions for Content Courses. We argue here that skills instruction for any given unit or course, or module and lessons within a unit, should be fundamentally content driven in two ways. First, the curriculum developer/teacher should identify the key ideas and concepts to be learned for a given segment of content. Second, the nature of that content should determine the sequence of the skills instruction. The concept of content-driven comprehension instruction emerged initially from the project, Collaboration to Improve Reading in the Content Area (CIRCA). The collaborating partners are the Chicago Public Schools and the Center for the Study of Reading at the University of Illinois at Urbana. The project seeks to develop U.S. history materials for grades seven and eight. In this project, the scope and sequence contain both content and skills objectives. However, the content objectives are determined first; then skills are selected based on the complexity of the content and the text structures involved. To elaborate, the writers begin a given unit of instruction by reviewing six or seven U.S. history texts and a summary text developed to determine the vocabulary and key ideas. These content "bullets" are then distributed over the number of lessons to be taught within the unit. If the texts discuss the interaction of two groups, for example, the Indians and Europeans, then the instruction must guide the students in compare/contrast and causal analyses, even though this is the first unit of instruction for the course. Thus, the instructional strategies and skills instruction are derived entirely to help the students understand the meaning of the text.

We call this type of instruction *content-driven comprehension instruction*, and skills instruction is always a means to comprehending the content. Moreover, in this type of instruction, a level of thinking skill is selected according to the content, not its location in Bloom's taxonomy or any other taxonomy. Consequently, if the beginning concepts in a course required inference and extrapolation, those skills should either be modeled or taught explicitly as a means to learning the content.

Does this principle mean that we abandon altogether earlier notions of sequencing instruction? No, it does not. It means that of the various skills that may be selected to teach a given segment of content, we should try to sequence the instruction for each skill from easy to difficult and to distribute skills instruction so that the student has time to assimilate a complex skill before being introduced to another. These concepts incorporate various strands of research in sequencing skills instruction (Stoll, 1981) as well as arguments that instruction should progress from teacher-directed to student-directed (Jones, 1980; Pearson and Gallagher, 1983). That is, every time a skill is introduced, instruction is teacher directed. As instruction progresses, the student takes increasing responsibility for applying it. (For further elaboration, see Jones and others, 1984, chap. 3.)

Solutions for Skills Courses. If the course in question is fundamentally a skills course, the curriculum developer/teacher can proceed along similar lines of reasoning. That is, the first step is to select the stories, genres, texts to be taught. Then, instruction is sequenced accordingly. Thus, reading may be conceptualized as a content area subject; only in this instance, since there is no established body of content to be learned, as in a science course, the developer is free to select the stories/poems/genre, to progress from easy to difficult along with the skills instruction. Additionally, for pure skills instruction that does not involve reading prose (for example, dictionary skills), the developer/teacher may cluster related objectives to teach a process or concept.

Examples of these solutions may be found in Chicago Mastery Learning Reading. For example, we clustered all of the grades five and six dictionary skills into a single, cohesive unit that was oriented to teaching the students each of the (initially) separate objectives as part of the *process* of reading a dictionary. Similarly, the two objectives on character traits were collapsed into one unit teaching a series of related concepts. These clustering procedures not only unified what would otherwise have been fragmented day-to-day instruction but also reduced the total number of units that were taught and tested from 271 objectives and tests to 150 objectives and tests. Thus, there are only twelve units in grades seven and eight and fourteen in grades five and six. This type of sequencing contrasts sharply with most mastery learning programs.

Solutions for Both Content and Skills Courses. Require publishers, subcontractors, consultants, and content experts, especially, to prioritize the information (content) to be learned and the instruction. Content may be prioritized by providing good reviews, summaries, outlines, and concept maps as advance or postreading organizers. Additionally, key ideas and vocabulary may be highlighted in various ways, such as boldfacing. Instruction may be prioritized by identifying key objectives, allotting greater amounts of time to high order objectives, and constructing test items to reflect the specified priorities. The emphasis on high order objectives is particularly important. Teach content and vocabulary as concepts. Teach skills as thinking processes and procedures.

Problem 2. Another reason why curriculum designers and developers do not specify high order objectives, such as analysis and reasoning, or high order concepts relates to their beliefs about the students. Unfortunately, many designers and developers and many school staffs believe that low achieving students are unable to attain high order objectives, or that high order thinking is not essential as long as the student demonstrates that he or she "knows the facts" or "does the job."

Recent developments in research suggest that these assumptions are not well founded. There is increasing evidence from reading research and learning strategy research that low achieving students are low achievers primarily because of limitations in prior knowledge (see Anderson, Spiro, and Montague, 1977) and the failure to develop effective reading and learning strategies (Levin, 1976; Rohwer, 1971). The same body of research indicates that low achieving students can indeed perform at markedly higher levels, which are equal to or approach levels of high achieving students, if they are trained to use appropriate strategies (Meyer, Brandt, and Bluth, 1980; Wittrock, 1984; Jones and others, 1984). Moreover, there has been a virtual revolution in the development of effective instructional strategies for learning from text (Bloom, 1984; Brown, Campione, and Day, 1980; Singer and Donlan, 1982; Sternberg, 1984; Tierney and Pearson, 1981). We also have available highly effective methods to teach procedures and rules, concepts, facts, and principles (see Anderson and Jones, 1981, summary). And we have already stated the argument that the learner should be taught higher order thinking skills as a means of comprehending the text and the information needed to do the job.

Vertical Sequencing

Recall that vertical sequencing refers to the order of instruction within a given lesson. There is a great deal of research on reading in the content area (Herber, 1978; Stauffer, 1975), on learning strategies (Anderson, 1980), and on schema theory (Anderson, Spiro, and Montague, 1977) that suggests the best learning occurs in three phases. In the phase before reading, students may review their prior knowledge so that they can link the new information to what they already know. They may also learn unfamiliar vocabulary at this time. Additionally, they may make predictions about the content, using the title, headings, subheadings, and graphics; or they may ask themselves questions to establish a purpose in reading. In the second phase of reading, the ideal student seeks to confirm the predictions, answer the questions, and monitor comprehension (that is, continually refine hypotheses about meaning, resolve contradictions, infer word meanings, and so on). After reading, the student seeks to correct predictions, identify or fill in gaps of information, organize any notes, and perform other activities to construct meaning from text.

Problem. There is nothing in mastery learning theory as stated by the early proponents to address these issues, except the critical notion that the learner should be ready for the instruction. Nowhere are there concepts or guidelines in mastery literature indicating to curriculum developers in the schools, military, or publishing companies how to develop instruction that deals with these stages of learning. This is one reason why we have argued that, powerful as ML is, it is primarily a scaffolding for instruction. New statements of ML should make provisions for this gap. In a large sense, a major purpose in developing our Army manual was to address that gap.

Solution. Conceptualize day-to-day instruction as occurring in three stages: *readiness instruction* to activate prior knowledge, preteach new vocabulary, and establish a purpose in reading; *comprehension instruction* to help students understand what they read and construct meaning from text; and *response instruction* to guide students in responding to questions about the content, summarizing the lesson, comparing and contrasting material, analyzing cause and effect, and so on. Jones and others (1984) have developed detailed definitions of each type of instruction as well as extensive guidelines regarding how to develop it. Figure 1 was developed for the CIRCA project. It illustrates all of the principles we have discussed regarding horizontal and vertical sequencing. Exhibit 1 illustrates how this two-dimensional sequencing is expressed in a lesson overview of the CIRCA project. The bullets for the political essay drive the instruction for that day. That is, the homework and activities are means of learning the content reflected in the bullets. Note also that the three phases of instruction are incorporated into this lesson. The previous day's homework requires the students to complete a chart. This activity provides readiness instruction. Activity A asks the students to analyze a cartoon. Note that the cartoon and the skills instruction for it are means to learning the content. Activity B provides response instruction. It asks the students to summarize what they have learned. The summary involves integrating information from the chart and from the cartoon. Again, notice that summarizing is used as a means of obtaining a high level understanding of the content.

Figure 1. Horizontal and Vertical Sequencing.

Horizontal Sequencing →

Lessons	1	2	3	4	5
Content	–gist of content Segment 1	–gist of content Segment 2	–gist of content Segment 3	–gist of content Segment 4	–gist of content Segment 5
Readiness Instruction	–question analysis –teacher directed –step-by-step prompt	–guided practice –content specific prompt	–independent practice –general prompt	–student directed –no prompt	
Comprehension Instruction	no new skills instruction →	no new skills instruction →	–new skill –teacher directed –step-by-step prompt	–independent practice –general prompt	–student directed –no prompt
Response Instruction	no new skills instruction →	no new skills instruction →			–summarization strategies –teacher directed –step-by-step prompt

content: simple ← content → complex

Vertical Sequencing ↕

Note: In content-driven instruction, *all* of the instruction for each lesson is devised to teach the content of that lesson.

Source: Board of Education of the City of Chicago, 1984. Reprinted with permission.

Exhibit 1. Example of Objectives Containing Both Content
and Learning Strategy Components.

Lesson 5 Overview

Content from the Political Essay, Part 2 (for Lessons 4 and 5)

England's monarchs become displeased with the way the colonies are run
and change some of them into royal colonies.

Royal control pushes the colonies toward a uniformity they do not want.

Attempts to unify the colonies lead to tension.

Instructional Information

The Summary Text contains a large number of cartoons which restate,
summarize, and/or enrich the information in the chapters. This lesson
begins with instruction on cartoon analysis. The students are taught to use
four questions to analyze a cartoon.

Activities

**Homework Corrections — Completing the Chain of Events Chart on
Political Tension between England and its Colonies** [5 min.]

The teacher directs the discussion and correction of the chain of events
chart. The students will use this information when they write a summary
of the Political Essay, Part 2 in Activity B.

**Activity A — Using a Cartoon to Understand the Political Interaction of
England and its Colonies** [15 min.]

This activity has two parts. The first is a teacher-directed explanation and
discussion of the reference box for Cartoon Analysis. In the second, the
teacher directs the students' analysis of a cartoon, which restates information on the colonial response to attempts to unify the colonies.

Reference Box: Cartoon Analysis (TM**, SN**)

**Activity B — Summarizing the Political Interaction of England and its
Colonies** [20 min.]

The students independently write a summary of the growing tension
between England and its colonies. The teacher directs a discussion of these
summaries.

Source: Board of Education of the City of Chicago, 1983. Reprinted
with permission.

Principle 2: Learning Unit Organization and Delivery

Four-Phase Cycle. To recall, according to Bloom (1968,
1976), ML instruction should be organized in terms of learning

units, each of which has four phases: teach, test, reteach/extend, retest. For the teach phase, Bloom emphasized these principles: teach to the objective; provide instruction only when the learner has the prerequisite entry knowledge and skills; sequence instruction within each learning unit to progress from factual to conceptual; and during instruction provide various opportunities to learn with frequent learning cues, feedback, and positive reinforcement. The reteach phase should employ a different teaching/learning strategy than the strategy or strategies used in the teach phase. The extension phase should truly extend the learner's skill and knowledge.

How are all of these instructional variables organized into a single unit using concepts of horizontal and vertical sequencing? The purpose of this section is to explain how these concepts define the sequence of instructional activities that may be used to organize all instructional materials. It is important to note that the format recommended here represents a synthesis of what the best ML programs typically offer for each learning unit. Some instructional materials, especially those written most recently, already contain many, if not most, of these elements. Thus, this section seeks to build on and systemize well-developed formats that already exist. The term *unit format* is used here to refer broadly to all of the various elements of instruction and assessment for the four-phase cycle for each learning unit.

Entry Information. Each lesson should begin by specifying the following information to the instructor and the student:

1. *Audience or user.* Each lesson should begin by identifying the audience or user.
2. *Unit objectives written for the learner.* Objectives should be written (not given orally) in easy-to-understand language. They should inform the learner of the content to be learned, as well as the conditions (time constraints, available materials, where appropriate), and standards (mastery criteria) for the tests at the outset of each lesson. Accordingly, the learners can orient themselves to appropriate study procedures from the beginning of learning and also establish a purpose for learning. The objective or overview should also identify the strategy to be used to teach/learn content.

3. *Lesson objectives.* The content, the strategy or skill identified to learn the content, and the sequence of instruction need to be specified.
4. *Materials required.* All equipment, including instructional materials, such as teacher manuals and field manuals, and other materials, such as pencils, compasses, needs to be listed.
5. *References.* Source materials that are not needed in the lesson but that may be used as additional source materials should be identified.
6. *Learning time.* A range of time that will accommodate faster and slower learners (for example, twenty-five to sixty minutes) should be stated.
7. *Prerequisites.* It is a waste of time, materials, and human resources to enter learners into a program for which they lack the prerequisite vocabulary, factual knowledge, and skills. This includes not only baseline skills but also reading level and prerequisite courses, where appropriate. It is also helpful to state *none* where there are no prerequisites. At the same time, there are numerous ways to provide prerequisite skills instruction either before entering a course or within a course: students go to a resource center before taking the unit; the instructor or curriculum materials provide prerequisite skills and content reviews and instruction; the instructor groups students within the classroom according to their readiness before a unit; and instruction is individualized so that each student progresses through a series of sequenced objectives tailored to his or her state of readiness.

Teach. Much has been said about the need for developing instruction that is not fragmented. What does this mean? Basically, it means that instruction about a topic should be sustained rather than "mentioned." The outline that follows integrates much of mastery learning theory and the theory of Hunter (1971), as well as instructional strategies developed by Anderson and Jones (1981) and reading in the content area specialists such as Herber (1978).

Overview. This includes the content to be learned and separately, when appropriate, the strategy or skill used to learn the content. It is extremely important, especially for informational and conceptual or category objectives, to be very clear about the content to be learned. Very often teachers and curriculum developers do not really know what information and ideas they want the students to learn until after they have taught or developed a unit. The content to be learned should be clear from the outset, and it should be used to drive instruction.

Readiness activities. These refer to efforts on the part of the teacher to motivate students to learn; to make clear the range of applications and practical uses of the instruction; to link the new information to prior knowledge to activate prior learning; to preteach difficult vocabulary; and to establish a purpose in reading. Of these functions, perhaps the most important is linking the new information to prior knowledge. A lesson on identifying friendly and threat vehicles, for example, might begin with a question asking the learners to recall what information and strategies they used to identify opposing sides in popular movies showing warfare in space. Another example would be to begin a lesson on the national debt with discussion of the factors involved when one person owes money to someone or to a bank. Other readiness strategies that are useful to activate prior knowledge include making predictions about the text (Stauffer, 1975), asking questions (Singer and Bean, 1983), or responding to declarative statements about the text (Herber, 1978).

Regarding vocabulary instruction, there are two types of vocabulary terms in any course. On the one hand, there are *technical terms* that are difficult to pronounce or difficult to learn and that may have no intrinsic meaning. Terms such as lensatic compass have intrinsic meaning because the words lens and compass are familiar. However, the word *Bezel* in Bezel ring may as well be nonsense syllables or a foreign language term since Bezel has no intrinsic meaning, or the term luminous may have intrinsic meaning but the learner may not know it. This makes the term itself and the link to its meaning difficult to remember. Pronouncing, preteaching, and where possible, providing a mnemonic, for such terms becomes critical. This applies also for abbreviations and acronyms that are new or seldom used. The CIRCA project has developed a special type of organized glossary, called a Glossary

Matrix, for teaching large groups of related words and relating them to what has been previously taught (see Jones and others, 1984).

On the other hand, there are what may be referred to as *nontechnical terms.* These are words that are uncommon for learners with a low vocabulary (for example, designated, deviation, accumulate) but are not content related. That is, they are basically function words and may appear in various content texts.

Caution: Preteaching vocabulary should be limited to key terms. If there are too many, the learner will be overwhelmed. Field testing should establish guidelines regarding number. Conservative estimates suggest that if the learners have to deal with more than five or six undefined, unfamiliar terms on a page, they are likely to be working at frustration level. The number can be considerably greater when definitions or context clues are provided in the text.

Instructional input. This is the basic instruction regarding the facts, rules, procedures, concepts or categories, and principles to be learned. Our fundamental thesis here is that elements of a given segment of content should be taught as concepts. This involves first identifying the various elements as key facts, ideas, or generalizations; principles or rules; procedures; categories; graphics; vocabulary terms; and so forth. Then for each element, there should be a definition or statement with the critical features clearly identified and labeled, if possible, followed by examples and nonexamples and applications when appropriate, and, finally, opportunities for comprehension monitoring. This is not to suggest that instruction should proceed in a fragmented way from element to element. To the contrary, a key function of the instructional input is to integrate the elements and to show explicitly the relationships between the parts. Additionally, Jones and others (1984) have described procedures for developing instructional input by using a concept called *frames.* Frames are questions or categories that identify the key information in a text. They often parallel the author's outline.

Examples and nonexamples. It is crucial to provide at least two examples or applications, either verbally or pictorially, where possible, for all elements of the content taught as concept. This is because examples and nonexamples establish the boundaries for a given concept. Moreover, many concepts are inherently abstract, complex, or "fuzzy." In such instances, examples may be the only means of really understanding the concepts. Obviously, sometimes this is not possible where events are unique. Similarly, nonexamples and incorrect applications are useful, provided they do not take too much instruction. However, it is often difficult to provide nonexamples, especially for history courses, which focus on unique events, and for procedures.

Explanation. An explanation of each example and nonexample should be provided. Often students do not know what they are to notice about an example. The text or teacher should explain how the example illustrates the point. In graphics, focus devices such as arrows may be used to highlight the key information.

Comprehension monitoring. These may be requests to paraphrase or summarize, add extra examples, explain why new examples given by the teacher or another student are correct, make predictions, or form hypotheses. They may also involve opportunities for students to ask questions.

Learning cues. These are hints, warnings, notes, or cautions regarding variations, errors, or problems.

Explicit learning strategy instruction. This means giving students step-by-step information regarding vocabulary learning strategies, text learning strategies, and metacognitive learning strategies. Strategies should be selected according to their appropriateness for learning the content. Thus, strategies are conceptualized as a means to learning a given content, not as ends in themselves. Also, note-taking, as a key learning strategy, should reflect the text structure.

Guided practice. This means monitoring student practice to see that all students understand the instructions and vocabulary as well as the content and strategies to be learned. Most good mastery learning instructors will stop the entire group from working to give additional instruction if more than a handful of students ask questions, seem puzzled about their assignment, or are making errors.

Independent practice. Independent practice is for reinforcement of what has *already* been learned. Students should *never* be given independent practice unless it has been ascertained through guided practice that they are able to do the work with confidence and fairly good accuracy. Moreover, independent practice should at some point involve the format to be used on the test. That is, if the test involves multiple choice, the independent practice format should somewhere invoke practice in a multiple choice format.

Correction of errors and positive reinforcement. The whole purpose of practice is to obtain feedback about one's performance. Also, recognition of correct answers may be highly motivating and rewarding for many students. And above all, the correction process should emphasize *why* a given answer is correct or incorrect.

Test. The test and the retest should be parallel in all of the dimensions given in the next section on assessment. Correct answers for the test should be given as soon as possible—again, with explanations as to exactly what was correct or incorrect about the answer. This is usually done in class through class discussion.

Reteach. The reteach phase is for nonmastery learners. Minimally, it should include a review of basic terms, content, and practical advice; a different teaching/learning strategy; and extra practice that builds up to the level and format of the retest. The different teaching/learning strategy may vary media selection, type of reasoning, and learning strategy. Methods of varying teach and reteach instructional strategies are given as an appendix to the checklist at the end of the chapter (see Appendix A).

Retest. The retest is for nonmastery learners only. The retest should be identical in structure to the test.

Extend. This phase is only for mastery learners. It is to coincide with the reteach and retest phases for the nonmastery learners. Mastery learners should either be advanced to the next unit of instruction, participate in an extension activity provided in the unit, or engage in peer tutoring nonmastery students. They may also engage in inferential reading; that is, reading at a higher level within the domain of the objective. The purpose of inferential reading is to give the interested learner an opportunity for somewhat more advanced work that does not involve preteaching vocabulary. This allows the learner to use his or her existing knowledge to work toward becoming an independent learner. While few learners may take this option, it is a means of identifying quicker learners and accelerating the pace of their instruction.

Answer Keys. All units should have written answer keys for all written practice problems. Where objective answers are not possible, guidelines for correct answers should be given.

Glossary. Every unit should list technical terms, acronyms, abbreviations, and key nontechnical vocabulary that is at a high readability level. Most glossaries are organized alphabetically. If this is the case, it is useful to have the students categorize and sort related words (for example, cluster all terms describing bodies of water). If the glossaries are teacher-made or developed locally, they should be organized, that is, related terms should be grouped together.

Principle 3: Testing and Curriculum Alignment

There are three different types of tests that are used in an ML program. First, ML programs must have the two sets of criterion-referenced tests (CRTs) that are used as the tests and retests for each learning unit. The first test is called a *formative test;* the second is called the *retest.* Second, an ML program may have *pretests* to establish which learners may bypass a given instructional unit. Pretests should be parallel in test content and format to the CRTs and to the test and retest phases. Third, there may be a *summative test.* A summative test is a test that is given for several purposes: to assess for long term memory of behavior(s) required by the objective; to integrate information, concepts, or principles across a series of learning units; and to give students quarter or semester grades for the course or course certification. Summative test items consist largely of selected items from CRTs administered previously as tests and retests. Summative tests may also have items seeking to assess for integration. Moreover, the type of content, test format, scoring procedures, test conditions, and available time should be made explicit to the learner for all tests well in advance of each test in an ML program.

Six issues are important to the development of tests in an ML program. First, there should be a close relationship between the objectives and tests. Second, the number of sets of CRTs available has important implications for the definition of the program and its effects. Third, the CRTs used for tests, retests, and pretests (if any) should also be aligned; that is, they should have parallel structure. Fourth, there are concerns about instruction for summative testing. Fifth, there are issues concerning the validity of the tests. Finally, there are issues of program evaluation.

Relationship between Objectives and Tests

In an objective-based program, it is critical that the tests are consistent with the objectives with regard to the nature of the content being taught and the level of thinking required. Content refers to the type of objective as requiring information, principles and generalizations, procedures and rules, or concepts. Level refers to the issue of high order thinking (application of generalization, inference, analysis) versus low order thinking (recognition, recall of facts). The objectives should state the content and the level of thinking. The tests should assess each of these. Test format should vary according to the type of objective.

Problem 1. Discrepancies between the skill levels of the test and the levels of thinking stated in the objective are a serious problem. Typically, objectives are stated without specifying whether the response requires recognition, inference, application, or other thinking levels.

Solution. Write objectives that specify the level of thinking for any performance components, such as laboratory work, as well as for written components; that is, state whether or not the objective involves information, concepts, procedures, or principles and the level of thinking.

Problem 2. Tests that focus on low order thinking are a serious problem because, whether we like it or not, tests drive instruction. This means that if the tests do not assess high order thinking objectives, instructional developers and teachers are not likely to focus on them. Moreover, a focus on low order thinking tends to fragment instruction and learning because there is no drive to integrate and relate what is read to prior knowledge or other bodies of knowledge. Instruction may be even more fragmented when test items seem to be selected at random. Both Durkin (1983) and Osborn (1984) indicate that this practice is widespread among basals. Certainly, it would seem to be widespread among the school-based materials we have seen in some of the less than successful ML programs (Anderson and Jones, 1981).

Before we can suggest solutions, it is important to ask why test developers focus on low order items. First, all too frequently test items may be developed by test developers in a research unit, and they may know very little about the content or structure of the instruction. Additionally, they may not be aware at all of how much integration and inferencing is required to comprehend what appears to be factual information. Second, they may not believe that low achieving students can master the high order items. Such beliefs may or may not be related to a desire to focus on low order items so that the school system can "look good." Third, those who develop the test items do not know how to develop good high order items.

Solutions. The first step toward a good solution is to understand clearly the relationships between the question and the text to which it refers. We strongly recommend that anyone interested in developing questions or test items examine and utilize the definition of question/answer relationships given by Pearson and Johnson (1978) and the research of Raphael (1982).

A second step toward solving the problems of developing high order text items would be to look at some recent efforts to provide guidelines. First, there is the excellent guide by Bloom, Hastings, and Madaus (1971) that provides instruction for developing items at every level of the Bloom taxonomy in various subject areas. Second, Herber (1978) has developed a variety of ways to teach vocabulary that require integrating information. These formats could be used as models for test formats.

Third, L. W. Anderson analyzed the relationship between objectives, instruction, and test format in materials used in schools throughout the United States (Anderson and Jones, 1981). He has defined the following test formats most often used for each type of objective:

- Information and principle objectives may involve any or all of the following types of test items: (a) verbatim recall; (b) paraphrases of the information or principle; (c) answers to questions about the information or principle (who, what, when, where, which, why, how); or (d) inferences based on the information including application of a principle or generalization.

- Conceptual objectives may involve any or all of the following: (a) identify new examples and/or correct illustrations of the concept; (b) identify the concept, give instances; (c) eliminate incorrect examples; (d) identify critical features of the concept; (e) identify related concepts and/or examples.
- Procedural and rule objectives may involve either or both of the following: (a) given a problem situation, select the correct procedure or rule; (b) apply the procedure or rule correctly to a given situation, including answering inference questions about the procedure.

Number of Criterion-Referenced Tests

Since ML has a four-phase cycle of instruction and assessment, there must be two sets of CRTs for each unit to implement the test and retest phases of each unit. These must be separate from any pretests provided in the program. A good example of the provision of tests is the course in map reading offered by Fort Sill; it provides a criterion test and two parallel retests for each part of a five-part series of programmed texts.

Problem. The failure to provide two sets of CRTs specifically for use as tests and retests is a very serious problem. Many programs of instruction offer only one set of CRTs or two sets, with one of them specified for use as a pretest in pretest, training, posttest design. Such programs preclude the effective implementation of the four-phase cycle of ML. Although these programs may be defined as *mastery-based* because they teach to the objective and assess with CRTs, they are not mastery learning because they do not facilitate systematic remediation of learning errors in the reteach phase or provide for a second opportunity for achievement in the retest phase. The diagnosis of errors in the test phase and remediation using a different teaching strategy in the reteach phase is the heart of ML. Without the reteach phase, learning errors accumulate and compound learning problems. The retest not only establishes what errors have been corrected but functions to reduce anxiety among low achieving learners and "high anxious," high achieving learners. That is, when a learner fails the formative test, if new instruction and a retest are available, this enhances self-confidence.

Moreover, the reteach and retest phases provide an additional opportunity to be equal to the mastery learners who passed the test. The retest phase, therefore, has great psychological benefits and provides a greater opportunity for educational equality than a program having only one set of tests.

The problem of having only one set of CRTs available is usually not solved by assuming or directing the classroom teachers to develop a second set of CRTs. This assumption is problematic for many reasons. First, there is the problem that different teachers develop a multiplicity of tests for the same objective; such duplication is a waste of time and energy. Second, many, if not most, teachers do not want to be responsible for developing tests. Either they do not perceive the need, or they feel it is not their job to perform what is essentially a curriculum or research and development function. Third, even if the teachers did want to develop a second set of tests, developing parallel tests is a specialized skill requiring not just scarce time but also training, close monitoring, and field testing, and it is unlikely that it would be possible for a large-scale program to provide consistent training and quality control across the set of instructors-cum-developers. Fourth, teachers should not be allowed to field test instructional or testing material in their own classrooms; it is a conflict of interest and should be explicitly eliminated as a possibility.

Solution. Develop a minimum of two sets of CRTs per learning unit at the outset. Then, it is possible to train appropriate personnel to control for parallel structure and to use appropriate field testing techniques.

Parallel Structure

Formative tests and retests should have parallel structure with regard to the level and content of the terms, test format, and readability. The rationale here is simple: If tests are not parallel, they are testing a different content or level of thinking.

Problem 1. The tendency to use different test content or formats for the test and retest is a problem that in all likelihood affects the level of thinking of the items as well. Examples of nonparallel structure are (1) a test that establishes steps in a procedure and a retest that asks how to solve a problem or apply a principle and (2) a test that uses a completion format with a retest using a multiple choice format. Most often such variations are not intentional, although sometimes it is argued that changes of format are helpful because they assess transfer. While changes of format do indeed test for transfer, transfer and tests for transfer should be built into the objective and instruction if they are desired.

Solution. Do not vary test format or type of content.

Problem 2. Use of traditional readability formulas that do not measure many of the factors that make a passage or diagram difficult to read has various consequences. The issue of readability is addressed at length in Jones and others (1984, chap. 1), and Osborn, Jones, and Stein (in press), and therefore will be discussed only briefly here. Basically, it is argued that differences in complexity (that is, number of component parts and levels of a graphic or prose text), explicitness, and density (memory load) markedly affect readability. Unfortunately, although the research base supporting that generalization is substantial, there are no formulas developed to apply readability guidelines for developing test items because these typically do not constitute extended prose.

Solution. The checklist at the end of this chapter refers the developer to lists for the general and specific factors that could influence parallel structure, including readability (see Appendix B).

Summative Tests

Summative tests are designed to test different skills than those tested for by the CRTs used for the test and retest phases in each learning unit. The latter are task or content specific and are given immediately after learning. CRTs therefore test for short term memory and comprehensive knowledge of one task or body of content. Summative tests often consist of selected items from CRTs used as tests and retests. However, summative tests may also cover many tasks or sets of content within a given level of instruction and are given weeks or months after the initial learning. These tests therefore assess long-term memory, the learner's ability to select what is important, and integration of knowledge across units of instruction. Accordingly, the learner needs to be notified explicitly of the differences between CRTs and summative testing. Additionally, he or she needs special preparation for such tests: training in selecting what is important and training in learning strategies that facilitate long term memory and integration of information, as well as training for any part of the test that varies from the CRTs upon which it is based. It is easy to see why many school districts are reporting very high scores on tests that measure low order objectives and low scores on tests that measure high order objectives.

Test Validation

Validation is essential to answer these questions: (1) Does the test really assess the performance indicated in the objective? This includes the level and content of the objective. (2) Will those passed by the test really be able to do the job or function well in the next level of instruction? (3) Does the test fail those who do not know how to perform the job?

Problem. A final problem is inadequate test validation. Some school administrators think that the primary means of validation occurs when subject matter experts judge the validity of the test simply by reading it and using professional judgment. While this type of validation is essential, it is important to validate the test in other ways. This is particularly important in jobs involving high risks of bodily harm or harm to equipment. Additionally, there are affective problems that arise when teachers and students perceive the tests to be unfair, inadequate, or inconsistent with the instruction.

A related issue is the tendency to adopt a "quick and dirty" scoring procedure (for example, 80 percent mastery on all tests) to establish mastery. Mastery levels should be decided on an objective-by-objective basis. According to Bloom (1984), having very high levels of mastery (for example, 95 to 100 percent) on initial units has a high payoff in cognitive and affective domains, provided that the instruction is effective. Cognitively, these high mastery levels establish a firm learning basis to support subsequent instruction. Affectively, low achieving and high anxious learners have rapid and dramatic evidence that they can be successful. Additionally, it is useful to establish very high levels of mastery for objectives that are critical to performance on important objectives.

Solutions. (1) Validate the tests by a survey that asks each subject matter expert specifically to examine the relationship of the objectives, tests, and instruction as well as the scoring. (2) Give the test to test masters (students known to have mastered the objective) and novices (those known to be unskilled) to establish that the test in fact discriminates between those who are skilled and those not skilled. (3) Conduct error analyses; errors should be distributed randomly over the items, unless some items have been deliberately made to be exceptionally easy or difficult. Generally, errors clustering disproportionately around an item or items disproportionately lacking errors indicate poor item construction or problems in instruction or both.

Program Evaluation

One final issue should be raised regarding assessment for mastery learning programs. It is fundamental to mastery learning theory that students should only be assessed using criterion-referenced tests that are closely aligned with the instruction and objectives. At the same time, schools need comparative, general measures to assess the extent to which a given program of instruction is effective. A school must be able to evaluate, for example, the effectiveness of a given program of reading by standardized and widely used measures. Thus, it seems entirely legitimate for schools to want to use some type of standardized test in addition to criterion-referenced tests.

The problem is that traditional norm-referenced tests have numerous limitations (Klare, in press). First, traditional tests typically do not test high order thinking and comprehension. Second, the reliability for such tests is relatively low. Third, norms are established by comparing students' scores to each other. Fourth, there is no norm, standard, or criteria to establish, other than by grade equivalents, that the sequence of items in such tests is progressively more difficult.

Fortunately, there is now a new standardized reading test called the Degrees of Reading Power (DRP) developed by the College Board (Cooper, 1982). This test utilizes a special procedure to develop passages that assess high order thinking and comprehension. Each passage is developed to assess comprehension of whole paragraphs so that the students must integrate information from various sentences in order to determine the correct answers. Then each passage is ranked using the Rasch model (Wright and Stone, 1979) so that each passage is increasingly more difficult than the preceding one in terms of variables related to inferential comprehension. Scores are normed in terms of DRP units. Thus, students are evaluated in terms of their ability to understand increasingly difficult passages, rather than compared to each other. Finally, the DRP is a highly reliable test. Therefore, if schools must use standarized comprehension tests, the DRP is a superior instrument, compared to norm-referenced tests.

Moreover, the DRP has a readability component making it possible to assess instructional materials and match them to levels of student ability using the same scale as the DRP comprehension test. This capability differs from traditional measures that assess students on one instrument and textbooks on another. Thus, the DRP allows for consistency between diagnosis and prescription of instructional materials to levels of student ability.

Principle 4: Recordkeeping—Unit by Unit

Most mastery-based programs focus on management by objectives (MBO). Typically, progress charts have the objectives or tests as column headings and the names of students as row headings. Management in such programs consists of recording and analyzing student mastery of each objective and grouping students in a classroom or course for instruction according to who has or has not mastered given objectives. Instruction and classroom organization varies objective by objective in such systems.

In contrast, we recommend that management in mastery learning programs proceed unit by unit, each unit consisting of the four-phase cycle of instruction and assessment (teach, test, reteach/extend, retest). In such systems, monitoring has two separate thrusts. On the one hand, it is possible to monitor the progress of students in each classroom using classroom progress charts, in each school using school progress charts, and in each school district (or subdistrict), using district progress charts. On the other hand, it is also possible to monitor the success of each instructional unit within a given course. For these reasons, we recommend conceptualizing the management of mastery learning as management by units of instruction (MBU).

Classroom Progress Charts. First, there is a Classroom Progress Chart in which the names of the instructional units are the column headings and the names of students are the row headings. Mastery of each instructional unit is indicated by darkening the cells. Nonmastery of the formative test is indicated by placing a diagonal line in a cell. Nonmastery of the retest is indicated by placing a second diagonal across the first diagonal, making an X. Student progress is analyzed by examining the rows. A series of darkened cells indicates repeated successes; a series of crossed diagonals (Xs) indicates repeated failures. Thus, a series of crossed diagonals is an immediate flag that the learner needs help, extra time, or reassignment to a lower level of instruction.

There are several advantages to using darkened cells and diagonals rather than the actual score of each test. First, the records of a student who fails the formative test (receiving a single diagonal) and then passes (receiving a darkened cell) look the same as those of a student who passed the first time. This equality generates a positive self-concept for the first type of student. Second, wall charts can be read at a glance even from across the room; the pattern of crossed diagonals and darkened cells is immediately obvious.

Moreover, instructional effectiveness, content covered, and time may be assessed quickly by examining the columns. That is, a series of darkened columns indicates that each instructional unit is successful. If, however, five of six columns contain darkened cells while the sixth contains many crossed diagonals, this pattern of outcomes suggests that there may be something wrong with the instructional materials in that unit. Similarly, if six teachers are teaching the same unit and five of them have darkened cells while the sixth has a series of crossed diagonals, this pattern of outcomes suggests that something is wrong in the instructional situation. Content covered is indicated simply by counting the number of columns containing darkened cells or crossed diagonals. Time is assessed by calculating the number of units covered in relation to the available time for the series of units. Thus, assuming that the test administration has been honest and competent, a manager or instructor can see if a class is behind schedule, on schedule, or ahead of schedule by looking at the number of units covered in relation to the available time. If an instructor has covered only one fourth of the units but one half of the available time has passed, the instructor needs to increase the pace of instruction in order to teach the remaining units in the remaining time.

School Progress Charts. These charts have the names of the instructional units as column headings and the names of classroom instructors as row headings. Progress is recorded by showing the number of students who passed each unit in proportion to the number who worked through the instruction. Classroom progress is assessed by reading the cells in each row. Effectiveness of the instruction for the whole school is assessed by reading the columns, unit by unit. Content covered for the whole school is assessed by counting the number of columns that are filled in. Time is assessed by counting the number of units covered in relation to the available time for each marking or grade period.

This system has a threefold capability. Instead of focusing exclusively on individual mastery, as most objective-based programs do, this system reflects individual, classroom, school, or district progress, as shown by analysis of the rows in each chart; the effectiveness of the instruction as shown by the columns of each chart; and content covered in relation to the available time, as shown by examining the number of units covered to date, relative to the total number of units in a given time period or program of instruction.

What is the difference between MBO and MBU? In MBO, the instruction is usually variable from teacher to teacher because teachers in such systems usually develop their own instruction, and there is only one test. In MBU, one knows whether one or two tests have been given and the materials for the instruction are the same from teacher to teacher. Thus, it is possible to assess instructional effectiveness and content covered precisely. In other words, if a learner fails to master a given test in an objectives-based system using MBO, there is no way to assess whether the problem is a function of student behaviors, teacher behaviors, or the instructional materials. By way of contrast, when a learner fails units using

MBU, it is possible over a period of time to assess whether the failures are a function of the student, the teacher, or the materials. These capabilities represent a strong argument for developing all of the instructional materials needed for the teach, test, reteach/ extend, retest cycle.

Mastery Learning Checklist

This checklist can be used for three entirely different purposes. First, the general concepts in this checklist can be used to evaluate existing materials. Second, the checklist can be used as the model to structure or plan the development of curriculum (the objectives), instruction, and assessment for the program as a whole. For this purpose, one should use all of Section B, the concept of the learning unit and the four-phase cycle of instruction and testing within each unit; the concept of varying instruction before and after the formative test; the concept of criterion-referenced testing; and the concept of assessing progress unit by unit (versus objective by objective). Third, the internal parts of the checklist can be used as a systematic step-by-step guide to develop mastery learning curricula: the objectives, tests, instruction, and recordkeeping components of each unit.

Traditionally, instruction is developed in the following way: First, the objectives are developed with little regard to the available content texts, focusing instead on "the needs of the district." This is based on the assumption that the instructor can adapt the content from various subject-related texts to apply to the objectives defined as important to the district. Often the objectives are "validated" by having panels of various people evaluate them for clarity and appropriateness for a given level of instruction. Second, the tests are often developed by a different group of people, usually persons with a background of testing and research who may not know very much about instruction. Third, the instruction may be left to the classroom teacher who probably has had little or no input into the objectives or the tests, who may or may not have the appropriate content materials, who may or may not be interested in or skilled at developing instructional materials to teach the content, and who may or may not want to spend the time needed to develop or align curriculum materials. Finally, the recordkeeping instruments are developed, sometimes by yet another group of people who had nothing to do with the objectives, the tests, or the instruction.

There are numerous problems associated with these procedures. Most important, it is not possible to validate objectives effectively until after the tests and instruction have been developed. All too frequently, an objective seems clear and appropriate at the outset but is interpreted quite differently by the test developer or the instructional developer. Worse still, it becomes clear in developing the test or instruction that the objective is full of problems, but it is too late to change the objective because it has been validated in the field or simply because it has already been published as the official curriculum. A similar situation arises when tests are developed separately from the instruction. That is, it is often impossible to tell how valid test items are until the instruction is developed.

Two methods of development are suggested to address these problems. One method, *simultaneous development,* is to develop all of the components of the program simultaneously by a team consisting of designers, teachers, testing experts, and instructional writers/consultants. That is, objectives would be developed first, but they would be only tentative, pending the development of tests and instruction. Then the team would proceed to develop whole units of instruction (that is, the instruction and tests for each objective), unit by unit. In this method, the objectives would be printed first in a limited edition, followed by the tests, followed by the instruction. The team would constantly align, sequence, and adjust the relationship between the objectives, the tests, and the instruction until all of the units for a given segment were ready to be field tested. Then they would be field tested, revised according to the field test, and printed or published for large-scale use as a whole segment (for example, level one in content area X, or first semester of year X). In this method, the only adjustments to be made would be level adjustments—if a given unit were too easy or too difficult in one level—relative to other levels.

A second method involves sequential development with revisions. Using this method, the objectives, tests, and instruction are developed and may be published sequentially, but each one is subject to revision, based on the development of the other. Thus, the objectives may be altered after the tests are developed, and both the objectives and tests may be revised as the instruction is developed. This method also involves teams of designers, curriculum developers, content teachers, and instructional writers/consultants who specialize in the given content area.

Of the two methods, the first will probably produce the more effective instruction because each unit is entirely content driven, but it will probably be more costly in terms of time. Either method, however, would solve many of the problems that arise from sequential development that is fragmented and unrefined without revisions to each component.

Exhibit 2. Mastery Learning Checklist.

A.   Mastery Learning
___ 1.   Does the school system support the philosophy and principles of mastery learning?
___   Are there stated objectives?
___   Is there a four-phase cycle of instruction and assessment?
___   Are the tests criterion referenced?
___   Are the objectives, tests, and instruction aligned?
___ 2.   Are school personnel aware of the program effects of mastery learning?
___ 3.   Is school staff aware of the distinction between mastery learning and other types of instruction?
___   traditional instruction
___   mastery-based programs
___ 4.   Are school personnel aware of problems of development and implementation?
___   the fragmentation of instruction resulting from teaching skills objectives as isolated and discrete skills
___   the low quality of instruction and lack of curriculum alignment resulting from the reliance on existing texts
___   the management problems that result from teaching multiple groupings in a single classroom in ungraded structures

B.   Objectives (Principle 1)
___ 1.   Does the objective specify the following components?
___   conditions (givens)
___   standards (goals)
___   test format for written components
___   level of learning
___   literal versus inferential
___   aided versus unaided
___ 2.   Does the objective specify the content of the task as involving
___   facts or information?
___   categories or concepts?
___   procedures?
___   rules?
___   principles?
___ 3.   Hierarchical sequencing refers to the overall sequencing of the instruction for a set of related concepts, procedures, and principles in a series of units, modules, courses, grades, or levels.
___   Does the instruction for a set of related concepts or principles begin with an overview of the hierarchy

    and then proceed to work through it from the lowest levels to the highest?

____ Does the instruction for procedures begin with an overview and then proceed to work through each step sequentially?

____ 4.   Horizontal sequencing refers to the order of instruction for each lesson in a unit and each unit in the module, course, grade, or level. Is the horizontal sequencing content driven?

    ____ Does each lesson and unit begin with an overview of the content? That is, an overview of the facts, concepts, principles, or procedures?

    ____ Are learning/thinking strategies sequenced as a means to learning the content?

    ____ Is the instruction for learning/thinking strategies sequenced to proceed from teacher directed to student directed?

    ____ Are learning/thinking strategies sequenced so that the student has time to have guided practice in one of them before being introduced to another?

    ____ Are related objectives integrated for the purposes of instruction?

    ____ Is there a focus on high order objectives?

____ 5.   Does the instruction for each segment of content provide vertical sequencing so that for each segment there is

    ____ readiness instruction?

    ____ comprehension instruction?

    ____ response instruction?

C.   Learning Unit Organization and Delivery (Principle 2)

____ 1.   Is each learning unit organized into a four-phase cycle?

    ____ teach

    ____ test

    ____ reteach and retest nonmastery students

    ____ extend mastery students

____ 2.   Is the following entry information specified for each unit?

    ____ the target audience

    ____ unit objectives

    ____ lesson objectives

    ____ materials required

    ____ estimated time ranges

    ____ prerequisite skills information

        ____ vocabulary

        ____ factual knowledge

        ____ skills

        ____ specific courses

        ____ reading level

____ 3.   Does the teach phase have the following?

    ____ overview
    ____ readiness activities
        ____ motivation
        ____ prior learning
        ____ practical application
        ____ difficult vocabulary
        ____ purpose in reading
    ____ instructional output
    ____ examples and nonexamples
    ____ explanation
    ____ comprehension monitoring
    ____ learning cues
    ____ explicit learning strategy instruction
    ____ guided practice
    ____ independent practice
    ____ correction of errors and positive reinforcement

____ 4. Is there a criterion-referenced formative test?

____ 5. Is there a reteach phase containing
    ____ a review of instruction?
    ____ a different teaching/learning strategy?
    ____ extra practice moving up to level of the retest?

____ 6. Is there a parallel retest?

____ 7. Are there extension options?
    ____ advancement to the next level
    ____ extension activity
    ____ inferential reading
    ____ peer tutoring

____ 8. Are there answer keys?

____ 9. Is there a glossary for
    ____ technical terms and their descriptors?
    ____ acronyms?
    ____ abbreviations?
    ____ nontechnical, difficult vocabulary?

D. Testing and Curriculum Alignment (Principle 3)

____ 1. Are the tests consistent with the objectives with regard to
    ____ the level of thinking relative to the available text (text explicit, text implicit, text inadequate)?
    ____ the content (information, generalization or principle, concept, or procedure)?

____ 2. Are the following types of tests available?
    ____ two sets of CRTs specified as tests and retests
    ____ pretests (optional)
    ____ summative tests (optional)

____ 3. Do all of the tests have parallel structure with regard to
    ____ level/content of terms?
    ____ test format?
    ____ readability factors? (See Appendix B)

____ 4. Are there summative tests?

___   Do the summative tests provide the following for all components?
      ___   definitions of the purpose and scope of the components
      ___   sample instructions, answer sheet format (where relevant), and scoring
      ___   sample questions or tasks
      ___   appropriate study indicators
___   Is there adequate preparation for the summative test with regard to
      ___   long term memory strategies?
      ___   integrating and/or reasoning strategies?

___   5.   Are all tests validated using
      ___   subject matter experts?
      ___   recent "experts" (graduates) and novices?
      ___   error analysis?

___   6.   Is there program evaluation using the Degrees of Reading Power Test?

E.   Recordkeeping: Unit by Unit (Principle 4)

___   1.   Is there a classroom progress chart?

___   2.   Is there a school progress chart?

Note: © Copyright by Beau Fly Jones, July 1984.

Appendix A: Examples of Teaching/Learning Strategy Variations

Initial Instruction (before the Formative Test)	Additional Corrective Instruction (after the Formative Test)
• verbal (printed materials)	• visual aids (pictures, movies) visualizing (mental pictures, drawings)
• verbal (lecture)	• discussion/debate/drama/ role play/interview
• self-instructional	• teacher-directed; teams/ groups
• inductive	• deductive
• verbal (print/lecture)	• concrete operation (manipulatives); constructive activity (make original survey, story, categorizing activity, and so on)
• focus on instructional content explaining the objectives	• focus on reading strategy to obtain the answer (scanning, use of fingers in reading tables); analysis of errors
• focus on reading applications	• writing explanations
• provision of factual information/rules (for example, spelling) formulae	• provision of mnemonic (associations); creative project (collage, game)

Appendix B: Parallel Structure

Formative tests and retests should have parallel structure. This means that they should be equal and consistent with regard to format, text structure, and other factors that affect readability. The list below is not comprehensive, but it is based on research on the factors that affect readability (Amiran and Jones, 1982).

____ 1.   test format (multiple choice, completion, and the like)
____ 2.   coverage of skills
       ____ test instructions and conditions
          ____ the amount of time given
          ____ whether or not an example is given
          ____ mode of presentation
              ____ oral versus read
              ____ oral versus written response
              ____ group versus individual testing
          ____ scoring
          ____ answer key criteria
____ 3.   level of processing (literal, inferential, and so on)
____ 4.   content difficulty with regard to
       ____ degree of concreteness (concrete versus abstract)
       ____ degree of familiarity of topic and vocabulary words
       ____ degree of explicitness (explicit, not requiring inferences, versus inexplicit, requiring inferences)
       ____ the distance between sentences or phrases which need to be integrated for comprehension; that is, ellipsis
       ____ the presence of effective context clues
____ 5.   difficulty of syntax with regard to
       ____ the number of compound and complex sentences
       ____ the number of syllables of unfamiliar words
       ____ the number of negatives
       ____ the distance between pronouns and indefinite articles (for example, it, this, some) and the nouns to which they refer
____ 6.   structure of test with regard to

___ the purpose of the text (narrative, expository, or argumentative)

___ the underlying organizational structure of individual paragraphs or sections as subordinate (for example, name/attribute), coordinate (for example, compare-and-contrast), and sequential (that is, steps in a series)

___ the text length

___ the number of component parts (simple versus complex)

___ the presence of organizational cues indicating sectional topics (subtitles, numbered paragraphs)

___ the presence of emphasis devices to highlight important information (for example, italicized words)

___ 7. design features

___ the presence of graphic or pictorical representations

___ the distance between the reference to the representation and the representation itself

___ the extent to which the representation reflects the meaning of the text

___ 8. graphics (maps, pictures, diagrams, charts, tables, cartoons)

___ the use of color and shading

___ the number of component parts of the graphic as a whole and in terms of each aspect

___ the size and shape of objects in the graphic

___ the degree of knowledge required to comprehend the graphic

___ the degree of inference required to understand the action, sequence of events, character relations, and so on

___ the levels of information (literal, inferred, figurative)

___ the use of numbers, statistics, or other technical information

___ the presence and location of labels

___ the amount and nature of the print in labels, cap-
tions, dialogues, and so on

Glossary

Phases of mastery learning (ML): teach, test, reteach/extend, retest

Stages of instruction for a given lesson

Readiness instruction: instruction devised to activate prior knowledge, establish mental set, preteach new vocabulary, and/or set a purpose in reading

Comprehension instruction: instruction devised to help students understand what they read

Response instruction: instruction devised to help students construct meaning from text and/or respond to questions about the text

Types of ML tests

Formative test: the first test *within* a learning unit, given after the initial instruction to assess learning against a pre-designated standard (the test phase of mastery learning)

Retest: the second test *within* a mastery learning unit, given after the corrective instruction (the retest phase of mastery learning)

Summative test: a test given *after* several units for one or more of the following purposes: to assess long term memory, to assess integration of information or skills across learning units, to assign grades to provide certification

Types of sequencing

Hierarchical: refers to the order of objectives/instruction over a series of related units, courses, modules, grades, or levels

Horizontal: refers to the order of objectives/instruction within a given instructional unit consisting of lessons and tests

Vertical: refers to the order of objectives/instruction within a given lesson

References

Abrams, J. D. "Mastery Learning in a Smaller School System." *Educational Leadership*, 1979, *37*, 136-139.

Amiran, M. R., and Jones, B. F. "Toward a New Definition of Readability." *Educational Psychologist*, 1982, *17*, 13-30.

Anderson, L. W., and Block, J. H. "Mastery Learning." In D. Treffinger, J. Javis, and R. Ripple (Eds.), *Handbook on Teaching Educational Psychology*. New York: Academic Press, 1976.

Anderson, L. W., and Jones, B. F. "Designing Instructional Strategies Which Facilitate Learning for Mastery." *Educational Psychologist*, 1981, *16*, 121-138.

Anderson, R. C., Osborn, J., and Tierney, R. J. *Learning to Read in American Schools: Basal Readers and Content Texts*. Hillsdale, N.J.: Erlbaum, 1984.

Anderson, R. C., Spiro, R. J., and Montague, W. E. (Eds.). *Schooling and the Acquisition of Knowledge*. Hillsdale, N.J.: Erlbaum, 1977.

Anderson, T. H. "Study Strategies and Adjunct Aids." In R. Spiro, B. C. Bruce, and W. F. Brewer (Eds.), *Theoretical Issues in Reading Comprehension*. Hillsdale, N.J.: Erlbaum, 1980.

Anderson, T. H., and Armbruster, B. B. "Content Area Textbooks." In R. C. Anderson, J. Osborn, and R. J. Tierney (Eds.), *Learning to Read in American Schools: Basal Readers and Content Texts*. Hillsdale, N.J.: Erlbaum, 1984.

Bailey, G. W., and Guest, H. "Gaining Staff and Board Support for Success Based Instruction." Paper presented at the Summer Instructional Leadership Conference of the American Association of School Administrators, Chicago, July 1980.

Barber, C. *Mastery Learning Through Involved Educational Leadership. Application for State Validation*. Denver Public Schools, August 1979.

Block, J. H., and Anderson, L. W. *Mastery Learning in Classroom Instruction*. New York: Macmillan, 1975.

Block, J. H., and Burns, R. "Mastery Learning." In L. J. Shulman (Ed.), *Review of Research in Education*. Vol. 4, Itasca, Ill.: Peacock, 1977.

Bloom, B. S. "Learning for Mastery." *Evaluation Comment*, 1968, *1, 2.*

Bloom, B. S. *Human Characteristics and School Learning*. New York: McGraw-Hill, 1976.

Bloom, B. S. "The Search for Methods of Whole Group Instruction as Effective as One-to-One Tutoring." *Educational Leadership*, 1984, *8*, 4–18.

Bloom, B. S., Hastings, J. T., and Madaus, G. F. *Handbook on Formative and Summative Evaluation of Student Learning*. New York: McGraw-Hill, 1971.

Bloom, B. S., and others (Eds.). *Taxonomy of Educational Objectives: The Classification of Educational Goals. Handbook I: Cognitive Domain*. New York: McKay, 1956.

Board of Education of the City of Chicago. *Chicago Mastery Learning Reading, Vocabulary Learning Strategies, Grades 5–8*. Watertown, Mass. Mastery Education Corporation, 1983.

Board of Education of the City of Chicago and the Center for the Study of Reading, University of Illinois. *United States History, CIRCA Teacher Manual: Era I, Units 1–3, Grades 7–8*. Chicago: Board of Education of the City of Chicago, 1984.

Brandon, R. K. "ISD: Is the System Out of Control?" Paper presented at the annual meeting of the American Educational Research Association, New Orleans, April 1984.

Brown, A. L., Campione, J. C., and Day, J. D. "Learning to Learn: On Training Students to Learn from Text." *Educational Researcher*, 1980, *10*, 14–23.

Brown, A. L., Campione, J. C., and Day, J. D. "Learning to Learn: On Training Students to Learn from Text." *Educational Researcher*, 1982, *10*, 14–23.

Bruce, B. "A New Point of View on Children's Stories." Reading Education Report No. 25, Urbana: University of Illinois, Center for the Study of Reading, July 1981.

Burns, R. B. "Mastery Learning: Does It Work?" *Educational Leadership*, November 1979, pp. 110–113.

Càponigri, R. (Ed.). *Summary, Second Annual Mastery Learning Conference (May 1981)*. Chicago: City Colleges of Chicago, 1981.

Carroll, J. B. "On Learning from Being Told." In M. C. Wittrock (Ed.), *Learning and Instruction*. Berkeley: McCutchan, 1977.

Cavert, C. E., and others. "Requirements and Recommendations for Learning Strategies in the U.S. Army Basic Skills Education Program." Department of the Army, November 1980.

Champlin, J. R. "Implementing Effective Mastery Learning Programs: Administrative Challenges and Rewards." Paper presented at the annual convention of the American Association of School Administrators, Atlanta, February 1981.

Champlin, J., and Mamary, A. "Effects of Mastery Learning Training." Unpublished report available from the Office of the Superintendent, Johnson City Public Schools, Johnson City, N.Y., 1982.

Cooper, E. J. "DRP Adopted in Boston." *College Board News,* Fall, 1982.

Durkin, D. "What Classroom Observations Reveal About Reading Comprehension Instruction." *Reading Research Quarterly,* 1978-79, *15,* 481-533.

Durkin, D. "Reading Comprehension Instruction in Five Basal Reader Series." In R. C. Anderson, J. Osborn, and R. J. Tierney (Eds.), *Learning to Read in American Schools: Basal Readers and Content Texts.* Hillsdale, N.J.: Erlbaum, 1983.

Ellis, J. A., Wulfeck, W. H., and Fredericks, P. S. *The Instructional Quality Inventory II. Users Manual.* San Diego: Navy Personnel Research and Development Center, 1979.

Herber, H. L. *GO: Reading in the Content Areas. Materials for Students.* New York: Scholastic Book Services, 1975.

Herber, H. L. *Reading in the Content Areas. Text for Teachers.* (Rev. ed.) Englewood Cliffs, N.J.: Prentice-Hall, 1978.

Hunter, M. *Teach for Transfer.* El Segundo, Calif.: TIT Publications, 1971.

Hyman, J. L., and Cohen, S. A. "Learning for Mastery: Ten Conclusions After Fifteen Years." *Educational Leadership,* November 1979, pp. 104-109.

Jenkins, J., and Pany, D. "Teaching Reading Comprehension in the Middle Grades." In R. Spiro, B. Bruce, and W. Brewer (Eds.), *Theoretical Issues in Reading Comprehension.* Hillsdale, N.J.: Erlbaum, 1980.

Jones, B. F. "Maximizing Learning for Low Achieving Students: An Argument for Learning Instructions." Paper presented at the

Summer Instructional Leadership Conference of the American Association of School Administrators, Chicago, July 1980.

Jones, B. F. "Key Management Decisions for Implementing Mastery Learning." *School Administrator,* March 1982.

Jones, B. F., Amiran, M. R., and Katims, M. "Teaching Cognitive Strategies and Text Structures Within Language Arts Programs." In J. Segal, S. F. Chipman, and R. Glaser (Eds.), *Thinking and Learning Skills: Relating Basic Research to Instructional Practices* Vol. 1. Hillsdale, N.J.: Erlbaum, 1984.

Jones, B. F., and others. "Content-Driven Comprehension Instruction: A Model for Army Training Literature." Arlington, Va.: Army Research Institute for the Social Behavioral Sciences, 1984.

Katims, M., and Jones, B. F. "Chicago Mastery Learning Reading: Instruction and Assessment in Inner City Schools." Paper presented at the annual meeting of the International Reading Association, New Orleans, April 1981.

Katims, M., and Jones, B. F. "N = 315,000: Mandating an Effective Mastery Learning Program." Paper presented at the annual meeting of the American Educational Research Association, Montreal, April 1983.

Kern, R. P., and others. *Guidebook for the Development of Army Training Literature.* Alexandria, Va.: Human Resources Organization, 1976.

Klare, G. "Matching Reading Materials to Readers: The Role of Readability Estimates in Conjunction with Other Kinds of Information About Comprehensibility." In E. J. Cooper and T. Harris (Eds.), *Reading, Thinking, and Concept Development: Strategies for the Classroom.* New York: The College Board, in press.

Klausmeier, H. J., and others. *Individually Guided Education and the Multiunit Elementary School: Guidelines for Implementation.* Madison, Wisc.: Wisconsin Research and Development Center for Cognitive Training, University of Wisconsin, 1971.

Klausmeier, H. J., Rossmiller, R. A., and Saily, M. (Eds.). *Individually Guided Elementary Education: Concepts and Practices.* New York: Academic Press, 1977.

Levin, J. R. "What Have We Learned About Maximizing What Children Learn?" In J. R. Levin and V. L. Allen (Eds.), *Cogni-*

tive Learning in Children: Theories and Strategies. New York: Academic Press, 1976.

Levine, D. U., and Stark, J. "A Study of the Chicago Mastery Learning Reading Program and Other Schoolwide Approaches for Improving Reading at Selected Schools in Chicago, Los Angeles, and New York." In D. U. Levine and J. Stark (Eds.), *Organizational Processes and Arrangements for Improving Academic Achievement at Inner City Schools.* National Institute of Education Report. Kansas City: University of Missouri at Kansas City, 1980.

Mager, R. F. *Preparing Instructional Objectives.* 2nd ed. Belmont, Calif.: Pitman Learning, Inc., 1975.

Markle, S. M., and Tiemann, P. W. *Really Understanding Concepts.* Champaign, Ill.: Stripes, 1969.

Meyer, B. J. F., Brandt, D. M., and Bluth, G. S. "Use of Top-Level Structure in Text: Key for Reading Comprehension of Ninth-Grade Students." *Reading Research Quarterly,* 1980, *16,* 72–103.

O'Neil, H. F. *Learning Strategies.* New York: Academic Press, 1978.

Osborn, J. "The Purposes, Uses, and Contents of Workbooks and Some Guidelines for Teachers and Publishers." In R. C. Anderson, J. Osborn, and R. J. Tierney (Eds.), *Learning to Read in American Schools: Basal Readers and Content Texts.* Hillsdale, N.J.: Erlbaum, 1984.

Osborn, J., Jones, B. F., and Stein, M. "The Case for Improving Textbook Programs: An Issue of Quality." *Educational Leadership,* in press.

Pearson, P. D., and Gallagher, M. C. "The Instruction of Reading Comprehension." Urbana: University of Illinois, Center for the Study of Reading, 1983.

Pearson, P. D., and Johnson, D. D. *Teaching Reading Comprehension.* New York: Holt, Rinehart & Winston, 1978.

Raphael, T. *Improving Questioning–Answering Performance Through Instruction.* Reading Education Report No. 32. Urbana, Ill.: University of Illinois, Center for the Study of Reading, 1982.

Reed, F. H. "A Comparison of the Effects of Staff Development/Curriculum vs. Staff Development Strategies On Student Achievement, Rate of Learning, and Retention in Group-Based Mastery

Learning." Paper presented at the annual meeting of the American Educational Research Association, New York, April 1982.

Reid, E. *Teaching Critical Comprehension Skills: Teacher Manual.* Salt Lake City: Cove Publishers, 1978.

Reigeluth, C. M., and Darwazeh, A. "The Elaboration Theory's Procedure for Diagnosing Instruction: A Conceptual Approach." *Journal of Instructional Development,* 1982, *3,* 22-32.

Reigeluth, C. M., and Merrill, M. D. *Extended Task Analysis Procedures (ETAP): User's Manual.* Hampton, Va.: U.S. Army, TRADOC, 1982.

Rohwer, W. D., Jr. "Learning, Race, and School Success." *Review of Educational Research,* 1971, *41,* 191-210.

Rosenshine, B. B. "Teaching Functions in Instructional Programs." *The Elementary School Journal,* 1983, *83,* 335-351.

Rubin, S., and Spady, W. G. "Achieving Excellence Through Outcomes-Based Instructional Delivery." *Educational Leadership,* 1984, *3,* 37-44.

Singer, H., and Bean, T. "Relationship Between Ability to Learn from Text and Achievement in the UC and the CSU Systems." Learning from Text Project, University of California at Riverside, 1983.

Singer, H., and Donlan, D. "Active Comprehension: Problem-Solving Schema with Question Generation for Comprehension of Complex Short Stories." *Reading Research Quarterly,* 1982, *17,* 166-186.

Spady, W. G. "Outcome-Based Instructional Management: Its Sociological Implications." *Australian Journal of Education,* 1982, *26,* 123-143.

Stauffer, R. G. *Directing the Reading-Thinking Process.* New York: Harper & Row, 1975.

Sternberg, R. J. "How Can We Teach Intelligence?" *Educational Leadership,* 1984, 42, *1,* 38-48.

Stoll, L. J. "Teach versus Test Reading Comprehension Skills: An Evaluation of Supplementary Materials." Paper presented at the annual summer conference of the American Association of School Administrators, Washington, D.C., July 1981.

Tierney, R. J., and Pearson, P. D. "Learning to Learn from Text: A Framework for Improving Classroom Practice." Urbana: University of Illinois, Center for the Study of Reading, 1981.

Weinstein, C. E., and Mayer, R. E. "The Teaching of Learning Strategies." In M. C. Wittrock (Ed.), *Handbook of Research on Teaching*. (3rd ed.) New York: Macmillan, 1983.

Wittrock, M. C. "Generative Reading Comprehension." *Ginn Occasional Reports*. Boston: Ginn, 1984.

Wright, B. D., and Stone, M. H. *Best Test Design: Rasch Measurement*. Chicago: Mesa Press, 1979.

6

∽ ✑

Establishing
a Management Plan
for Implementing
Mastery Learning

Phyllis R. Pringle

As the competency movement gathers momentum, mastery learning, in one form or another, is being adopted by school districts because its use has produced verifiably good learning results. Regardless of the form of mastery learning adopted (Reid, Bloom, Keller, or a homespun variety), an underlying concept is adopted along with the teaching system and that is responsible for the quality of learning that occurs. The search for quality and excellence in education is meaningless, however, without a standard against which they can be measured.

Quality is defined as "conformance to requirements" (Crosby, 1979, p. 17). If the requirements are high and if they are met, the quality will be high also. Mastery learning is a teaching/learning technique that can be applied to any educational requirements. A school district establishes its own standard of quality by preparing courses of study or curriculum guides that say what students in each grade level or course are required to learn. Such curriculum development exercises have been going on for many years but it is only recently that competency and mastery learning concepts have led to the verification of the actual quality of learning against the stated curriculum requirements. It is this verification of learning conformance to curriculum requirements that leads school districts to establish Management Plans.

Foundations of the Management Plan

A Management Plan is a district-wide document that guides the district in verifying that its learning product conforms to its curricular requirements—thus assuring that the desired level of educational excellence is met (Grove, 1983). The plan itself establishes "inspection points" where those students whose learning behaviors differ radically from the requirements can be identified and treated. Of necessity, the plan is virtually useless without courses of study or curriculum guides that state the learning requirements, valid and reliable verification measures, treatment program specifications, and proven classroom teaching techniques—most often mastery learning. All four of these steps are found to be present in the nation's most effective schools (Squires, Huitt, and Segars, 1984). It is possible, however, to have all these steps in place accompanied by a Management Plan and still not achieve excellence. The program's quality lies in its learning requirements first and in its verification measures second.

Learning Requirements. Designing excellent learning requirements is difficult because, unlike the metric or foot ruler, there is no nationally recognized curriculum standard. Writing learning requirements is usually done by a curriculum committee of teachers. Experienced teachers of first through third grades usually know quite well what skills their students actually learn. Above third grade, however, experienced teachers know more about what they "do" or "cover" during the year than which skills students actually master. Often textbooks and standardized tests are used during curriculum writing sessions to eliminate some of the guesswork. Neither of these tools can be relied upon exclusively for answering what the curriculum will do to produce excellence. Textbooks, which are designed for such supermarket states as California and Texas, have become simpler so they can be used with the middle and bottom thirds of those states' students. For example, one arithmetic series has compressed the study of decimals and percent into eight to ten pages in both seventh and eighth levels of their series and incorporated geometric figures into almost two thirds of each book. Adequate numerical and verbal practice exercises are notably missing throughout the series (Pringle, 1982).

Standardized tests are also being designed for the masses. A close examination of one major test revealed that seventh grade students who missed *all* items on the math subtests that dealt with arithmetic computations, concepts, or applications beyond multiplication of whole numbers scored at 6.9 grade-level equivalency in math. Most districts work toward the mastery of division of whole numbers by fifth grade at the latest (Pringle, 1982.)

The district's learning requirements cannot be established without coordinating them with textbooks and standardized tests, but, even using these tools, the first writing should not be considered final until it has been field tested for at least one year in that district. The field test should provide both objective and subjective data, which the curriculum committee can use to decide whether each learning objective meets the desired level of excellence for the district.

Verification Measures. Designing verification measures that match the learning requirements is an essential component of the Management Plan. Most districts are using a combination of criterion-referenced mastery tests and norm-referenced tests to verify conformance with learning requirements and to identify, for early intervention, those students whose learning behavior is above or below grade level. The district that develops a standard set of learning requirements also develops a standard set of criterion-referenced tests and field tests them to assure their content and construct validity, their test/retest reliability, and their levels of difficulty (Tuckman, 1972).

Treatment Programs. Treatment program specifications, customarily left to teachers' discretion or to special programs, are carefully planned to include both in-class and out-of-class interventions for students displaying unusual learning behavior. The treatment program for in-class intervention generally includes extra practice exercises in the form of ditto sheets, enrichment activities, tutorial techniques, counseling techniques, or reteaching strategies.

Out-of-class treatment programs include counseling, summer school sessions, Saturday study, reassignment to more appropriate learning groups, cross-age tutorial techniques, and program or schedule modifications.

Teaching Techniques. The classroom management/teaching technique most often adopted by districts that use a Management Plan is mastery learning. Usually, a standard technique is adopted by the district for all of its teachers to use. Forest Hills School District, for example, after becoming knowledgable about both Exemplary Center for Reading Instruction and Chicago Mastery Learning, prepared its own *Steps in Mastery Learning.* The steps call for teachers to (1) diagnose; (2) teach; (3) test, using Form A of the district's criterion-referenced verification measures; (4) provide intervention for those who mastered; (5) reteach those who failed; (6) retest, using Form B; (7) provide application activities; and (8) maintain profile sheets and communicate progress (Deighan, 1983, pp. 16-17).

Developing the Management Plan

Who writes the Management Plan? When is it written? What does it say?

The district's Management Plan is a comprehensive document. It is different from the course of study because it describes in detail how the learnings specified in the course of study will be verified and managed. Board policies and procedures establish the basis for the district-wide Management Plan to be used by curriculum supervisors, principals, and teachers. As a working document, it may be revised as the need arises.

As a management document, it is most often written by the district's management team with ample opportunity for input from teachers. Teachers are, in terms of learning production, members of the management team. They are responsible for learning in their classrooms. Principals are responsible for learning in their schools and the superintendent's office is responsible for learning in the district. All three management levels are involved in planning for learning, but the superintendent's office usually assumes responsibility for preparing the actual working document. In most school districts it seems to work best for the superintendent's leadership team to collect suggestions from all the other involved parties, organize them, draft the plan, circulate it for further input, revise it, and have the plan approved by the board of education.

Some of the topics to be addressed before writing the Management Plan include:

- Goals to be accomplished in a specified time period
- Subject areas to be included
- Time period for the plan
- Provision for special students
- Grading and promotion procedures
- Teachers' involvement in verifying effectiveness
- Interventions to be provided for students who do not master skills—stating length of time and who is responsible
- Individual school's customization of the plan
- Principals' role in verifying curriculum effectiveness
- Principals' reporting procedures and time lines
- Central office's use of reports and data
- Reports to board of education and community—procedures and time lines
- Course design and materials acquisition
- Assistance to be provided to principals and teachers based on their needs
- Course of study revision from data gathered
- Revision and update of Management Plan

These areas all must be planned for before or during the field test year. As the superintendent's leadership team, along with other district educators, begin their planning, they may develop a first-year draft plan and then move directly into a five-year Management Plan.

Goals for Students and Staff. Goals are stated for a specified implementation period. The goals cover student learning, staff development, treatment provisions, reporting procedures, and materials acquisition. These goals were stated by the management team for Lockland School District in its five-year Management Plan for the K–12 language arts program:

1. Seventy percent or more of the students at each grade level will demonstrate mastery of the required grade level language arts objectives (required objectives are shown with an * in the course of study) as demonstrated by achievement of 90 percent or better on the district's criterion referenced tests.
2. One hundred percent of the language arts, reading, and English teachers will be proficient in using mastery learning.
3. All students who are behind or ahead of grade level will be identified and will receive treatment as needed.
4. Report of students' learning will be computer-managed to provide program effectiveness information to teachers, principals, counselors, the superintendent's office, the board of education, and the community. These reports will be used to make decisions about materials, students' matriculation, and staffing needs.
5. All language arts objectives will be matched to adopted texts, workbooks, and supplementary materials; if needed, materials will be purchased to provide teaching tools where none now exist (Stamm, 1982, p. 1).

Baseline data gathered during the field test year were used to establish the first goal. In large, diverse districts, each school may develop its own Management Plan goals in order to meet or exceed the district's standards.

Standards for Decision Making. Standards include definitions for providing treatment and to promote or retain students. Examples of such standards are:

1. Students who are working on the objectives for the grade in which they are enrolled but who fail to demonstrate mastery of 70 percent of the objectives studied by the class must be identified for treatment by November 5th of each school year.
2. Students who are working on the objectives for the grade in which they are enrolled must demonstrate mastery of the required objectives to be considered for advancement to the next grade or course.
3. Students who, after the second attempt, fail to demonstrate

mastery of a given objective must be identified for in-class treatment by teachers.

4. Students who are working one grade below grade level must demonstrate mastery of the required objectives for the grade level in which they are working and must receive small group or individualized treatment to bring them along the continuum into the objectives for the grade in which they are enrolled.

5. Students who are working more than one grade below grade level must master the required objectives for the grade level in which they are working and must receive individualized treatment to bring them along the continuum into the objectives for the grade in which they are enrolled.

6. Students may be considered for retention after June 1984 if they are working on the objectives that are more than one grade below the one in which they are enrolled.

7. Students may work on the objectives for one or more grades above the grade in which they are enrolled and may be considered for advancement to courses or grades commensurate with the level at which they are working. To do so, they must demonstrate mastery of 100 percent of the objectives for the grade or grades in between the grade in which they are enrolled and the grade to which advancement is being considered (Stamm, 1982, p. 2).

Procedures to be Followed. Procedures listed and explained for teachers are: use the learning requirements as the primary planning tool; use the mastery learning teaching technique; use the district's criterion-referenced tests to verify learning; report mastery to students, parents, and the principal; identify students who are working below or above grade level; provide in-class treatment; and report treatment results to the principal when steps taken have failed to produce the desired learning results.

Principals are expected to follow procedures such as monitoring teachers' use of the learning requirements and criterion-referenced tests; assisting classroom teachers to become proficient in mastery learning; providing out-of-class treatment programs; providing learning materials and treatment strategies as needed; reporting learning and treatment results to the central office;

communicating learning requirements and students' accomplishments to parents; and participating with the superintendent's
leadership team to update or revise the learning requirements,
verification measures, or Management Plan.

Procedures listed and explained for others in the district,
such as the central office, assist principals and teachers in the
use of learning requirements, criterion-referenced tests, and mastery
learning techniques; summarize and report learning data received
from principals; assist principals to provide out-of-class treatment
strategies; and coordinate revisions to the learning requirements,
criterion-referenced tests, or Management Plan (Stamm, 1982).

Management of Students' Learning

Using the Management Plan provides teachers, principals,
and other district personnel with objective data derived from proven
criterion-referenced measures that have content validity with the
learning requirements. The learning requirements have been field
tested and represent the district's level of excellence. When computer resources are available, districts are mechanizing the gathering
and reporting of their learning data and using it to manage the
quality of learning achieved by individual students, classrooms, and
schools. This type of management results in upgraded learning
requirements, efficient intervention programs, and cost-effective
materials acquisition.

Teachers. Traditionally, teachers are familiar with the district's learning standards as stated in courses of study, but they are
guided more by their textbooks than by the district's documents.
This is neither surprising nor irrational since courses of study are
often developed, typed, and distributed without field use and
revision and frequently are not articulated among grade levels.
Many courses of study say more about what the teachers should do
than what the students will learn. Having to conform to or exceed
the district's own standards will be new to the teachers. Most of the
time, teachers appreciate having such standards set because it is
rarely possible to "get through" the textbook let alone to hold
students accountable for learning all that it contains.

Using the Management Plan, teachers may have to change the way they plan and deliver courses, in that their lessons must now show which district learning requirements are being taught. The textbook, which may have been the primary planning tool, now becomes the support material used to accomplish the learning requirements. Since the learning requirements rarely demand every minute of the classroom year, there is still ample opportunity for the incidental curriculum that develops from current world events, students' personal interests, and teachers' areas of special expertise.

Teachers have always given tests to verify that students learned what was taught. Generally, teachers prepared their own tests after teaching had occurred. The Management Plan calls for teachers' use of the district's tests to verify the objectives. Teachers must learn how to design their teaching to match the objectives and to use district-wide standards for verifying learning. This is, however, a very important step because these tests are fairer for students and give more accurate results than can be gotten when the several teachers at grade level have each developed their own measures. Some tests and grading systems used individually were undoubtedly easier or more difficult than others.

Elementary teachers, coaches, vocational instructors, and band directors are among those educators accustomed to organizing their classes to produce verified learning all along the way. They are notorious for using classroom management techniques that provide for ample amounts of practice followed by mastery testing. Many are accustomed to diagnosing and treating learning behaviors. Reporting treatment and learning results in ways other than report cards is not new to them and many already practice the desired classroom management techniques. Many teachers who are unaccustomed to holding students responsible for the learning requirements will need both time and efficient teaching techniques as they adjust to new routines such as administering and using diagnostic and mastery tests.

Management plans usually provide a specific district-approved teaching technique that is to be used, and this becomes quite a change for some teachers. The teaching technique adopted by one district may be the Exemplary Center for Reading Instruction's mastery learning. Another may adopt certain steps that teachers are expected to follow, that is, diagnose, teach, test (Form A), reteach, test (Form B), and so forth. From about the fourth grade up, teachers are less and less accustomed to diagnosing, reteaching, or retesting.

Teachers may also be unaccustomed to dealing with individuals or small groups of students who are either ahead or behind by providing interventions for them and seeing to it that they learn one thing successfully before going on to the next. Some Management Plans ask teachers to perform specified interventions and to report that they have done so, when, and with what results. It may be that none of the teachers' interventions work, and the student must receive other forms of intervention from outside the classroom.

Another aspect of classroom management that may be new to teachers will be the manner in which students' learning is reported. Traditionally, teachers graded students and turned in those grades. But each teacher usually used a different set of grading criteria so that there could be no interpretation of learning results based on the grades. Under the Management Plan, teachers use the standard mastery tests and pass along the test results. Some districts provide for use of the mastery tests in determining grades while others do not. Grading systems are usually maintained, as students and parents expect them. Verification measures used by all teachers in the district assure that interpretable data are generated.

Principals. The district's Management Plan often helps principals become the educational leaders of their school. Principals receive more information from teachers on students' learning than ever before. Most of the time, teachers pass on the scored tests to the principal as well as almost-daily intervention reports. The principal organizes, records, and uses this data. Many do so using microcomputers. Others use handcompleted charts, folders, or other means. The mastery tests, which must be kept secure, are generally filed by the principal, who has them destroyed at the end of the school year. Often principals keep a student-by-student record of learning mastery and use it to counsel both students and their parents when the need arises. Such records are useful for scheduling classes, designing courses, and assigning students to classrooms. Some principals use the students' learning records to help determine eligibility for extra-curricular activities.

Principals are responsible for communicating students' learning progress and the school's programs to the parents. The Management Plan may easily provide how this is to be done. In one district, principals send, at the beginning of the school year, a list of the learning requirements for each student. At each reporting period, in addition to A-B-C grades, parents also receive a new copy of the skills list showing what their child has mastered to date.

A prime responsibility of principals is staff development. The Management Plan generally contains a staff development section that requires the principal to make sure the teachers know how to implement the Management Plan. Principals work with teachers or arrange for persons with expertise to work with them in areas where there is a demonstrated need.

Through their recordkeeping, principals become aware of weaknesses in the curriculum. If most students in a grade are having difficulty with the same objective, the principal begins to question why. Is the objective weak? Is the test weak? Are the materials inadequate? Should the objective be shifted to a lower or a higher grade? By finding answers to these questions and working with teachers, other principals, and the district curriculum staff, the principal is continuously working directly with learning.

The principal is responsible for helping teachers do the best possible job. Spelling out a mastery learning teaching technique in the Management Plan helps principals identify what kinds of help to give teachers. Some teachers just need better diagnostic tools; others would be more successful if initial teaching/practicing were more thorough so that fewer students require treatment after failing the first mastery test. Better treatment materials or activities may need to be provided or better classroom management techniques may need to be instituted. Principals use their learning data to spot teachers whose students learn faster. By studying the techniques used by these teachers and having other teachers learn from them, many teachers can and will improve.

The Management Plan helps to improve materials acquisition by requiring that recommended material be reviewed against the learning standards and the students' verified learning needs. A textbook should match the district's objectives and those persons making recommendations for buying a particular text should identify how well the text supports the skills to be taught. Many principals, when beginning to implement a mastery learning Management Plan, take the first year to match up all existing materials with the objectives. When everything is matched, teachers have references to use and the principal has a list of objectives that no materials match. Materials can then be effectively reviewed and purchased to match the documented need.

In decentralized districts, each school may prepare its own Management Plan. The school's plan is based on the district's plan but has parts that are particularly suitable to the school's population. In this case, the principal is responsible for the entire action plan and for reporting results in a standard way to the superintendent's office.

Teachers report test and treatment results to the principal's office where the data are organized and summarized by the principal's staff so that learning reports are generated for individual students, classes, and grades within the school. Results are reported for individual students, and success rates are computed for each identified type of intervention. Mechanized data collection also allows learning results to be reported against objectives.

Individual learning reports show what learning requirements have been selected for the student based on diagnostic data, what the student has mastered to date, what intervention, if any, has been used and with what results, and what learning requirements remain for the student to learn that year. Reports by learning requirement show the names of students who have demonstrated mastery, who are developing mastery, who have tried and failed, and who have not yet begun on this requirement. Other mechanized reports can show, for each requirement, the textbooks, supplementary books, audiovisuals, paper and pencil interventions, kits, and programmed materials that exist at the school and the specific location within the resource that applies to this requirement. These reports provide important help to both the principal and teachers.

Central Office. The central office focuses on verifying curriculum excellence for the entire district by using the learning data to manage course of study development, direct staff development activities, coordinate testing, authorize materials acquisition, and evaluate treatment programs. The person responsible at the central office may be an assistant superintendent for instruction or a program coordinator.

Principals send to the central office the learning results they have gathered from their teachers. The results are analyzed against the objectives in terms of the percent of students who mastered each objective. Intervention reports are also analyzed by the central office to determine what is being done to help students who have failed and how well each intervention is working. The central office may help principals and teachers spot students who have special learning behaviors.

The central office uses the Management Plan to help principals improve learning in their schools. In-service programs are built into the plan to provide professional assistance to principals and their staffs in how to better manage the mastery learning program.

As more knowledge is gained and the plan is used for at least one year, revisions can be made based on data gathered. Learning achievement should be reported by the central office to the board and the community even though the Plan may be in its first year stage.

Effective Treatment Systems

When the school district accepts responsibility for students' learning, it designs a treatment system for youngsters who either cannot pass the mastery tests or who pass them very early and need to go on to the next step. The goal for any treatment system is that it be effective for producing the desired learning results.

Designing Treatment Systems. There are two major types of treatment for students with unusual learning behavior: that which is provided in the students' classroom by the teacher and that which is provided outside of the classroom by someone other than the students' teacher. Many districts are now designing treatment strategies for students who are below grade level *and* those who are above grade level.

Students Who are Below Grade Level. Using mastery learning techniques, all students can master the learning requirements (Bloom, 1980). Perhaps the single most effective treatment for below-grade level students is practice or over-learning before testing. The Exemplary Center for Reading Instruction's mastery learning calls for more efficient practice using directives to help these students learn how to learn and to increase their learning rates over time (Reid, 1980). Some Mastery Learning strategies call for treatment to be administered *after* students have failed a formative test. Some below-level students, however, gain learning confidence by succeeding on the mastery test the first time they take it and will, if they experience early failures, give up altogether. School districts have done time-on-task studies and found that the average teaching/practicing time for mastery tests that 75 to 80 percent of the students failed the first time was only fifteen minutes (Pringle, 1984). An important treatment strategy is to allow more than enough practice *before* mastery testing.

Other treatment strategies for below-grade level students include tutoring in and out of school, Saturday study, counseling, and computer-assisted drill and practice programs.

Students Who are Above Grade Level. In many districts above-grade level students are allowed to continue advancing along the continuum of skills and to use the next grade's materials to do so. This means that, the next year, the teacher continues to move them along and, eventually, advanced placement courses are provided in both junior and senior high schools. In other districts, these students are given enrichment projects or "deep" studies to perform until others in the class can join them, and the entire group is moved along together. Using the above-grade level students as tutors has an effective learning result for both the tutor and the students being tutored.

Evaluating the Treatment System. The principals and the central office staff are responsible for evaluating the treatment programs. Data are collected about what works with particular students, which tutors are most effective, and which materials or paper/pencil interventions work best. Teachers and parents may also provide data about the type of homework that is successful with students.

Following data collection and analysis of the treatment system, revisions are made. Successful treatments are expanded and unsuccessful ones are revised.

Reporting Learning Results

The Management Plan includes a procedure for reporting regularly to students, parents, board of education, and community about the learning results.

Reporting to Students. Students are told what their learning requirements are going to be at the beginning of each year, semester, quarter, or unit—depending on their age. They are always able to tell in their own words what it is they are learning and how they will be required to demonstrate their mastery. As soon as they have achieved mastery, they receive both verbal and written reports on their accomplishments. In some districts the written report is a computer printout. In others, the teacher has specifically designed report forms to give students as soon as their tests are scored. Or a written report is given in the form of a grade for that marking period. Some teachers have found that the more immediate the positive feedback, the better the students' learning. Hence, short interim reports are given to students during weekly teacher conferences.

Reporting to Parents. Parents are kept informed through the formal grading reports established by the district. They receive the usual A-B-C grades and printouts or profile sheets showing the students' accomplishments. Parents like to know how their children are progressing, and some teachers set up weekly reporting forms that are given to students who take them home for parents to see. It has been found that when students and parents receive more frequent learning reports, learning improves—especially when those reports are positive.

Reporting to the Board of Education. The board of education receives monthly reports from the superintendent in many school districts, especially when mechanized data analysis systems are available. Most boards receive a complete annual evaluation of learning performance, as measured against learning requirements, in reports that come from each school principal. Some districts combine these and issue to the board the school report. Some districts' annual reports are comprehensive. Other districts use a series of charts and graphs to report data. Line graphs show, for each subject and for the total population, the desired level of excellence and the learning levels produced. Another graph may show the national norm with one line and the local achievement with another, for each subject. Some districts, in their annual reports, also evaluate students' achievement against aptitude. This, of course, can best be done if the district is using a standardized instrument, such as the *Comprehensive Testing Program* distributed by the Educational Records Bureau.

Reporting to the Community. In most communities, the annual report that goes to the board of education is also provided to the community. Some districts mail their report directly to all parents in the community. Other districts prepare annual fact sheets and distribute them to all households in the community. The reports may be placed in banks, dentists' offices, pediatricians' offices, and real estate offices, and they may also be provided to such organizations as Kiwanis, Rotary, and the Chamber of Commerce. Newspapers may also carry a summary of these annual reports.

Managing Program Materials and Equipment

Management Plans need to justify expenditures against learning requirements and achievement. The largest expenditure for educational materials is usually textbooks, which are adopted every five to seven years in most districts.

Procedures for evaluating textbooks and other educational materials are related by the Management Plan to the customary forms of teacher review plus justification of their purchase based on their ability to support the learning requirements. One district, preparing to adopt new reading textbooks, for example, narrowed its selection to five publishers whose series all met the subjective evaluations performed by teachers, including ratings for the teacher's guide, the illustrations, the story contents, the print size, and page layout. Then all five were evaluated against the reading objectives, the selected vocabulary lists, and the adopted readability levels. Two of the five contenders were found to be quite well matched with the district's requirements and the one adopted was the most cost-effective (Pringle, 1983). The district had developed a comprehensive way to assure that materials purchased are those that do support what students are to learn.

Conclusion

Most districts begin the process of using a Management Plan by establishing or reconfirming their educational goals. These goals, which justify every course of study, provide the foundation upon which learning requirements are based. Once the goals are in place, a long-range plan is prepared for each area to show when it will be developed, field tested, implemented, and provided with support materials. As a K–12 subject, for example, mathematics or language arts, reaches its implementation, the Management Plan is simply revised. Some school districts manage only the basic subject areas (reading, composition, and mathematics) and others combine all subjects under the Management Plan. Most often districts add one subject area each year to their Management Plan.

The Management Plan is a proven way to map out what is to be done with learning in a district. Since the plan calls for collecting data, decisions can be made about personnel, materials, and strategies based on solid information. This takes the guesswork out of decision making.

Budgeting for the instructional program can be projected over a five- to ten-year period for each subject area to include personnel, materials, equipment, and staff development. The long-range plan eliminates much crisis management by establishing data-collecting and analyzing check points on the district's own educational goals and learning requirements.

References

Bloom, B. S. "The New Direction in Educational Research: Alterable Variables." *Phi Delta Kappan*, 1980, *61* (6), 382–385.

Crosby, P. B. *Quality Is Free: The Art Of Making Quality Certain.* New York: McGraw-Hill, 1979.

Deighan, W. P. "Field Test Guide, Language Arts/Reading Curriculum: Competency Project, 1983–84." Document prepared as management plan for Forest Hills School District, Cincinnati, August 1983.

Grove, A. S. *High Output Management.* New York: Random House, 1983.

Pringle, P. R. "Developing Outcomes-Based Curriculum Systems to Improve Students' Learning." *Outcomes,* 1982, *1* (4), 12–18.

Pringle, P. R. "Outcomes Based Program Implementation." *Outcomes,* 1983, *2* (3), 31–35.

Pringle, P. R. *Summary of Data Analysis.* Cincinnati: Educational Services Institute, 1984.

Reid, E. R. "Another Approach to Mastery Learning." *Educational Leadership,* November 1980, pp. 170–172.

Squires, D. A., Huitt, W. G., and Segars, J. K. *Effective Schools and Classrooms: A Research-Based Perspective.* Alexandria, Va.: Association for Supervision and Curriculum Development, 1984.

Stamm, G. "Implementation Guide for the Language Arts and Reading Course of Study, August 1982 through June 1987." Document prepared as management plan for Lockland City School District, Cincinnati, July 1982.

Tuckman, B. W. *Conducting Educational Research.* New York: Harcourt Brace Jovanovich, 1972.

7

Teacher Reactions
to Use of Tests
for Accountability

Mary M. Kennedy

A large part of teaching consists of reacting to what one sees. Teachers spot bewildered faces and respond accordingly; they comfort children who have skinned their knees; they correct grammar throughout the day, not just during language lessons; and they can usually gin up a spontaneous lesson on earthworms when one is found on the playground. The extent to which teaching is or should be *reactive,* as opposed to *directive,* has been a matter of debate for centuries. There are those who believe that the best teaching is entirely reactive, capitalizing on student interests or on the moment. But the more prevalent view today is that teaching should be more directive than reactive. The contemporary preference for this point of view may be stimulated less by pedagogical considerations than by an increasingly popular argument that schools should be able to guarantee a common set of knowledge and skills to all children, and that they should be accountable for what students learn.

This is a management consideration, not a pedagogical one, and it does not preclude the possibility of spontaneous or reactive teaching in the classroom. But it does require the interaction between teachers and students to be more focused. Indeed, the two most popular tools for installing substantive direction into the classroom are both designed to focus the instructional efforts of teachers. These are systems of management-by-objectives (MBOs), and tests that not only measure learning but by their very existence also inform teachers and others of what the instructional content should be. Mastery learning (ML) is among the instructional approaches that place significant emphasis on both these tools. Objectives to be taught, tested, and retaught must be clearly specified as part of a system for planning and delivering effective instruction, and assessment of mastery is a key element in managing the instructional system. However, despite the management rationale for employing these tools, they are often introduced into a school system on the (untested) assumption that they will positively influence pedagogical practices as well; that is, that they will improve teaching.

When these two tools are adopted by a school system (as part of ML or related approaches), two things happen. First, administrators become zealous advocates of the tools. This attitude is not, of course, completely a result of the tools: Since it was the administrators' decision to develop and use these tools, they were no doubt convinced prior to adoption that the tools would be valuable. But adoption does increase their advocacy. The second thing that happens when these tools are introduced is that teachers become afraid.

These two attitudes—zealous advocacy and fear—are not a good combination. While many administrators expect teachers to be nervous, and some even want to encourage that response, their own enthusiasm may inhibit their ability to correctly gauge teacher fear. Too much teacher anxiety can induce counterproductive behavior, and an over-zealous administrator may not be able to see the signs of damage. This chapter reviews several of these counterproductive options that are available to teachers who feel threatened by such management tools and the reasons why teachers prefer these to more productive responses. It then reviews some of the options available to administrators who wish to curb counterproductive behaviors and to encourage productive responses among their teachers.

Options Available to Teachers

Management systems that are designed to increase accountability or to tighten the focus of instruction are usually based on tests. Tests define the content to be taught, measure what students currently know, and are used to infer improvements or changes in student knowledge. All forms of tests—norm-referenced, criterion-referenced, objectives-referenced, and so forth—have been used for all of these purposes, but none of these forms of tests are direct measures of student knowledge or skills in the sense that a yardstick is a direct measure of length. Instead, test scores are *indicators* of these characteristics. Just as dark clouds indicate the possibility of rain and changes in the average price of Dow-Jones Industrial stocks indicate larger economic trends, test scores indicate what students know and do not know or what they can and cannot do. The job of the psychometrician is to improve the veridicality between the indicator and the indicatee, so to speak, but no one knows better than teachers, who see students perform every day, how unreliable and inaccurate test scores can be.

Furthermore, test scores are *corruptible* indicators: They can be manipulated, and they are very likely to be manipulated if the people responsible for gathering the test data, that is, the test administrators, are also the people who are responsible for the outcomes being measured, that is, the teachers. Teachers have available to them a variety of options for manipulating student test scores. How much effort they devote to these options will depend on how desperate they are to have high-scoring students and on how easy it is for them to manipulate the scores. The options listed below are presented in order of their relative ease.

The Test Items. Some accountability systems are built from teacher-made, rather than store-bought, tests. Committees of teachers responsible for common grade levels or common subject areas meet to hammer out a core curriculum and an associated set of test items. The object of these exercises is to develop agreement regarding what students *ought* to know, but teachers also realize that some portions of the course content are easier to teach than others. To the extent that they feel threatened by the proposed accountability system, they can use this opportunity to restrict both course objectives and test items to the knowledge and skills they know they can easily transmit to students. Administrators who are unaware of this defensive action may later feel a false sense of satisfaction with their management system: The majority of students will have acquired all the material outlined for each grade level or subject area. What they fail to realize is that students may not have learned some of the things they should have learned because teacher did not want to accept the risk of being held accountable for difficult-to-teach content.

The Objectives. Some systems are designed so that each teacher must prepare a set of his or her own objectives at the beginning of each year. For instance, a teacher who notices that his or her students have not done well in abstract mathematical thinking over the past few years, may set an objective of improving scores in that area this year. Defining objectives is not unlike defining test items, however. Teachers can emphasize the areas in which they are most likely to succeed, rather than the areas in which there is more need. Or they may interpret the test data as indicating that they have no pressing problems at all, and that they therefore have no need for demanding objectives.

Note that these judgments are not necessarily devious. Test scores have no meaning by themselves. They need human beings to judge whether they are too high or too low. Likewise, collections of scores lack meaning until a human being perceives a pattern in them. And reasonable educators may reasonably disagree as to what the most pertinent aspects of any given pattern are.

The Testing Equipment. Whether or not teachers are involved in developing test items, they are inevitably involved in test administration. They have as much freedom to structure the test environment as they have to structure the classroom learning environment. To the extent that they feel a need to assure high test scores, they can read items more slowly, repeat more often, use intonations that hint at how to respond, move about the room pointing their fingers at right answers in individual test booklets, give helpful hints to baffled students, and overlook conversations among the students themselves. Conversely, if the accountability system includes a pretest, teachers can be brusk during pretesting, overlook instructions, cut the time short, and engage in noisy and disruptive activities while students are taking that test.

And teachers need not wait until the day of the exam to influence the testing environment. They can prepare students for the posttest by reminding them daily that it is pending and that it is important, and tell them not to worry about the pretest, or fail even to mention that a pretest is forthcoming.

Note again that these behaviors may not be done with the conscious intent of undermining the system. Teachers care about their students and want them to do well. Much of this behavior may be done with good or at least benign intentions. After all, in the teachers' eyes, the pretest is not an important exam for the students, and therefore students should not have to be anxious over it. And, after all, we all want our friends to look good and to do well.

The Tested Population. Teachers are also sometimes able to affect the composition of their student body so that their classes contain only the more able students or so that only the more able students will be present on posttest day. This they do by such legitimate means as referring less able students to special education or remedial education programs, or by such illegitimate means as counting the slower students absent on testing day and discarding their exams. At the secondary level, they can impose prerequisites on their courses. The biology course with a chemistry prerequisite receives an already-screened group of students. But so does the chemistry course with a biology prerequisite, and secondary teachers can get themselves embroiled in serious squabbles when it comes to what constitutes a legitimate prerequisite for what.

The Timing of Instruction Directed Toward Specific Test Items. None of the preceding options entails any changes in actual instruction, yet each of them has the capability of altering a classroom's aggregate test score, sometimes dramatically. Assuming that teachers will also devote some portion of their instructional time to the specific items that are on the test, the next option available to them is to rearrange their teaching schedule so that the weeks immediately preceding testing are converted to a cramming period for the test. By itself, this is not necessarily a counterproductive activity. But it can be if it results in students memorizing answers only to forget them after the exam.

The Quantity of Instruction Directed Toward Specific Test Items. If teachers perceive last-minute cramming as insufficient to attain the scores they feel are needed, they also have the option of altering the overall proportion of their teaching time that is devoted to specific test content. Some teachers devote the entire school year between pretest and posttest to test items. Some feel no need to teach at all during the first and last three weeks of the school year, that is, before the pretest and after the posttest. Those who are more conscientious will use the last three weeks to convey context and nuance, the substantive glue that holds the test items together.

The Quality of Instruction. Teachers can also attempt to improve the quality of their teaching so that students are more likely to acquire the knowledge and skills they need. Notice that, while this option is the one administrators hope to encourage when they establish accountability systems, it is the last option listed here. This is because it is the most difficult option for a teacher to implement, and consequently it often is the option of least preference. There are several reasons why this option is difficult.

One is lack of knowledge regarding how to improve teaching, a condition that is not unique to teachers. Despite volumes of educational research, there are still very few propositions regarding what constitutes good teaching that the entire research community would agree to. A second reason has to do with native ability. Some teachers have a knack for it; others do not. And the intuitive sense for such things as timing and pace is not readily transferable from one teacher to the next. A third reason it is difficult for teachers to improve the quality of their teaching is that teaching is heavily dependent on context. Teachers can be only as good as their environmental circumstances will allow. If they teach youngsters whose parents threaten to sue after each disciplinary action, if their lessons are interrupted regularly by the public address system, if textbooks are old or missing altogether, if other teachers present no professional challenge or expectations, then the quality of teaching will be low.

A considerable volume of research literature is beginning to accumulate now regarding the nature of everyday teaching. These studies indicate that, at least from the teacher's point of view, teaching is not a rational activity. Teachers do not plan their lessons around objectives, as these management systems assume, but instead plan around activities (Clark and Yinger, 1977). Their first consideration in lesson planning and lesson implementation is not subject matter but crowd control (Hargreaves, 1979); they do not depend on normative propositions as researchers do, but instead build their knowledge base from the particulars of their own situation-specific experiences (Bolster, 1983); and they base their assessments of students' knowledge and abilities more on their own observations and experiences than on test data (Kennedy, 1984). In other words, teaching is not a rationally planned exercise but is instead a craft, where experience in analogous situations gives the teacher a feel for what to do next. Note too that the criteria for a successful lesson are not those associated with instructional effectiveness but rather those of a successful group activity: It follows an orderly process, and everyone is involved.

Furthermore, several investigators have found that the things teachers value in their craft are not the things that managers and researchers value. Their goals for students are more often social than cognitive, (Salmon-Cox, 1984), they strive as much or more to be liked and admired by students as they do to instill specific knowledge in students (Lortie, 1975), and they are not at all confident that they are having the impact they hope to have. When they look for evidence of success, they aren't impressed by aggregate test scores or even by impressive individual scores. What they seek is evidence of their craftsmanship—of their *personal* impact. They look for particular impacts on particular students or particular events (Lortie, 1975).

For all of these reasons, then—informational, motivational, situational, and conceptual—teachers will not be inspired by accountability systems to change their pedagogical practices. Their pedagogy is derived from a craftsman's experience, and test scores frequently have little to do with the personal and social goals they hope to achieve with their students. Even if they recognize the test as a threat they must deal with, regardless of its relevance to their craft, they may not be able to change their behaviors for the several reasons cited above. Consequently, teachers will generally prefer one or more of the other options available to them to raise their test scores, rather than trying to change their method of instruction.

Options Available to Administrators

Most administrators do not think of teaching as a craft acquired by experience, nor do they consider the possibility that teachers might not be impressed by an accountability system. But they do realize that teachers may try to manipulate test scores. And just as there are many different ways teachers can attempt to manipulate test scores, there are also several ways in which administrators can try to prevent or minimize these teacher behaviors. Administrators' options fall into two broad categories: those designed to reduce the corruptibility of the measures and those designed to improve the quality of teaching so that corruption may not be necessary.

Reducing Corruptibility. Corruptibility can be reduced either by changing the people who design and administer the test, or by changing the structure of the test itself, or both. If administrators feel that teachers cannot write adequate test items or that teachers cannot administer tests using fair and uniform procedures, then administrators can choose someone else to perform these tasks. This is not to say that teachers might not be involved at all but merely that their role would be modified. For instance, a team of teachers, curriculum specialists, and psychometricians could work together to develop test items. Perhaps these three types of participants could operate in a mutual check and balance system.

With respect to the structure of the test itself, administrators might try using item banks rather than single-version tests and comprehensive exams rather than unidimensional scales. Item banks can convey to both students and teachers what the generic content areas are while still discouraging them from focusing on specific items within a general area. Comprehensive examinations accomplish a similar end. Because they measure multiple outcomes, attention cannot become too riveted on a limited area.

If these two options are combined so that administrators change the composition of the staff responsible for developing and administering the tests and change the composition of the tests themselves, the result is likely to be a far less corruptible measure of educational outcomes and consequently a far stronger base on which to build an oversight system. But these changes alone will not stop—nor perhaps even discourage—teachers from their interest in counterproductive behaviors if the teachers feel they have no other alternatives.

Improving the Quality of Teaching. I mentioned earlier three broad classes of variables that influence the quality of teaching. These are knowledge regarding what constitutes effective teaching, individual differences among teachers in their ability to teach effectively, and the immediate teaching context. Assuming that the second variable is out of the administrator's control, there are two general strategies for improving the quality of teaching. One is to provide training regarding proven pedagogical principles; the other is to adjust the teaching context so that it is more conducive to good teaching.

There are two mistakes that administrators often make when they choose to develop or purchase training programs. The first is to assume that training in what should be taught is the same as training in how to teach it. But the fanciest, glossiest set of materials ever created is no help to teachers if it reviews content only. And most do review content only, in part because acknowledged principles of good teaching are so rare. Teachers often cite the value of these materials for new teachers, who need to learn what the curriculum is, but also point out that the materials are not helpful to floundering teachers, who know the curriculum but simply cannot get students to learn it. The second common administrator error is to assume that a generic set of procedures can be used effectively by all teachers in all contexts. An off-the-shelf training package on lesson planning, question asking, grouping, or any other topic is not likely to address every teaching situation equally well. Techniques can vary in their effectiveness across subject areas, grade levels, and kinds of students. Even if administrators purchased training programs that were tailored for particular grade levels or subject matters, the craft nature of the profession, at least as teachers see it, would permit them to reject any of the lessons that did not "fit" their own experiences. Again, the over-zealous administrator may assume that simply purchasing a training package is sufficient and fail to find out from the teacher if or when it was helpful.

The importance of context has only recently been acknowledged. Many of the current reports on the status of education have pointed to outdated or absent textbooks, burdensome paperwork requirements (often associated with management-by-objectives), intrusive public address systems, and the lack of opportunity for professional support among teachers. None of these variables can be completely controlled by administrators, but administrators exercise more control over them than teachers do.

Even professional support systems are more controllable by administrators than by teachers. Those few occasions when teachers have an opportunity to interact are usually staff meetings in which new policies are presented, new rules are outlined, or assignments for lunchrooms and hall duty are allocated. Teaching techniques and students' needs are not routinely a part of these meetings. Perhaps converting these group meetings to some form of quality circle would prove useful. Since teachers trust particular experiences more than the general propositions and seek recognition for unique accomplishments more than for general student performance, quality circles could provide teachers with a vehicle for sharing their particular experiences as well as with a professional recognition and support system.

Conclusion

I have tried to describe here both the teacher's perspective and the administrator's perspective toward that class of management systems that is intended to focus instruction and to increase accountability. I am more sure of the behavioral options available to teachers than of those available to administrators. In a recent investigation (Kennedy, 1982), I found all of these options employed. But because administrators tend to be advocates of their accountability systems and consequently to overlook evidence of their malfunctioning, they rarely consider many of the options I have described for them. However, the administrative practices I have seen lead me to two conclusions. First, teachers are not persuaded to improve their practices by rational arguments or by fear. Second, belief in how a management system *ought to work* does not make it work that way. If teachers feel threatened, they will engage in counterproductive behaviors regardless of how often or how well the administrator recites platitudes about accountability, the importance of a common curriculum, or the efficacy of MBO. And unless administrators are watchful they will never know that their teachers have undermined their systems. In fact, they will interpret the improved test scores as further evidence of the rightness of their approach. The most difficult task facing the administrator who uses tests to increase accountability is that of determining how it is *actually* working, as distinct from how it ought to be working.

References

Bolster, A. S., Jr. "Toward a More Effective Model of Research on Teaching." *Harvard Educational Review*, 1983, *53*, 294–308.

Clark, C. M., and Yinger, R. J. "Research on Teacher Thinking." *Curriculum Inquiry*, 1977, *7*, 279–304.

Darling-Hammond, L., Wise, A. E., and Pease, S. R. "Teacher Evaluation in the Organizational Context: A Review of the Literature." *Review of Educational Research*, 1983, *53*, 285–328.

Hargreaves, D. H. "A Phenomenological Approach to Classroom Decision-Making." In J. Eggleston (Ed.), *Teacher Decision-making in the Classroom*. Boston: Routledge & Kegan Paul, 1979.

Kennedy, M. M. *Working Knowledge and Other Essays*. Cambridge, Mass.: Huron Institute, 1982.

Kennedy, M. M. "Uses of Tests in School Districts." In L. M. Rudner (Ed.), *Testing in our Schools: Proceedings of the NIE Invitational Conference on Test Use*. Washington, D.C.: National Institute of Education, Mass.: 1984.

Lortie, D. C. *School Teacher: A Sociological Study*. Chicago: University of Chicago Press, 1975.

Salmon-Cox, L. "Elementary Teachers and Achievement Tests." In L. M. Rudner (Ed.), *Testing in our Schools: Proceedings of the NIE Invitational Conference on Test Use*. Washington, D.C.: National Institute of Education, 1984.

8

Assessing Mastery of Basic Skills Through Summative Testing

Huynh Huynh

Recent developments and interest in adaptive instruction and mastery learning call for new testing procedures focusing on the evaluation of individual performance in terms of some competency criteria. Given that a domain of behavior is uniquely defined by the mastery of some unit of instruction, a test is deliberately constructed to reflect the degree of competency in these behaviors. At the end of the period of instruction, the test is administered to the individual student, and, on the basis of the observed test score, the student is classified in one of several achievement categories. In typical instructional situations, there are two such categories, which are usually labeled *mastery* and *nonmastery*.

The fundamental purpose of mastery testing resembles those purposes of minimum competency and basic skills assessment programs. In attempting to reverse the decline in student achievement over the last decade, several states have implemented statewide testing programs testing for minimum competency in the basic skills. Many of these programs aim to insure that high school graduates possess a minimum level of academic achievement or have acquired the skills required to function effectively as adults in American society. Minimum competency, in this sense, acts as a high school exit examination or what has been called a certification exam. When used in this manner, minimum competency examinations do not have the positive connotation of some other basic skills assessment programs. The latter programs are specifically designed for a continuous monitoring of the acquisition of the basic skills (namely reading, writing, and mathematics) across succeeding grade levels. The results of these continuous monitoring programs are used to diagnose a student's deficiencies in the basic skills and to provide for instructional remediation.

Although sometimes differing in their ultimate purposes, mastery testing, minimum competency, and the monitoring of the basic skills are similar in many aspects of test development and other technical problems. The selection and construction of test items rely heavily on a thoughtful specification of the educational objectives or domain of skills to which scores are to be referenced via performance on the test items. The specification of the items themselves must, in most instances, be worked out in considerable detail so that there will be a high degree of congruence between the test items and the educational objectives. Technical aspects held in common include such major issues as setting passing scores, reporting objective-referenced data for the purpose of instructional remediation, and assessing the quality of decisions. In addition, in mastery testing and basic skills assessment, it is of considerable interest to track the progress of individual students across several years of schooling and to plot the results of instructional emphasis that a school or school district places on several succeeding grade levels.

This paper provides a discussion of the major technical issues in testing for mastery as mentioned above. Several of the procedures that address these issues have been conceptualized and worked out in conjunction with the development and implementation of the South Carolina Basic Skills Assessment Program (BSAP).

Setting Passing Scores

There are a variety of ways to set passing scores for a mastery or minimum competency test in a basic skills assessment program.

Most procedures can be classified as content-based or data-based. Variations of content-based approaches have been proposed by Nedelsky (1954), Angoff (1971), and Ebel (1972). These typically focus on some type of subjective judgment regarding the expected performance of the examinees at the borderline of achievement on the content of the items or on the objectives that underline the test.

Data-based procedures, on the other hand, utilize the examinees' responses to the items. Most of these procedures rely on an external classification (which is independent of the test data) of examinees in nonoverlapping groups and seek passing scores that sort these examinees in categories consistent in some sense with the external classifications. When examinees can be classified in the two groups (high and low) independently of test data, the contrasting-group procedure as described in Ziesky and Livingston (1977) may be used. This procedure seeks a passing score that will maximize the number of students correctly sorted by the test scores. (These are students in the high group who pass the test and those in the low group who fail the test.) In instances where the borderline (or undecided) group is added to the external classifications, a summary measure (such as the median) of this group may be used as passing score.

Since most procedures currently used for setting passing scores are judgmental, there appear no compelling reasons to suspect that one procedure would provide passing scores that are better or more valid than those derived from others. Thus, to set a passing score for a particular test, any of the currently available procedures may be used; the choice for a particular technique would depend on the availability of appropriate data and the acceptability of the procedure as perceived by the practitioner.

In a large testing program, such as the South Carolina BSAP, passing scores are sometimes required for different subject areas and at different grade levels. For the passing scores to be defensible, it seems reasonable to expect that these passing scores should be derived from procedures that are compatible with each other. Where several approaches can be used, it may be desirable to try most of these procedures first and then select the one that provides acceptable passing scores for all situations under consideration. (This may seem like a fishing expedition; however, the task of defending a set of consistent passing scores is far less arduous than the effort to combine seemingly unrelated passing scores.) The process of setting passing scores for the South Carolina BSAP is used as an illustration of the various issues raised in this section.

For the South Carolina BSAP tests of reading and math for grades one, two, three, six, and eight, the setting of passing scores was based on a combination of students' responses and teachers' judgments. Since most standards are judgmental in nature, the fairness and credibility of those who make the judgment determine the extent to which the resulting passing scores are acceptable to the public. For the BSAP tests, it was felt that teachers who had been teaching the students for almost a year would be in the best position to make judgments regarding the performance of the students in the subject areas under study.

During the May 1981 statewide BSAP testing, samples of slightly under 3,000 students were selected for each of the grades one, two, three, six, and eight. A few weeks prior to testing, teachers were asked to classify as *Adequate* or *Nonadequate,* the achievement of each of their students. In the case of uncertainty, the student was to be placed in the category labeled *Undecided* (the borderline group). The classifications of the teachers were, of course, independent of the students' test scores on the BSAP. Three approaches were then considered in the setting of passing scores based on these classifications and the students' BSAP test scores. They were subsequently described as the Contrasting-Group Procedure, the Equal-Percent-Failing Procedure, and the Undecided-Group Procedure.

In the Contrasting-Group Procedure, the Undecided group was ignored, and the passing score was set at the test score at which the number of students correctly classified was maximized.

More specifically, let $N_1(x < c)$ be the number of Nonadequate students with test score less than c. Likewise let $N_2(x \geq c)$ be the number of Adequate students with test scores of at least c. Then the total number of students correctly classified is $N_1 + N_2$. The Contrasting-Group Procedure seeks the passing score c at which this sum is maximum.

Table 1 illustrates an application of the Contrasting-Group Procedure. For each score c, this table respectively lists the frequencies of students in the Nonadequate group and in the Adequate group, the quantities N_1, N_2, and the sum $N_1 + N_2$. It may be noted that this sum is maximized at the score $c = 3$, which is the solution of the procedure. The Contrasting-Group Procedure can be generalized to situations in which differential weights are given to the identification of students in the Adequate and Nonadequate students. For example if it is three times as important to fail a Nonadequate student as to pass an Adequate, then the passing score is at the place where the weighted sum $3N_1 + N_2$ is maximized.

In the Equal-Percent-Failing Procedure, the Undecided students were also ignored. For the remaining students, the percent of Nonadequate students was determined. A passing score was then sought that would yield a similar percent of statewide students who scored below this minimum standard. (These were students who would fail the test.) Since all BSAP test score distributions were discrete, the percent of Nonadequate students and the statewide percent of students who would fail the test could not usually be made equal. However, since the BSAP tests aimed at detecting students who would need help, the passing score was set at the first test score at which the statewide percent of failing students exceeded the percent of Nonadequate students.

Finally, in the Undecided-Group Procedure the passing score was set at the median of the test score distribution of the Undecided group. This approach presumed that the category *Undecided* was comprised of students who were on the borderline between adequacy (passing) and nonadequacy (failing). The Undecided-Group

Table 1. An Illustration of the Contrasting-Group Procedure.

Score c	Frequency Non-adequate	Adequate	N_1	N_2	$N_1 + N_2$
0	10	2	0	65	65
1	8	2	10	63	73
2	5	4	18	61	79
3	3	6	23	57	80
4	4	12	26	51	77
5	2	18	30	39	69
6	1	21	32	21	53

Procedure thus split this group into two roughly equal subgroups, one consisting of those with low scores and the other those with high scores, and set the passing score at the line from which these subgroups parted. It may be noted that the median was preferable to other summary measures, such as the mean, because of its resistance to extreme data that may be common in large testing programs.

Table 2 reports the passing scores for the 1981 BSAP tests of reading (thirty-six items) and math (thirty items) derived from three procedures.

The data of Table 2 indicate that for grades one, two, three, and six the discrepancies among the three procedures are no more than two units for each test. For grade eight, however, the discrepancy stands at six units for reading and four units for math.

Except for the math test of grade eight, all three procedures appear to provide passing scores that are intuitively defensible. The passing scores of 11 and 12 produced by the Contrasting-Group and Equal-Percent-Failing Procedures for the eighth grade math test appear too low considering that, with four options, the chance score is already 7.5. The passing score 15 of the Undecided-Group Procedure seems more acceptable. These observations seem to indicate that if one unique procedure is to be selected for the setting of passing scores for all the situations presented here, the

Table 2. BSAP Passing Scores Based on Three Procedures.

Grade	Subject	Contrasting Group	Equal Percent Failing	Undecided Group
1	Reading	22	23	22
2	Reading	24	25	26
3	Reading	28	28	26
6	Reading	23	24	24
8	Reading	20	22	26
1	Math	22	24	25
2	Math	23	25	25
3	Math	20	22	22
6	Math	15	16	17
8	Math	11	12	15

Undecided-Group Procedure would be the best choice. For various illustrations described in the remainder of this paper, the Undecided group passing scores will be used as the actual passing scores for the BSAP tests.

Linking Content-Based Passing Scores
with Data-Based Passing Scores

In a large testing program it may not be feasible to apply the same procedure for setting passing scores to all grades. If procedures vary from grade to grade, it may be desirable to have a way to link the resulting passing scores so that these can be compared in terms of leniency or difficulty.

For example, in addition to testing at grades one, two, three, six, and eight as previously mentioned, the South Carolina BSAP also consists of the reading and math tests for the eleventh grade. Any of the three previously mentioned procedures for setting passing scores is deemed not applicable because of the difficulty in obtaining an independent classification of students in various groups. (Not all eleventh graders take math or English; hence, teachers' judgments as previously used may not be available.) A content-based procedure similar to the Angoff technique was used to elicit judgments from members of a committee convened for the purpose of setting passing scores for the grade eleven tests. In order to link their judgments on this grade with the current passing scores established via the Undecided-Group Procedure for grades six and eight, the committee was asked to pass the same type of judgments on the tests for these two grades. The median of the passing scores judged as acceptable by members of the committee for grades six, eight, and eleven are listed in Table 3. This table also lists the Undecided group passing scores for the two lower grades.

It may be interesting to note that the median passing scores based on the committee judgments were equal to or smaller than the data-based passing scores for grades six and eight. If the passing scores were set at 35 for reading and at 24 for math at grade eleven, it would be concluded that, as judged by the committee, these passing scores are somewhat more lenient than the passing scores adopted from the Undecided group for the two lower grades.

Table 3. Median of Passing Scores of Committee Members
and Undecided Group Passing Scores.

Source	Test	Grade 6	Grade 8	Grade 11
Committee Median	Reading	23	23	35
Undecided Group		24	26	Not applicable
Committee Median	Math	16	15	24
Undecided Group		17	15	Not applicable

Adjusting Passing Scores To Reflect New Priority

In some instances passing scores may have to be revised to reflect new emphasis on detecting (failing) students who truly need additional instructional help. For example, if greater emphasis is put on the identification of these students, then it becomes desirable to adjust the passing score upward in order to increase the chance of homing in on these students.

Let us denote Q as the ratio reflecting the importance of passing an Adequate student to the importance of failing a Nonadequate student. (For example, if passing an Adequate student is less important than failing a Nonadequate student, then the ratio Q should set at less than one.) In addition let z be the $100/(1 + Q)$ percentile of the standard normal distribution. Now let c_1 be the passing score set at the priority ratio Q_1 at which the normal percentile is z_1. If the priority ratio is then set at Q_2 at which the normal percentile is z_2, then the new passing score is given as $c_2 = (z_2 - z_1) \times SEM$, where SEM is the standard error of measurement for the group to which the passing scores are appropriate.

As an illustration, let $c_1 = 28$ and $Q_1 = 4$. The z_1 score is the $100/(1 + 4) = 20$th normal percentile; in other words $z_1 = -0.84$. Now let the new priority ratio be $Q_2 = 1/2$ at which $z_2 = 0.44$. With the standard error of measurement at 1.8, for example, the new passing score now becomes $28 + (0.44 + 0.84) \times 1.8 = 30.3$. If only integral test scores are used, the new passing score is to be set at 31.

Reporting Objective-Referenced Data

The methods previously presented are useful in setting or adjusting a passing score on an overall test. Such a passing score helps to determine whether a student has attained the minimum standard on a broad content area, such as reading or math. For any student whose achievement is not up to par, instructional remediation is needed. For efforts of this endeavor to be effective, however, details regarding the student's performance on each part (subtest) of the content area are essential. For example, if a student does not pass the reading test, then it seems reasonable to probe the various subareas of reading in which the student is weak. Thus, there appears to be the need for translating the passing score of the overall test down to each of the relevant parts of this test.

There are many ways to accomplish the above task given the constraints of the testing program and of the test itself. For example, from the purely instructional point of view, it may be necessary to give equal consideration to each part of the overall test. In this case, the passing score for each part should be set so that the passing percent stays close to the passing percent on the overall test. As an illustration, let us consider the BSAP reading test for the first grade. The test has thirty-six items that are allocated equally across the six objectives (subtests) of Decoding and Word Meaning (DW), Main Idea (MI), Details (DE), Analysis of Literature (AL), Reference Usage (RE), and Inference (IN). At the overall passing score of 22, the percent passing is 61.1; hence, on each of the six-item subtests, the passing score would be set at approximately $6 \times 61.1\% = 3.7$.

The rounding of the quantity 3.7 to an appropriate integer presents some subtle problems. If the nearest integer 4 is taken as the passing score for each of the six subtests, then the sum of all the subtest passing scores will be 26 and, hence, larger than the passing score of 22 on the overall test. This fact implies that for a student who barely passes all the six subtests the total reading score may be more than is needed to pass the overall reading test. On the other hand, if 3.7 is rounded downward to 3, then the subtest passing scores will add up to only 18, a sum which is far below 22. For this case students who barely pass all the subtests will not pass the overall test.

The above elaboration seems to indicate that the passing scores on the subtests should be set so that they would sum up to the passing score on the overall test. This will insure that a student who barely passes all the subtests is only at the borderline on the overall test. We will refer to the condition imposed here as the *constant-sum constraint*. For the reading test previously discussed, this restriction will result in the passing scores of 4 for four subtests and the passing score of 3 on the remaining two. The interesting question, of course, is the identification of the objectives at which the passing score is set as 3.

Aside from instructional emphasis, the setting of passing scores on the subtests should probably take into account the level of difficulty at which the subtest items are located. It is conceivable, for example, that one subtest is considerably harder than another one and that the passing scores should reflect this variation in difficulty. In other words, it seems to make sense to require that the passing score on a difficult subtest be smaller than or equal to (but not larger than) the one proposed for an easy subtest.

There are other considerations regarding the nature of the items in the subtests. The unavoidability of error of measurement implies that on a six-item subtest, for example, the passing score probably should not be set at the maximum score of 6. In addition, if multiple choice items with (say) three options are used, the passing score perhaps should not wander too close to the chance score of $6 \times 1/3$, or 2.

In the context of the South Carolina BSAP, two seemingly different procedures were tried out for the translating of the passing score on the overall test to each of its (objective) subtests. The constant-sum constraint was adhered to in all situations. The first procedure was based on the latent trait Rasch model (Wright and Stone, 1979), and the other constituted an application of the minimax framework in decision theory (Huynh and Casteel, 1983).

The Rasch Procedure. In the Rasch model, the probability that a student will answer an item correctly is a function of the difference between his or her ability and the difficulty of the item. Given a test with predetermined Rasch item difficulty, it is possible to find a cutoff ability that corresponds to a specific passing score on the raw score scale. The number of items that a borderline student is expected to answer correctly on the subtests can be computed; the rounded results may then be used as candidates for the subtest passing scores. Details regarding the Rasch procedure may be found in Huynh and Casteel (1983). It may be noted that as in most unidimensional latent trait models, the Rasch technique presumes that all the items tap the same dimension of achievement; in other words, the various (objective) subtests measure a common trait, each with a different level of difficulty. While it may take a heavy dose of conviction to assume that two objectives such as Decoding and Word Meaning and Analysis of Literature can be placed on the same continuum, the Rasch model may at least provide an approximate framework under which the setting of subtest passing scores takes into account the differing difficulty of the subtests.

As an illustration, let us focus on the BSAP first grade reading test. At the passing score of 22, the Rasch cutoff ability is 0.542. The expected numbers of correct responses for a student at this borderline ability are listed as follows: 5.23 (DW), 3.95 (MI), 2.68 (DE), 2.26 (AL), 4.38 (RE), and 3.50 (IN). (Note that they add up to the overall passing score of 22.) The next task is to round these expected frequencies to appropriate integers under the constant-sum constraint and in such a way that each integer is not 6 and is not too close to the chance score of 2. It seems obvious that the passing scores should be set at 5 for DW and 3 for both DE and AL. That will leave a total of 22 – (5 + 3 + 3) = 11 for the three remaining objectives. Given that the expected frequencies are 3.95 (MI), 4.38 (RE), and 3.50 (IN), the subtest passing scores may be taken as 4, 4, and 3.

The Minimax Procedure. As indicated above, the Rasch procedure (and other unidimensional latent trait models) relies on rather strict assumptions regarding the student's ability, the characteristic of the item, and the actual response to the item. In some instances, it may be difficult to support these assumptions. In addition, the Rasch appears foreign to situations where instructional consideration should take a significant part or when responses to the items are not coded simply as correct or incorrect. The minimax procedure provides one way to fill this gap.

Let us focus on the BSAP first grade Reading test with the overall passing score of 22. This score divides the students into the Passing group (those with scores of at least 22) and the Failing group (those with scores of 21 or less). There are six reading objectives, each measured by a six-item subtest. Let the passing scores on these subtests be c_1 through c_6. On the first subtest (DW) the passing score c_1 separates students into the Adequate group (those with subtest scores of at least c_1) and the Nonadequate group (those with subtest scores of $c_1 - 1$ or less). At each feasible c_1 the combined proportion P_1 of students who are in the Passing/ Adequate and Failing/Nonadequate categories may be computed. The repetition of this process for the remaining five objectives will yield the proportions $P_2(c_2)$ through $P_6(c_6)$.

For each allowable configuration C of the subtest passing scores c_1 through c_6, the six proportions $P_1(c_1)$ through $P_6(c_6)$ are available. Let $P(C)$ be the smallest of these proportions; this represents the minimum degree of consistency between the overall classifications of Passing and Failing and the subtest classifications of Adequacy and Nonadequacy that the configuration C can afford. The minimax principle asserts that a configuration C (minimax) may be found that will make this minimum as high as possible.

As applied to the BSAP tests of reading and math for grades one, two, three, six, and eight, the minimax procedure provides subtest passing scores that are identical to those derived from the Rasch model in about 70 percent of the cases. For the remaining 30 percent of the cases, the discrepancy between each minimax passing score and the Rasch-derived cutoff score is one unit on each of the six-item subtests. Thus, for all practical purposes, the minimax procedure and the Rasch model provide essentially the same passing scores for the South Carolina BSAP tests of reading and math.

Thus in the setting of passing scores for the subtests the minimax procedure is a viable alternative to a procedure based on latent trait models, such as the Rasch, when both approaches are applicable. Unlike latent trait models, the minimax approach does not impose strict assumptions on the way students respond to the items and is applicable to simple 0-1 or more complex scoring systems. It is also applicable when instructional consideration leads to various restrictions on the passing scores for the subtests.

However, the minimax procedure is population-dependent in the sense that it requires the administration of the entire test to a group of students. The Rasch and other latent trait models, on the other hand, rely on very strong assumptions on the way students respond to the items. However, once all the items that form the test are calibrated, the Rasch model can be used to allocate passing scores to the subtests without requiring a new administration of the entire test.

Reporting Objective-Referenced Data as Percent of Correct Responses

The previous sections described ways to classify student achievement on each (objective) subtest. The classification is binary; that is, achievement in each subtest is assessed only as Adequate or Nonadequate. Classifications of this type may be useful in the identification of the subareas in which instructional remediation may be needed.

In a number of situations it may be informative to report the percent of correct responses on each subtest. When only one test form is used for each grade throughout several years, the proportion of correct responses may be determined by dividing the number of correct responses by the number of items in each subtest. However, due to factors such as test security, a different test form may be needed for each new test administration. Although concerted efforts are typically exercised to insure that alternate test forms are comparable, strict equivalence among these forms is rarely accomplished due to differences in item content and difficulty. In other words, the raw percent of correct responses may not have the same meaning across alternate forms. Hence, if test scores are to be reported as percent of correct responses, procedures must be developed that take into account variation across different test forms.

Rather than using the proportion of items that are answered correctly on an objective, it may be more meaningful to relate student performance to the pool of items from which the subtest for the objective was assembled. If the item pool can be taken as the operational definition of the instructional domain for the objective, then it may be of interest to report student achievement as a percent of the domain that has been successfully accomplished. In this way, percents of correct responses across alternate test forms are anchored on a common domain; they are thus independent of the specific test forms from which they are derived.

Formally speaking, let the item pool for the objective consist of M items with characteristic functions $P_1(\theta)$ through $P_M(\theta)$. Each function elicits the probability that a student with ability θ will answer the item correctly. From the pool L, items are selected to form the test for the objective. (Without loss of generality, it may be presumed that these are the first L items of the pool.) For the entire item pool, the characteristic function represents the number of items that a student with ability θ is expected to answer correctly. It is given as the sum $E_M(\theta)$ of all the probabilities $P_1(\theta)$ through $P_M(\theta)$. For the test of L items, this function takes the form $E_L(\theta)$, which is the sum of the probabilities $P_1(\theta)$ through $P_M(\theta)$.

For a student with x correct responses on the test, the equation $E_L(\theta) = x$ yields the ability θ_x. At this ability, the number of items in the pool that are expected to be answered correctly are $EM(\theta_x)$; hence the (expected) proportion of correct responses in the pool is the ratio $E_M(\theta_x)/M$. For the special case of $x = \theta$ or L, the abilities are $-\infty$ and $+\infty$; hence the (pool) proportions of correct responses stand at θ and 1. If percents of correct responses are preferable, all proportions must be multiplied by the factor 100.

The procedure so described requires that all the items in the pool are calibrated on a common ability dimension. This may be done via the Rasch or most other latent trait models.

As an illustration, let us consider the Decoding and Word Meaning objective of the reading test for grade one. There are twenty-one items in the pool; their 1981 Rasch item difficulty levels are listed in Table 4. For the 1981 BSAP statewide test administration, the DW objective was assessed via the subtest consisting of the items DW01, DW04, DW10, DW14, DW16, and DW20. At the DW scores of 1 through 5, the Rasch abilities are -3.024, -2.098, -1.394, -0.689, and 0.238. The corresponding expected numbers of correct responses in the pool and their percents (listed in parentheses) are 3.56 (17 percent), 6.77 (32 percent), 9.88 (47 percent), 13.05 (62 percent), and 16.52 (79 percent). As previously mentioned, the percents are taken as 0 and 100 for the DW scores of 0 and 6.

Table 4. Item Pool for the DW Reading Objective of Grade One.

Item Name	Rasch Difficulty	Item Name	Rasch Difficulty	Item Name	Rasch Difficulty
DW01	-1.365	DW08	-1.441	DW15	-1.922
DW02	-1.667	DW09	-1.503	DW16	-1.682
DW03	0.677	DW10	-1.704	DW17	-1.701
DW04	-1.446	DW11	-0.070	DW18	-2.595
DW05	-0.421	DW12	-2.595	DW19	-1.922
DW06	-0.924	DW13	-1.102	DW20	-1.169
DW07	0.243	DW14	-0.994	DW21	-0.686

The percents reported in the previous section have straightforward interpretation. At the DW score of 5, for example, the student would be expected to answer correctly 79 percent of the items in the pool if the entire pool were administered.

Tracking Student Progress Through Several Grades

In a number of situations, it may be of interest to track the progress of an individual student in academic areas such as reading or math through several succeeding grade levels. For example, if it is feasible to map the entire reading curriculum of the first three primary grades through a common item pool, then it may be helpful to track the percent of the curriculum that a student has achieved through each of these grade levels. Through the Rasch model and the process of vertical equating (Slinde and Linn, 1978), for example, it may be possible to link the reading tests developed for these grades together to form an item pool. This pool operationally defines the reading curriculum for primary school. Then the raw scores on the tests for various grades may be expressed in terms of percents of correct responses in the item pool. The fact that these percents are expressed by use of a common item pool will help to assess the amount of progress that a student has made from year to year. As an illustration, let us presume that a student makes the scores of 20, 21, and 31 on the reading tests of grades one through three, and that these correspond to the percents of 50, 70, and 80 in the item pool. It may then be said the student has progressed twice as much from grade one to grade two as from grade two to grade three. If this conclusion is acceptable, then questions would be raised regarding the level of motivation or the quality of instruction that the student has been or is exposed to at the third grade.

Tracking School Progress Throughout Several Years

The method just presented for tracking student achievement may also be used to plot the pace of achievement that students at a school display from year to year. Again, it may be presumed that the instructional content covered at several grades (say of primary school) can be put on the same dimension (such as reading or math) by linking together the tests designed for these grades. Then the student mean achievement, as measured by the test raw scores, may be converted to a percent in the item pool. A comparison of these percents would reveal the differential rate at which students at the school have progressed from one grade to the next. Such comparison would be helpful in plotting ways to improve schools. For example, if the percents of student achievement stay at 50, 70, and 80 at grades one through three, then speculation may be made on the reasons for the smaller student progress during the second grade.

Summary

This chapter touches some of the basic technical issues in mastery testing and basic skills assessment programs. These issues deal with ways that test data can be used effectively to make decisions regarding student achievement and to assist in the identification of the academic areas in which instructional remediation might be fruitful. The chapter also describes a general outline on the tracking of the rate at which students at a given school progress in a given curriculum, such as primary school reading through succeeding grades. Tracking of this type may be of considerable importance in the search for ways to improve school effectiveness or to allocate instructional effort and resources equitably in the teaching of a subject area through several succeeding grades.

References

Angoff, W. H. "Scales, Norms, and Equivalent Scores." In R. L. Thorndike (Ed.), *Educational Measurement.* (2nd ed.) Washington, D.C.: American Council on Education, 1971.

Ebel, R. L. *Essentials of Educational Measurement.* Englewood Cliffs, N.J.: Prentice-Hall, 1972.

Huynh, H., and Casteel, J. "Technical Works for Basic Skills Assessment Programs." Unpublished Report to National Institute of Education. Columbia: University of South Carolina, College of Education, 1983.

Nedelsky, L. "Absolute Grading Standard for Objective Tests." *Educational and Psychological Measurement,* 1954, *14,* 3-19.

Slinde, J. A., and Linn, R. L. "An Exploration of the Adequacy of the Rasch Model for the Problem of Vertical Equating." *Journal of Educational Measurement,* 1978, *15,* 23-35.

Wright, B. D., and Stone, M. H. *Best Test Design.* Chicago: Mesa Press, 1979.

Ziesky, M. J., and Livingston, S. A. *Manual for Setting Standards on the Basic Skills Assessment Tests.* Princeton, N.J.: Educational Testing Service, 1977.

9

Flexible and Heterogeneous
Instructional Arrangements
to Facilitate
Mastery Learning

Albert Mamary
Lawrence A. Rowe

The educational system that evolved out of the Industrial Revolution of the 1800s was a product designed to fit the needs of a society shifting from an agricultural to an industrial base. These needs called for a dramatic change in the behavior pattern of millions of people, which in turn demanded a reorganization of the process for educating young people. Children had to be prepared for factory life and prefitted to the industrial system. While the basics of math, reading, and writing were taught, the latent curriculum consisted of punctuality, obedience, and rote repetition. Thus, the mass educational system and type of current grouping (namely, thirty students to one teacher) was born and continues to flourish today.

John Goodlad's recent book (1984) on elementary and secondary education in the United States supports the conclusion that schools are still guided by the basic principles undergirding an industrial society. These principles include, among others, the practices of standardization, synchronization, concentration, and specialization (Toffler, 1980).

Standardized tests often are used to measure intelligence and achievement, which in turn leads to the concentration of various ability groups within classrooms organized around a synchronized time schedule designed to ensure that learning begins and ends at the same time for all students. These principles are coming under heavy attack by forces in society and the educational profession. One only has to read about and view the millions of assembly line workers who have either lost their jobs or anticipate losing them due to the technological advances sweeping industrial societies to see that the needs of the emerging society call for much more than mere rote learning, obedience, and punctuality. They call for all students to enter society with the ability to create, solve problems, and converse competently within the sciences and math. Additionally, educational research over the past fifteen years has produced new knowledge that questions the use of standardized tests in assessing performance and in grouping students.

But schools, taking their cue from society and industry, still frequently group students according to some type of standardized (norm-referenced) measure. Findley and Bryan (1975) estimated that over 77 percent of the school districts in the United States group students by ability. Many teachers and administrators generally believe that grouping students by ability will allow the teacher to be more efficient in planning and will provide for individual differences within the classroom. It is also generally believed by many teachers and administrators that high-aptitude students will learn more than low-aptitude students, that low-aptitude students will not be frustrated by the progress of the high-aptitude students, and that mid-aptitude students will learn to their potential if they are all placed in separate groups. Many teachers and administrators also believe that it is easier to teach and that there are fewer discipline problems with homogeneous classes than with heterogeneous classes. Students assigned to groups in primary school frequently stay in those groups throughout their elementary grades.

Robert Rosenthal, a Harvard social psychologist, is chiefly responsible for developing the field of psychological inquiry dealing with the effects of experimenter expectancy on human and animal behavior. Research by Rosenthal and Jacobson (1968) suggested that teachers' expectations may have an important effect on students' intellectual development. Other studies (Rothbart, Dalfen, and Barrett, 1971; Beez, 1968; Brophy and Good, 1970) also support the belief that students perform in a manner that teachers expect of them. Clarke (1960) reported a positive correlation between students' academic performances and their perception of the teachers' academic expectations of them. Homogeneous grouping is one of the ways that teachers communicate low expectations to their low achieving students.

Bloom, Hastings, and Madaus (1971) stated that each year teachers begin their courses or school year with the belief that about a third of their students will learn adequately what they want them to learn, about a third will just "get by" or fail, and another third will learn much of what is to be learned but not enough to be regarded as good students. They also concluded that "This set of expectations which fixes the academic goals of teachers and students is the most wasteful and destructive aspect of the present educational system" (p. 43).

The result of teachers' categorizing students in this way may be to convince some students that, from the teacher's viewpoint, they are able, good, and desirable and other students that they are deficient, not good, and undesirable (Bloom, Hastings, and Madaus, 1971). To be continually sorted, categorized, and labeled and to continually receive negative feedback for long periods of time can have an unfavorable influence on many students' self-concept, reducing or destroying their motivation for learning (Stringer and Glidwell, 1967; Bloom, Hastings and Madaus, 1971). Since most schools group students according to ability, they are systematically setting expectations and convincing some students that they are worthy and capable and others that they are inferior and incapable.

The purpose of this chapter is to describe the approach to mastery learning—particularly the grouping practices—in the Johnson City, New York, public schools. The overall approach is intended to provide more effective instruction while avoiding or reducing homogeneous grouping. A mastery learning approach to learning relies heavily on the powerful assumption that under favorable learning conditions most students can learn well what schools want them to learn and that learning can be improved substantially. These favorable learning conditions are embedded in

Figure 1. Johnson City, N.Y., Model and Components for Sequencing and Delivering Mastery Learning Instruction.

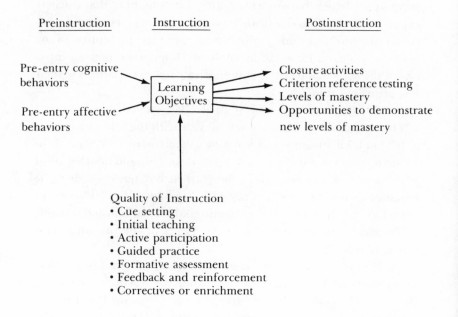

Source: Adapted from Bloom, 1976.

Figure 1, depicting three stages of instruction and some of the instructional components emphasized in implementing mastery learning in the Johnson City public schools. While each stage will be discussed separately, it is not intended that they be mutually exclusive.

Preinstruction

Students cannot be expected to learn a given set of unit objectives unless they possess the necessary concepts, procedures, and information needed to learn these objectives. This being the case, the need to predetermine and to state appropriately these prerequisites is critical. Additionally, the need to either formally or informally assess students as to their possession of the prerequisites must be accomplished. Finally, opportunities for students to recall, reinforce, relearn, or learn the prerequisites must be provided.

Students approach a course of study or set of objectives within a course with feelings ranging from extreme confidence to total despair. Therefore, students should be led to realize that they will not be expected to learn objectives they are not ready for, and if they need to learn prerequisite objectives, corrective help will be provided.

Instruction

This section attempts to define what quality instruction represents. Though distinctive behaviors and acts will be described, we are not assuming or arguing that there is one immutable sequence. Teachers could well change the order, emphasize one over another, and repeat one or more steps. However, to ignore one or more of these behaviors or acts reduces the possibility of some students learning the intended objectives.

Initial Teaching. Formal instruction of the unit objectives is initiated through an overview. This overview should focus student attention by explaining or demonstrating what is to be learned, how it is to be learned, why it is important, and how it can be used now and in the future. Initial instruction should also consider the many and varied ways students learn. Therefore, it is important, whenever appropriate, to provide at least two modes of presentation (for example, visual and verbal; lecture and discussion). This will help reinforce learning as well as contribute to effective teaching. Furthermore, by receiving different modes of instruction, students may develop skills in new learning styles.

Guided Practice. A critical point in students' learning is when they attempt to put into practice what has been taught during the initial teaching phase. These initial attempts should be made under the careful guidance of the teacher, who can then reinforce understanding or correct any misunderstandings that students may have. The guided practice phase helps ensure that students' independent practice will be correct.

Correctives/Enrichment. Throughout the instructional process informal assessments are made. In addition, formal, formative assessments are given to determine which objectives students have or have not mastered. Those students found not mastering certain objectives are given corrective help through the use of alternative learning activities. Those students who have mastered the objectives being measured at that time are given opportunities to explore other topics in the discipline, engage in investigations, and pursue other in-depth, higher cognitive level experiences.

Prior to the end of the unit the teacher should engage all students in closure activities that attempt to review the various parts of the unit and to correlate the parts to the whole. A great many strategies that elicit student participation are used in these activities.

Postinstruction

Students are given a criterion-referenced test at the end of the unit only when mastery of the unit objectives has been demonstrated. Thus, the unit test attempts to confirm learning as well as to reveal who did not learn. The most appropriate and timely correctives given to eliminate learning errors should be done when such errors are ascertained through assessment during the unit. Yet, the criterion-referenced test may still be used as a diagnostic tool to determine which students need additional help on certain objectives. The opportunity for students to demonstrate higher levels of mastery should almost always be available.

Teaming and Grouping Models

Teachers' implementation of the instructional process described above forces schools to rethink their organizational arrangements. To clarify this notion, three possible teacher-teaming models are presented.

Model I: Multi-Age Performance Groups

Among the characteristics of this model are the following teacher responsibilities:

1.   Organizing small group instruction.
2.   Teaching the same subject at different grade levels.

3. Teaching during a common period of time.
4. Creating multi-age groups by performance.
5. Providing cooperative teaching, learning, and scheduling.

Teachers using this model usually teach different grade levels but group students according to the objectives the students are studying. Teachers form and schedule the multi-age groups according to student performance. Students may be from the same grade level or different grade levels. Students cooperate in peer learning teams. Additionally, instructional aides and volunteers are utilized. This model is used primarily in elementary schools. Implementation arrangements might be as follows:

1. Number of teachers—3 or 4.
2. Approximate number of students—80 to 110.
3. Grade and subject—2-3-4, or 2-3-4-5, or 5-6, for any subject, but usually reading, mathematics, and language arts.
4. Curriculum organization—by objectives, units, or chapters.

Figure 2 illustrates one approach to forming and managing instructional groups within a multi-age performance model. Teachers decide who will teach each performance group and when the group will be taught. Every effort should be made not to have a larger number of performance groups than can be managed feasibly. Usually, three to four per teacher is the maximum number. Individualized instruction can be viewed as an extreme version of this model.

Formation and Management. There are generally three critical decision points for forming multi-age groups within the instructional process. Decisions for grouping must be made when dealing with prerequisites and guided practice and in the corrective and enrichment phases.

1. Prerequisites and Grouping. Since each teacher has a different instructional group, he or she must teach or recall the prerequisites that students in his or her group do not know. Students who know the prerequisites may engage in enrichment activities or be a member of a cooperative learning team. Students who continually learn more quickly may be allowed to accelerate.

Figure 2. Multi-Age Performance Grouping.

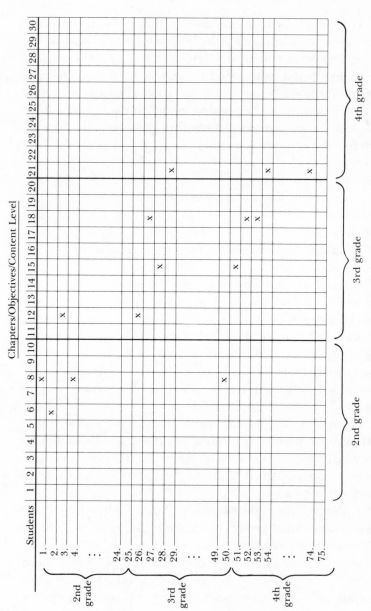

Chapters/Objectives/Content Level

Note: Team teachers use this planning chart to identify the students within the same performance level. Students appearing in the same chapter, objective, or content level would thus be taught in the same group regardless of grade level.

To save time, it is not always necessary to formally assess knowledge of prerequisites but rather review each as needed.

2. Guided Practice and Grouping. Each teacher must ensure that students are practicing correctly before practicing independently. Cooperative student learning groups might be formed during the guided practice phase of the instructional process.

3. Correctives, Enrichment, and Grouping. Generally, each teacher using this model provides his or her own correctives and enrichment. Students who don't need correctives work independently or cooperate with peers on enrichment activities. However, some students who need enrichment may be grouped with any one of the teachers to receive instruction. Classic books, nonroutine mathematics problem solving, scientific experiments, and historical investigations are just a few of the themes and activities used in the enrichment phase. Teachers can cooperate by acquiring different expertise and teaching one of the activities listed above to a group of students.

Mastery Learning Principles. There are generally two critical considerations for forming groups according to mastery learning principles. These two important principles are: (1) given enough time, most students can learn what teachers in schools want them to learn and (2) students should receive credit and be assigned to a group based on performance (that is, mastery). Therefore, time for learning and student certification and assignment must be carefully considered and managed:

1. Time and Grouping. A block of time, usually two and a half to three hours a day, is generally available for mathematics, reading, and language arts instruction. Teachers cooperatively plan scheduling and share in the responsibility for teaching different performance groups for each subject. Students who have learned the objectives more quickly than others in their instructional group may receive extra help and be placed in an instructional group that is studying another set of objectives. Students may also form cooperative groups or work independently, investigating some topic within the subject. Students who need more time to learn the objectives can get extra help at other times during the day. Teacher aides, cooperative peer groups, after school help, and additional time during the day are a few of the ways students may receive extra

help. If extra help is not sufficient, students may be placed in another instructional group that is studying the appropriate set of objectives.

2. Assignment, Certification, and Grouping. Students are assigned to instructional group levels according to performance, not potential. Credit is only awarded a student when he or she demonstrates mastery of a unit. Whether or not a student then continues to the next unit is determined by the teacher. However, a student does not get credit until he or she eventually demonstrates learning. Periodically teachers will allocate more time from other subjects for some students. Teachers may not find it necessary to teach social studies and science every day for every student in the elementary school.

Advantages. The multi-age performance group model provides many important advantages. The formation of cooperative peer learning groups and of varied instructional groups enabling continuous progress are but two of these advantages.

A third advantage of this model is the flexible use of time. Time for correctives, enrichment, prerequisites, and guided practice is available. Acceleration and enrichment are enhanced. Constant changing of groups within this model avoids pullout programs and stereotyping. Students stay within the multi-age team population from three to four years; thus retention in its usual sense is avoided. Students who need more time in the group do not repeat but continue learning a set of objectives that must be learned. Since parents should be informed at all times of their child's progress along the continuum of objectives, they should easily understand their child's need for more time to learn.

Another advantage is that teachers do not need to assess each student's knowledge for group placement at the beginning of each school year. They already know the student's performance level. Students are not labeled but are assigned by performance to an instructional group. Students of various aptitudes may be in the same performance group.

Disadvantages. Since there are usually three different grades and three different teachers, cooperative planning of curriculum is not generally convenient. This is a major disadvantage, since each teacher must plan unit guides around the curriculum for each grade. A second disadvantage might be in the cooperative teaching phase. Usually each teacher provides his or her own prerequisites, guided practice, enrichment, and correctives, without much help from other teachers.

Model II: Interdisciplinary Teaming

Among this model's general characteristics are the following teacher responsibilities:

1. Organizing whole class instruction.
2. Teaching different subjects at the same grade level.
3. Teaching during a common period of time.
4. Creating groups within the team by performance.
5. Providing cooperative teaching, learning, and scheduling.

Teachers using this model teach different subjects but within the same grade level. Teachers cooperate in scheduling but generally do not cooperate in teaching the same subject. Although this model is generally used in the middle or junior high school, it can be used in the intermediate elementary grades. Implementation arrangements might be as follows:

1. Number of teachers—4.
2. Approximate number of students—100 to 115.
3. Grade and subject—4 through 8, mathematics, English, social studies, and science.
4. Curriculum organization—by objectives, units, or chapters.

Figure 3 illustrates one approach to forming and managing instructional groups within an interdisciplinary team model.

Formation and Management. Grouping practices related to the instructional sequence may be as follows:

1. Prerequisites and Grouping. Since teachers each have a different subject to teach, they must teach or recall the prerequisites that students in their classes do not know. However, a teacher may group students from the classes of the four teachers for this purpose. Students who know the prerequisites may engage in enrichment activities or negotiate with the teacher for other types of activities.

Figure 3. Interdisciplinary Teaming for Four Teachers and One Hundred Students.

Daily Time Period	Monday				Tuesday				
9:00 - 9:20	T-1 NG 15 Students	T-3 RC 25 Students	T-4 RC 25 Students	RR, Lib IS	T-1, 2, 3, 4 LGI 100 Students				RR, Lib IS
9:20 - 9:40	T-2 Lab 20 Students								
9:40 - 10:00	T-1 NG 20 Students	T-3 RC 25 Students	T-4 RC 25 Students	RR, Lib IS	T-2 Lab 20 Students	T-3 NG 15 Students	T-4 RC 25 Students	T-1 RC 25 Students	RR, Lib IS
10:00 - 10:20									
10:20 - 10:40	T-1 NG 20 Students	T-3 RC 20 Students	T-4 RC 25 Students	RR, Lib IS			T-4 RC 25 Students	T-1 RC 25 Students	RR, Lib IS
10:40 - 11:00									
11:00 - 11:20	T-1 NG 25 Students	T-3 RC 15 Students	T-4 RC 25 Students	RR, Lib IS	T-2 Conf	T-3 RC 25 Students	T-4 RC 25 Students	T-1 RC 25 Students	RR, Lib IS
11:20 - 11:40	T-2 Lab 20 Students.								
11:40 - 12:00	T-1, 2, 3, 4 LGI 100 Students				T-1, 2, 3, 4 Lib, C, IS, Conf				
1:00 - 1:20	T-1, 2, 3, 4 Lib, C, IS, Conf				T-2 NG 10 Students	T-3 RC 25 Students	T-4 NG 12 Students	T-1 RC 25 Students	RR, Lib IS
1:20 - 1:40									

Key: T-1 - Math Teacher
T-2 - Science Teacher
T-3 - English Teacher
T-4 - Soc. Studies Teacher
NG - Needs Group (Enrichment or Correctives)

LGI - Large Group Instruction
Lab - Lab
RR - Resource Room
Lib - Library
IS - Independent Study

RC - Regular Class Instruction
C - Corrective Help
Conf - Conferencing
IE - Intensive Education
Comp - Computers

Note: This chart encompasses only two days of planning to demonstrate the concept. Obviously it could be extended to include the remaining days of the week.

2. Guided Practice and Grouping. Cooperative groups may be formed for peer interaction during the guided practice phase of the teaching process. Each teacher ensures that students are practicing correctly before independent practice is assigned.

3. Correctives, Enrichment, and Grouping. Generally, each teacher provides his or her own correctives and enrichment but can cooperatively schedule these activities with the other three teachers. A science teacher, for example, may conduct an experiment with the students assigned to enrichment, while the other teachers schedule corrective learning opportunities for the rest of the group.

Mastery Learning Principles. Time and certification implications for grouping are as follows:

1. Time and Grouping. A block of time, usually three hours a day, is generally available for mathematics, science, social studies, and English. Teachers plan cooperatively in scheduling these four subjects, but do not generally share responsibility for teaching them. Teachers negotiate more time with their colleagues for those students who need it. Students can also get extra help during other times of the day. Another period of time in the day may be set aside for teachers to work with students who need correctives or enrichment. Generally, there is not much acceleration in this model except when groups of students are accelerated to begin high school algebra, a language, or sciences in the eighth grade.

2. Assignment, Certification, and Grouping. Teachers must determine and teach their own performance groups. However, credit is only awarded when a student demonstrates mastery of a unit. Most teachers using this model try to keep their entire class together by providing enrichment and correctives as needed. While a teacher may begin the next unit of study, a student who has not mastered a unit must receive extra help. Cooperative peer groups and extra sessions during and after the school day are a few of the ways students receive this extra help. Some extra help can also be provided in a learning center if one exists.

Advantages. The major advantages of this model are teacher cooperation and the flexible utilization of time. The allocation of time for subjects is negotiable among the four teachers, which can provide large amounts of time for intensive learning or small amounts for review, drill, or correctives. Cooperative peer help, class meetings, team government, teacher consistency, and high expectations also can be easily advanced within this model. Students in this model tend to have high self-esteem through a feeling of belonging, acceptance, and participation.

Disadvantages. The major disadvantage of this model is that it becomes difficult to manage too many different groups and hence acceleration may be hindered. Since each teacher teaches a separate subject, lack of cooperative curriculum planning is a disadvantage. But teachers of the same grade level and subject may plan, develop, and implement units containing grade level objectives. Finally, each teacher must provide his or her own review, correctives, and enrichment.

Model III: Intradisciplinary Teaming

Among this model's general characteristics are the following teacher responsibilities:

1. Organizing whole class instruction.
2. Teaching the same subject at the same grade level.
3. Teaching during a common period of time.
4. Creating groups within the class by performance.
5. Cooperating in teaching and planning.

Teachers using this model generally teach their own classes, but group students according to learning needs within a subject. Teachers cooperate in planning units and teaching small groups of students within the instructional process according to the performance of students. While this model is used with secondary schools, it can also be used in the intermediate grades. Implementation arrangements might be as follows:

1. Number of teachers—2.
2. Approximate number of students—50 to 60.
3. Grade and subject—can be used with any grade within the same subject.
4. Curriculum organization—by units or chapters.

Figure 4 illustrates one approach to forming and managing instructional groups using intradisciplinary teaming.

Formation and Management. Grouping practices related to the instructional sequence may be as follows:

1. Prerequisites and Grouping. One teacher may teach the group of students that does not know the necessary prerequisites for the unit while the second teacher may provide enrichment activities for the group that does.

2. Guided Practice and Grouping. Cooperative groups may be formed for peer interaction during the guided practice phase of the instructional process. This may be done by each teacher. A teacher may circulate within the class to ensure that each student is practicing correctly prior to any independent practice.

3. Correctives, Enrichment, and Grouping. One teacher may teach the group of students that need correctives while the second teacher may provide enrichment activities for the group of students that does not.

Mastery Learning Principles. Time and certification implications are as follows:

1. Time and Grouping. While time during the day is generally available in forty- to fifty-minute periods, teachers may share responsibility within the teaching period. Students who have learned the objectives of the unit more quickly than others may form cooperative groups and pursue an investigation or can work with one of the teachers on an enrichment activity. Students who need more time to learn or to practice the objectives of the unit can be grouped according to their needs and be taught by one of the teachers.

2. Assignment, Certification, and Grouping. Generally teachers using this model want to keep both classes together when starting a unit and giving a test at the end of the unit. While teachers may begin the next unit of study, no credit is awarded until the student demonstrates mastery of the unit. The formation of cooperative groups within a classroom and the utilization of learning centers staffed by teachers during and after the school day are but two of the ways students receive extra help. Some computer-assisted instruction is becoming effective for remedial purposes.

Figure 4. Intradisciplinary Teaming for Two Teachers and Fifty to Sixty Students.

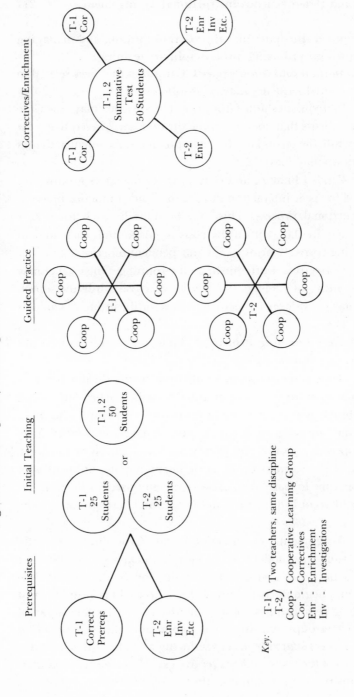

Advantages. Teachers share in the responsibility for planning and teaching. They cooperatively plan the prerequisites, the motivation for the unit, the objectives to be learned, and the different modes of learning. They also plan for group participation, for guided practice, and for correctives and enrichment. They share in writing test items for each objective. Another advantage of this model is its manageability. Teachers can keep groups together within the start-stop curriculum that is outlined. This procedure avoids fragmentation of the class and in practice can ensure that every child will learn within a given time frame.

Disadvantages. The major disadvantage is that time is fixed. Teachers must find extra time during and at the end of the school day. Since the groups start and end each unit at the same time, acceleration is sometimes limited within this model. Enrichment activities are used in the place of acceleration. However, if a segment of the group begins to move much more quickly than the rest of the group, one of the teachers can take that segment and move it through the curriculum at a more accelerated pace.

The preceding models offer choices to minimize homogeneous grouping in implementing a mastery learning program. Each model has its advantages and disadvantages, and the teachers or teams of teachers must determine which is best for them. Clearly, a combination or a modification of the models is in order, and each will yield its own advantages and disadvantages. Furthermore, a teacher may not wish to be a member of a team or to cooperate in teaching or grouping but can still organize the classroom according to many of the same principles described.

Since their expectations of students are frequently transmitted to teachers by the kinds of groups assigned to them, schools must be sensitive to grouping decisions. While most groupings have some degree of homogeneity, labeling, sorting, and categorizing of students must be kept to a minimum. The grouping of students should be flexible to allow for changes in student performance.

The Johnson City Central School District has used the above models with much success. As shown in Table 1, student achievement scores have improved so that students are performing almost two and a half years above grade level in reading, and more than three and a half years above grade level in mathematics by the end

Table 1. Johnson City, N.Y., Central School District California Achievement Test Results Over Six Years.

Grade	National Norm	Reading						Math					
		1978	1979	1980	1981	1982	1983	1978	1979	1980	1981	1982	1983
1	1.8	1.6	1.9	1.9	2.1	2.2	2.1	1.7	2.2	2.0	2.1	2.2	2.3
2	2.8	3.0	3.2	3.1	3.1	3.2	3.4	3.0	3.4	3.3	3.3	3.2	3.3
3	3.8	4.0	4.1	3.9	4.0	4.1	4.5	4.1	4.5	4.3	4.4	4.3	4.6
4	4.8	5.3	5.5	5.7	5.7	5.6	5.8	5.0	5.7	5.7	5.5	5.4	5.5
5	5.8	6.8	6.8	7.8	7.6	7.1	7.0	7.1	7.2	7.5	7.4	7.0	6.9
6	6.8	7.2	8.0	8.1	8.5	8.3	8.3	7.6	8.0	8.6	8.4	8.1	8.1
7	7.8	8.7	9.3	9.2	9.7	10.0	10.0	8.5	9.3	9.2	10.0	9.9	9.8
8	8.8	8.7	9.3	10.8	10.6	11.0	11.1	10.7	11.1	12.5	11.9	12.5	12.5

of the eighth grade. We are proud of these results. We are even more proud, however, of the improvements we have seen in interactions and relationships between teachers and students, thus diminishing the very stereotyping of expectations for students by teachers that homogeneous grouping promulgates.

References

Beez, W. V. "Influence of Biased Psychological Reports on Teacher Behavior and Pupil Performance." *Proceedings of the 76th Annual Convention of the American Psychological Association,* 1968, *3,* 605–606.

Bloom, B. S. *Human Characteristics and School Learning.* New York: McGraw-Hill, 1976.

Bloom, B. S., Hastings, J. T., and Madaus, G. F. (Eds.). *Handbook on Formative and Summative Evaluation of Student Learning.* New York: McGraw-Hill, 1971.

Brophy, J., and Good, T. L. "Teachers' Communication of Differential Expectations for Children's Classroom Performance: Some Behavioral Data." *Journal of Educational Psychology,* 1970, *61,* 365–374.

Clarke, W. E. "The Relationship Between College Academic Performance and Expectancies." Unpublished doctoral dissertation, Michigan State University, 1960.

Findley, W., and Bryan, M. *The Pros and Cons of Ability Grouping.* Phi Delta Kappan Educational Foundation, Bloomington, Ind., 1975.

Goodlad, J. I. *A Place Called School, Prospects For the Future.* New York: McGraw-Hill, 1984.

Rosenthal, R., and Jacobson, L. *Pygmalion in the Classroom.* New York: Holt, Rinehart and Winston, 1968.

Rothbart, M., Dalfen, S., and Barrett, R. "Effects of Teacher's Expectancy on Student-Teacher Interaction." *Journal of Educational Psychology,* 1971, *62,* 49–54.

Stringer, L. A., and Glidwell, J. C. *Early Detection of Emotional Illnesses in School Children.* St. Louis: St. Louis County Health Department, 1967.

Toffler, A. *The Third Wave.* New York: William Morrow, 1980.

10

Improving Reading Ability
Through a Mastery
Learning Program:
A Case Study

Marsha Menahem
Leon Weisman

The 1970s marked a decided shift in thinking and research on educational change strategies. While the previous decade focused on top-down models of change (usually accompanied by federal money and external technical assistance) evaluators of the 1970s favored changes at the local building level in a bottom-up model of mutual adaptation and innovation (Berman and McLaughlin, 1978; Berman and Pauly, 1975; Farrar, DeSanctis, and Cohen, 1980). Recently, however, evaluation experts have begun to challenge the "mutual adaptationists" and have found positive results associated with federally inspired top-down projects (Chabotar and Keel, 1978; Kaplan and Stevens, 1978). In re-examining the empirical studies of the bottom-up conceptualists, some scholars have concluded that although research does support mutual adaptation and local program-solving, the data do not build a substantial case against the top-down, technically assisted model of educational innovation (Datta, 1981).

Perhaps we can liken the top-down model to a "filtration" analog and its counterpart, bottom-up, to having a "percolator" effect on educational innovation. What has resulted from this dichotomy in the literature has been polarization of educators in the field as to the best strategy for instituting change. This chapter suggests an alternative model for introducing mastery learning (ML) that attempts to bridge the two philosophical camps—hence the top-down, bottom-up model of change. It will also add to the current research on implementation in order to assist local educational leaders in selecting the appropriate strategies in bringing their goals to fruition.

The Case Study

The most critical elements generally accepted in instituting change are local commitment, the content of the innovative program, the instructional context, and the program's management. The interrelationship among these variables is illustrated by the following case study in which a local district opted to remodel its reading skills instructional program. The various strategies developed to attend these variables elaborate and illustrate the top-down, bottom-up model of change.

Local Commitment

In the summer of 1979, Community School District 19, in Brooklyn, New York, hired Frank C. Arricale, II, as its new superintendent. His first weeks in office were devoted to a general needs assessment, an attempt to prioritize the needs of his schools, and an effort to identify the desires of the various constituencies that impacted on the local educational unit. The twenty-six schools in the district at that time provided services to 23,000 students, 90 percent of whom were minority children and 70 percent of whom were reading below grade level. Historical analysis of the district's reading scores indicated a steady decline in reading achievement since 1969.

The neighborhoods that surrounded the schools were plagued by high crime, high unemployment, and the third highest poverty rate in the city. Many of the community's problems extended into the schools' domains, which made professional staff hardpressed to meet both the educational needs and the general welfare considerations of their students, and it was more than intuitive that one set of needs directly impacted the other.

The organizational framework of the school district resembled fiefdoms—each principal maintaining rights of territoriality over his or her dominion. This type of situation has been described in the research of Cohen, March, and Olsen (1972), who wrote about "organized anarchies." The organizational framework typified the "loosely coupled systems" identified by Weick (1976). The District Office maintained a communication system among the schools and acted as liaison between the district and the Central Board of Education. (The Central Board maintains quasi-authority over the educational system for the entire city.)

Acknowledging the difficulty inherent in the district's organization, Arricale's first decision was to focus on the primary need of the district. His needs assessment ranked reading achievement as the top priority; a comprehensive change was needed in reading skills instruction. To facilitate this end, administrators, teachers, students, parents, and community activists would be mobilized towards the common objective (reading achievement) through an innovative instructional program using a mastery learning approach and a carefully designed implementation plan to bring the loosely coupled district organization under more direct supervision.

This decision marked the beginning of the school district's entry into the world of educational change. Arricale was an experienced public administrator and educator, and he assumed his office determined to put into effect at the grassroots level many of the ideas and strategies he had acquired during his previous years in public administration. Arricale inherited a district characterized by a decade of declining reading scores. The Community School Board, which appointed him, was eager to see reading improvement in a district that had ranked among the lowest in reading of the thirty-two school districts that comprised New York City's educational community.

Commitment from the local school board was easy to extract, because Arricale's priority to upgrade the level of reading in the district was in consonance with the goal of the board. Gaining the cooperation of local building leadership and the individual teachers, however, would be a major obstacle in the path of innovation (Cohen, March, and Olsen, 1972). A number of studies had demonstrated that unless building personnel shared goals, strong leadership, and high expectations for students (Edmonds, 1979; Duckett and others, 1980) any innovation was doomed to failure.

In addition, shrinking economic resources created pressures for programs with minimal costs—a factor that would dictate the selection of the appropriate instructional program.

The Instructional Program

Foremost in Arricale's plans was to incorporate the instructional design of mastery learning, a structured approach to curriculum, instruction, evaluation, and management. His research into effective instructional strategies had generated a number of ideas that underscored mastery learning.

John Carroll, a professor of education at the University of North Carolina, proposed that the degree of learning time associated with skill acquisition equalled the time actually spent on a task divided by the time needed to learn the specific skill. This model indicates that if students devote sufficient time to learn a task, they will master it. In addition, students must master prerequisite skills before they may proceed to another. This implies that a hierarchy exists among skills or objectives in a content area. Bloom (1976) proposed that skills be taught in a traditional group setting and only the remediation of weaknesses be individualized, making this approach relatively cost efficient. Students should be given two opportunities to demonstrate skill mastery, thus increasing their success rate and bringing achievement levels to 80 percent. According to Block and Anderson (1975), three quarters of the students in forty studies of mastery learning programs have achieved at the same rate as the top 25 percent of students learning under traditional methods.

The importance of engaged time has been the subject of much study (Denham and Lieberman, 1980). Engaged time is actually composed of two units, allocated time and engaged rate. Allocated time is the period set aside by the teacher for specific subject areas. Engaged rate is the percentage of time students actually spend in a subject area. Engaged time is the actual minutes per day in which a student is actively involved in a subject area. The work of Stallings and Kaskowitz (described in Denham and Lieberman, 1980) indicates that of the programs they observed the strongest variable in student achievement was engaged time.

Other researchers (for example, Bloom, 1976) have introduced into this concept a third component—success rate. Their conclusions indicate that a stronger correlation exists between engaged time and student achievement when the engaged time is spent with tasks that yield high success rates on the part of students. More recent studies (Denham and Lieberman, 1980) have demonstrated that academic learning time (ALT), which integrates engaged time with high success, is the most critical variable in achievement. Mastery learning as an instructional strategy attempts to ensure high ALT for all students.

Convinced that mastery learning was an appropriate strategy, Arricale found that the Chicago Public Schools had developed reading materials to deliver mastery learning instruction. The Chicago Mastery Learning Reading program (CMLR) consists of curriculum guides, in which 1,400 instructional objectives were categorized and sequenced; criterion-referenced tests that correspond to various objectives in the guides; and a variety of activities called learning packets for each objective. Supported by both academics and practitioners, the mastery learning approach utilizing the CMLR program was the instructional approach that Arricale would introduce into the school district in order to bring about some standardization of methodology and to increase engaged time on reading skills instruction (Levine and Stark, 1981).

The Instructional Context

A major dilemma soon arose. Mastery learning is a process of instruction, a philosophically based methodology to be used by teachers in the instruction of content. But the adoption of the CMLR materials by the district office did not guarantee that the new ML process would be accepted, understood, or used by the district's teachers.

Underlying the ML approach is the belief that teachers who utilize it will develop more positive attitudes regarding student ability and, at the same time, build confidence in themselves as professionals capable of achieving results. In addition, the district had been subject to warring building leadership, and teachers were reluctant to accept another packaged panacea after having experienced many such "cures" and their resulting failures. The tremendous need of the district and the unstable instructional context demanded that Arricale formulate some innovative strategies to make his program succeed.

The superintendent opted for a bottom-up/top-down implementation plan in which middle management (building principals) would be the link between the commitment and motivation of the superintendent and the adaptation and acceptance of the instructional design by the district's teachers. The management program demanded that teachers be trained off site, at least for the initial round, and that the entire professional staff of the school district be immersed in the philosophy, literature, and materials of CMLR. In addition, Arricale sought a liaison with New York's United Federation of Teachers (UFT) whose backing for the planned realignment would be construed by teachers as a positive force. The UFT entered into this commitment and initial CMLR materials would be printed in the district with the UFT's logo emblazoned on the early editions.

Program Management

A district office team was organized, which consisted of a director of reading and five staff developers. Based at the district office, this team appeared in the schools regularly for follow-up of off-site training and continued on-site development of the program. They distributed CMLR materials, and they developed non-threatening and supportive relationships with building administrators, but at the same time, they monitored implementation and provided feedback to the superintendent on problems or obstacles developing in the schools.

By the end of the first year, third, fourth, and seventh grade teachers were trained in the use of the materials. Many of these teachers were trained off site through the use of Chicago Board of Education personnel, publishers, consultants, and a trainer from the teachers' union. Building principals accepted the new project, but viewed it with guarded optimism. Teachers involved in the pilot grades had ambivalent feelings towards the materials, not yet sure if this was a disguised system for their own accountability, or an innovative whim of a new superintendent. Whatever their feelings, CMLR provided them with field-tested and completed lesson plans for the year, which relieved them of much detailed planning, along with on-site technical assistance from the staff developers.

Observing the implementation arena, Arricale had identified four major obstacles to his plans: building administrator resentment toward a district office-mandated reading program, the possible "loose-coupling" effect of co-opting a program mandated internal to the school, organized teacher opposition to the demands of the new program, and the presence of conflicting priorities with the absence of long-range educational goals. His strategy entailed meeting each obstacle before it disrupted the objectives of the program (Mann, 1976).

In effect, building principals had been asked to assume responsibility for a curriculum change for which they had had no input and, at best, viewed with suspicion and concern. A mandated innovation inevitably results in a disjuncture in the supervisory process linking principals and assistant principals with the teachers they supervise. To some degree, problems arise because teachers who have received a high degree of training for a particular innovation may often develop a greater expertise at the outset than the administrators who supervise them. Therefore, provision had to be made to realign the supervisory process.

The standardization of the reading curriculum mandated by the district office established the superintendent as the instructional leader. From his office emanated the design, the implementation arrangements, and the evaluation of the new program. He grouped his principals into small groups, met with each group separately, and related directly to their concerns and criticisms. At times he had to be arbitrary, but he tempered his new mandate with all the fiscal and staff support he could muster. The teachers' union had been part of the program from the beginning. It had some deep concerns about rigidity and structure of CMLR. Compromises were made where necessary, and the channels of communication that were opened remained so for the next three years.

Previous superintendents, while dedicated to their positions, had been more crisis-oriented than synoptic. Thus, Arricale, for the first time, established long-range objectives, a timetable of change, and a continuous assessment of implementation effects. The district had specific objectives and a comprehensive plan for implementation.

By the beginning of the second year, it appeared that five staff developers housed at the district office were insufficient to monitor the program at the building level as the program expanded from kindergarten to eighth grade. Therefore, a teacher trainer was established at each school site. The trainer was responsible for distribution of materials, monitoring program implementation, and linking the district office to building adaptation of CMLR. The teacher trainer as a linking agent was critical to the program, in line with the conclusions of the bottom-up evaluations of the 1970s. As long as the trainers demonstrated that they understood the dynamics of mutual adaptation, teachers generally were accepting of external technical assistance.

The trainer's job was ambiguous. Though not a supervisor, the trainer had to comprehend and utilize the strengths and weaknesses of the staff. In addition, part of the trainer's job was demonstrating mastery lessons to former colleagues. Though loyal to building staff, the trainer was responsible for reporting co-option by local forces. The trainers were selected by the director of reading, via district recruitment of applicants in conjunction with input from the building principal and were continuously trained by him and the staff developers. Their overriding professional characteristics had to be their ability to be multifaceted. Their roles were the focal point of the implementation for the second year. Because each school and each staff was unique, each trainer had to create the role that served the school and the program best. As the year developed, their sophistication in dealing with teachers and building staff grew. This was evidenced at teacher trainer meetings in which their questions and reports became more comprehensive and global. They appeared to have gained two perspectives: the uniqueness of their particular school and how their school was an integral part of the district organization.

By the end of the second year, three aspects of the program were evaluated by the director of reading, and the director of evaluation: supervisory response to the CMLR program, teacher response to the implementation of the program, and the impact of the program on student achievement.

Supervisory Response to the CMLR

In May of the second year, a questionnaire was completed by twenty-four of the twenty-six principals. Sixty-eight percent of the respondents were in favor of the new program. Seventy percent of the principals perceived the program as increasing their workload, but an equal number claimed they would not return to their previous reading instructional program even if given the option to do so. Sixty-nine percent of the respondents stated that school climate during reading skills instruction was improved. Sixty-nine percent of the respondents stated that the new program had improved the teaching of reading skills in their building.

In January of the third year, a similar questionnaire was completed by principals and assistant principals. As shown in Table 1, 85 percent of the principals stated that the quality of reading skills instruction had improved in their schools. This was a 16 percent increase over the previous survey in May 1980. Of the assistant principals, (Table 2), 77 percent felt similarly. More than 75 percent of both principals and assistant principals stated that the benefits of the new program were greater than any of the administrative or supervisory problems associated with its implementation. More than 75 percent of the principals found that the CMLR increased their monitoring capabilities concerning reading skills instruction. The most interesting result, however, is that, again, more than 50 percent (60 percent principals, 77 percent assistant principals) of the principals and assistant principals stated that they would select CMLR even if given the option to return to their previous programs.

Table 1. Community School District 19 Principal Response to Survey
Regarding Chicago Mastery Learning Reading Program (CMLR).

	Percent disagree	Percent undecided	Percent agree
1. The quality of reading *skills* instruction has improved through the addition of CMLR.		15	85
2. The CMLR has increased my *supervisory* responsibilities.	20		80
3. The CMLR has increased my *administrative* responsibilities.	20	5	75
4. As a result of the CMLR, there is an increased amount of *time*, (time-on-task) devoted to reading instruction.	10	10	80
5. As a result of the CMLR, there is a more positive attitude toward pupil success on the part of the teacher (expectancy).	5	40	55
6. For *skill development*, I prefer the Bloom model of instruction to other learning models used in the past.	15	35	50
7. The CMLR has increased my monitoring capabilities vis-a-vis reading skills instruction at each grade level.	20	5	75
8. I have observed a more positive school climate during reading skills instruction since the introduction of CMLR.	15	35	50
9. My CMLR data-collection system has enabled me to improve my evaluation of teacher performance.	10	50	40
10. My CMLR data-collection system has enabled me to improve my evaluation of pupil performance.		35	65
11. The standardized reading skills curriculum (mastery learning) has diminished my role as a decision maker.	50	15	35
12. I have experienced an increased dependency on the services of the teacher trainer vis-a-vis CMLR during the current school year (81–82).	30	20	50
13. The standardized reading skills curriculum (CMLR) has diminished my administrative flexibility.	50	10	40
14. With respect to the administration of the school program, the problems resulting from the implementation of the CMLR are greater than the benefits.	95	5	
15. With respect to the supervision of instruction, the problems resulting			

Table 1 (Continued).

	Percent disagree	Percent undecided	Percent agree
from the CMLR are greater than the benefits.	90	10	
16. As a result of the CMLR, I have worked more closely with the teachers in my school than in past years.	55	20	25
17. I would continue to use the CMLR if given an option to return to my previous methodology.		40	60

Teacher Response to Program Implementation

In May of the second year, a teacher questionnaire was distributed to over 600 of the district's teachers. Four hundred and eighty completed questionnaires were returned to the district office. Sixty-eight percent of the respondents stated that the district should continue to use the CMLR materials for the next school year. Over 72 percent of the teachers claimed they had received sufficient teacher training for CMLR. Over 60 percent of the teachers stated that CMLR materials had increased their ability to teach reading skills. The most favorable responses concerned the materials. The teachers perceived the materials as appropriate, sequenced in a logical fashion, and relevant to their student body. They found the formative test structure a positive form of feedback, and more than 50 percent stated that more students were successful on the formative tests as the year progressed. In general, the teachers' responses were more favorable than anticipated. With some changes, based on teacher feedback, the program was continued for the following year.

Student Impact

Student achievement is recorded in a number of tests mandated by the city, district, and federal categorical program units. The city administers a New York City Reading Test each April of the school year. The 1980 test revealed that overall achievement had substantially increased, and scores increased again in 1981. Table 3

Table 2. Community School District 19 Assistant Principal Responses to Survey Regarding Chicago Mastery Learning Reading Program (CMLR).

	Percent disagree	Percent undecided	Percent agree
1. CMLR has improved the quality of reading skills instruction in my school.	3	19	77
2. My school's CMLR data collection system, for monitoring unit progress, has increased my assistant-to-principal's capability for teacher supervision.	16	29	54
3. Standardizing the reading skills instruction via CMLR has increased my knowledge of specific skills objectives at each grade level.	16	6	67
4. As a result of the CMLR, I have observed an increased amount of instructional time devoted to reading instruction.	9	9	77
5. I have observed a more positive school climate during reading skills instruction since the introduction of CMLR.	9	38	48
6. With respect to the administration of the CMLR, the problems resulting from its implementation are greater than the anticipated benefits.	77	19	3
7. With respect to the supervision of instruction, the problems resulting from the CMLR are greater than the anticipated benefits.	77	19	3
8. Standardizing the district's reading skills program has diminished my role as a decision maker in the area of reading instruction.	45	29	25
9. The CMLR has created in my school higher levels of expectancy concerning reading skills achievement.	16	16	67
10. I would continue to use the CMLR if given an option to return to my previous methodology.	6	16	77

Note: Percentages sometimes do not total 100 due to nonresponses.

summarizes the improvement over two years of program implementation.

Absolute achievement, however, can be deceptive. Student achievement in the local district was then compared to student

Table 3. Community School District 19 Reading Scores, Grades 2-8, 1979-1981.

Year	Percent at or Above Grade Level	Percent 0-1 Year Below Level	Percent 1-2 Years Below Level	Percent 2 or More Years Below Level	Percent LEP[a]
1979	29.8	25.0	25.2	20.0	6.8
1980	36.3	26.6	21.0	16.1	7.4
1981	40.7	26.2	20.5	12.1	5.6
Difference	+10.9	+1.2	-4.7	-7.9	-1.2

[a]LEP means "limited English proficiency."

Table 4. New York City Reading Scores, Grades 2-8, 1979-1981.

Year	Percent at or Above Grade Level	Percent 0-1 Year Below Level	Percent 1-2 Years Below Level	Percent 2 or More Years Below Level	Percent LEP[a]
1979	40.3	20.1	19.3	10.9	9.4
1980	46.7	20.2	15.6	10.5	7.0
1981	50.8	19.6	15.0	10.0	4.6
Difference	+10.5	-0.5	-4.3	-0.9	-4.8

[a]LEP means "limited English proficiency."

achievement throughout the city. Table 4 indicates that student achievement in Community School District 19 was consistent with city-achievement at all levels except for those students who were two or more years below reading level. The decline in the number of students at this level in the district was dramatic in comparison to city achievement. The consistency at the other levels of reading achievement was also revealing. Never in the recent past had achievement in the local district kept pace with the progress of the city.

Table 5 shows that reading scores in Community School District 19 have continued to improve since the first two years. During four years of implementation of the CMLR program, the percentage of students with scores two years or more below grade level fell from 20 percent to 8 percent, and the percentage at or above grade level increased from 20 to 45 percent.

The results of the criterion-referenced tests (CRTs) inherent in the CMLR also revealed individual differences among schools within the district, and among classrooms within a school. Future evaluation will focus on the relationship between the CRTs of the CMLR program and the standardized norm-referenced test given throughout the city. While the CRTs evaluate what is being taught at the classroom level, the norm-referenced instrument indicates/ evaluates our students' abilities relative to the general population. Whatever the failings inherent in standardized tests, they are the

Table 5. Community School District 19 Reading Scores, Grades 2-8, 1979-1983.

Grade Level	1978-1979	1979-1980	1980-1981	1981-1982	1982-1983
Percent at or above	29.8	36.3	40.7	40.1	45.3
Percent 0-1 year below	25.0	26.6	26.2	28.8	28.3
Percent 1-2 years below	25.2	21.0	20.5	20.7	18.0
Percent 2 or more years below	20.0	16.1	12.1	10.5	8.3

most adequate evaluative device school systems administer to gain information concerning their primary goal—to provide students with the skills to function in the mainstream of American society. For this reason, we need more information on relationships between the CRTs and standardized test scores.

Conclusion

Several conclusions can be drawn concerning the Chicago Mastery Learning Reading program, implementation of educational change, and teacher education and instruction.

The CMLR program contains a number of components that reflect recent research in education. It is systematic, organized, objective-based, and evaluation oriented. It introduces two concepts essential for student achievement and the survival of school systems in times of diminished resources: high expectancy and cost-effectiveness. The high expectancy rate is developed from the philosophical base of mastery learning. The underlying philosophy of mastery learning is that *all* children can learn. Reflecting this, the CMLR program supports high expectancy on the part of the teacher. The cost effectiveness is accomplished by the emphasis on group instruction. The prepackaged material reduces planning overload on the part of the teacher and redirects teacher energy to instruction, assessment, and engaged time.

In addition, the built-in formative test structure reinforces student success, which is directly related to student achievement. The utilization of CMLR brought schools into more contact with one another, thereby creating a commonality among schools and reducing the "organized anarchies" that were assessed three years earlier. Yet each school's adaptation was unique to the school's particular needs and structure.

More authoritarian principals mandated that the CMLR program be taught at 9:00 each morning and each lesson be taught in a lock-step approach. Less authoritarian principals mandated that the CMLR program be used one period during the day. A suggested time sequence was distributed by the district office, but each school and teacher was given the flexibility to pace lessons as class needs demanded.

The strategy of implementing the CMLR program in Community School District 19 used a top-down/bottom-up scenario. Perceiving the implementation arena as hostile to new programs and assessing middle management as the most reactionary element, the superintendent partly bypassed middle management and directed his energies toward teacher education. Taking teachers off site in this regard was most productive. Appointing a teacher trainer at each school, whose allegiance was to the district office, was also helpful. By the end of the second year, teachers were so motivated to use the new program that, contrary to much of the literature in the field, the administrators at each school had to involve themselves in adapting their supervision to the new program. The CMLR program placed administrative burdens on building supervisors but, at the same time, supplied data as part of the continuous assessment component, which became invaluable and was applauded by local administration.

The objective of the superintendent was not to subordinate local administration, but to bring about innovation and implementation. This implementation scenario indicates that building administrators may not be as critical to initiating educational change as previously thought. However, caution must be added. Though building-level administrators were not the initial focus of the implementation, great care was taken not to antagonize them. The third year of the program was refocused on building-level supervisors. They have been the subject of in-service training in supervising and administrating the new program. The long-term goal is to prepare local administration to replace the teacher trainer if resources are drastically reduced. One goal for the fourth year will be to have building administrators purchase their own materials and monitor their own staff.

It is somewhat difficult to align the events in Community School District 19 with much of the research that has placed primary emphasis on bottom-up introduction and planning of innovations. It appears that another model for educational change has been developed by Community School District 19 that is replicable and cost-efficient. The top-down/bottom-up strategy can succeed given an instructional context in which building administrators initially may not be the most effective agents to bring about change. Their long-range acceptance of this innovation, however, is critical in successful implementation.

The most important conclusions that educational systems can cull from the District 19 experience is that implementation strategies should address and reflect the situation and problems in a school district. Because each school district is somewhat unique, implementation arenas are equally different. Therefore, innovators should spend their energies in appropriately assessing the forces and pressures that will be uncovered during the implementation process. It can be concluded further that the innovative program selected must be appropriate to the needs of the district. There must be commitment from the local school board, as well as from other local constituencies, not to interfere with the implementation of the new program. In addition, the implementation strategies that are selected must be compatible with the innovative program. The CMLR program is a structured and systematic approach to reading skills instruction. It demands a structured and systematic organizational framework in order to succeed. The top-down effort of the superintendent and the district office staff provides the structure. The bottom-up strategy (going directly to the teachers) links the efforts of the district office directly to classroom instruction.

References

Berman, P., and McLaughlin, M. W. *Federal Programs Supporting Educational Change: Implementing and Sustaining Innovations.* Santa Monica, Calif.: Rand Corporation, 1978.

Berman, P., and Pauly, E. W. *Federal Program Supporting Educational Change: Factors Affecting Change Agent Projects.* Santa Monica, Calif.; Rand Corporation, 1975.

Block, J. H., and Anderson, L. *Mastery Learning in Classroom Instruction.* New York: MacMillian, 1975.

Bloom, B. S. *Human Characteristics and School Learning.* New York: McGraw-Hill, 1976.

Chabotar, K. J., and Keel, D. S. *Linking R & D with Schools: An NIE Policy and Its Policy Context.* Cambridge, Mass.: Abt Associates, 1978.

Cohen, D. L., March, J. G., and Olsen, J. P. "A Garbage Can Model of Educational Choice." *Administrative Science Quarterly*, 1972, *17*, 1-25.

Datta, L. "Damn the Experts and Full Speed Ahead." *Evaluation Review*, 1981, *5*, 5-32.

Denham, C., and Lieberman, A. (Eds.). *Time to Learn, A Review of the Beginning Teacher Evaluation Study*. Washington, D.C.: National Institute of Education, 1980.

Duckett, W., and others. *Why Do Some Schools Succeed?* Bloomington, Ind.: Phi Delta Kappa, 1980.

Edmonds, R. "Effective Schools For the Urban Poor." *Educational Leadership*, 1979, *37*, 15-24.

Farrar, E., DeSanctis, J. E., and Cohen, D. K. "The Lawn Party: The Evaluation of Federal Programs in Local Settings." *Phi Delta Kappan*, 1980, *62*, 167-171.

Kaplan, C., and Stevens, G. *Report of the Dissemination Sessions of the Second Annual EBCE National Network Conference*. Washington, D.C.: National Institute of Education, 1978.

Levine, D., and Stark, J. *Instructional and Organizational Arrangements and Processes For Improving Academic Achievement at Inner City Elementary Schools*. Kansas City: University of Missouri at Kansas City, 1981.

Mann, D. *Policy Decision-Making in Education*. New York: Teacher's College Press, 1976.

Weick, K. E. "Educational Organizations As Loosely Coupled Systems." *Administrative Science Quarterly*, 1976, *21*, 1-19.

11

Incorporating
Testing and Retesting
into the Teaching Plan

William J. Smith

In the implementation of mastery learning strategies, the concept of testing and retesting generates a special concern in the minds of teachers. They worry that the paperwork may be excessive, that students will not prepare for the first test if they know they will be offered the opportunity of a retest, and that there is an over-emphasis on testing in general. Based on my experience implementing mastery learning (ML) at Young Junior High School in Bayport, New York, I believe that the following procedures and strategies will minimize these teacher anxieties.

A Formative Testing Strategy

A retest is a constructed device that allows a teacher to determine if all of the students have attained mastery of a learning task. In a mastery learning process, the teacher thoroughly instructs and explains a learning unit composed of specific learning objectives. Often such units require a period of five to ten days of instruction. On the last scheduled day of the unit, a teacher designs a formative test to determine student success. For those students who indicate nonmastery (usually a grade of less than 80 percent), the

241

teacher develops corrective instruction so that students get another opportunity to master the objective and demonstrate their improved learning on a parallel retest.

To implement the general testing strategy outlined above on a practical basis in working with the large number of students some teachers confront each day, I will propose several realistic suggestions that may be of help.

The First Formative Test. As the first step in the testing process, the teacher must prepare a short fifteen- to twenty-five-minute formative test that carefully assesses mastery of the learning objectives for the specific instructional unit. If possible, teachers should direct students to exchange papers. Since teachers usually do not assign credit for formative tests, motivation for collusion is greatly lessened.

Teachers must explain to students that their cooperation is greatly needed in performing their best because they, the teachers, are genuinely concerned about their learning. In fact, teachers must convey their determination that their students will learn even in spite of themselves. Teachers can assure themselves that most students will respond to such a sincere commitment on their part.

Initial Period of Correctives. After correcting the test, or through a show of hands, teachers must identify those questions that baffled most students. For example, on a twenty-five-question test, a teacher can expect that most students will miss from four to six questions, particularly when the mastery process is first introduced. On the same day or the day following the formative test, teachers must reteach these four to six items using expressions, diagrams, or techniques different than those used in the original instruction. This will expose students to different methodologies that may be more appropriate for their learning styles. It also is helpful to have students go to other teachers in the same department for a short period of extra help. This increases the odds of students encountering a teaching style that may be more appropriate for their learning styles. To do this, each department should organize its extra-help schedule so that teachers can draw on each other's styles and techniques.

After reteaching the nonmastered objectives on a large-group basis, teachers should meet with several of their best students after class or after school to brief them on how they can serve as group leaders during the following day's class. During this instructional period, the teacher should divide the class into four or five groups with each captained by a student who has demonstrated mastery of the instructional unit and who has already been briefed on the techniques needed for directing the group. This technique has the advantage of exposing students to still another style of explanation. Many students will benefit from this type of peer interaction because this technique better complements their learning styles. In addition, this experience also enriches the group leaders in that they have an opportunity to demonstrate, explain, and enhance their own learning. To teach is to learn.

As students work with each other, the teacher has an opportunity to work with those students who are experiencing the most difficulty. A variety of group activities may be needed for several more days before the class is ready for the second formative test. Yet, as the teacher more thoroughly accustoms his or her students to the mastery process, less and less time will be needed for correctives. In addition, when this approach is used regularly, teachers find that students develop more of a compassion for each other over a period of time. The desire to attain a competitive edge generally wanes because students are not competing against each other but rather against the learning objectives.

The Targeted Second Formative Test. After one to five days, the second formative test is given. Students are ready for this test when persistent oral feedback indicates that they are ready. A teacher can approach this test by retesting all students but only on those parallel questions that students did not master as determined by the first formative test.

Since this brief test is not counted for credit, it can again be corrected by the students. At this point, the teacher may assign students who have demonstrated mastery to reteach those students who again missed several items. Nonetheless, the teacher should probably proceed to the next instructional unit even if several students have not attained mastery. Teachers should not be surprised if students show little or no progress the first time they move through the process. Teachers may have to go through several instructional units before students become thoroughly accustomed to the format.

More time for correctives will probably be needed in the initial phases of mastery instruction, but as students master the necessary prerequisites, less and less time will be needed for correctives. Once students master the necessary prerequisites, teachers will generally find that in a relatively short time (eight to ten instructional units), the learning rate will almost double. From the viewpoint of managing the program, teachers will find that the time needed for learning will lessen, as will the time needed for correctives. Thus, there will be a more expeditious use of time, which invigorates the entire process.

Readiness is the persistent theme that permeates mastery instruction. In an ML format, teachers see to it that students master the learning objectives in order to be *ready* for the next learning task. The deep-rooted concept that a student must receive a grade by a certain date virtually eliminates the chance that many capable students have of attaining a rich and successful experience in school. Retesting in the ML context offers many more students a golden opportunity of succeeding in school.

Diagrams of the Process. In a nonmastery process, instructional units follow instructional units according to a predetermined time allocation regardless of student mastery. Following such a format, the so-called fast learners excel, while the medium fast and slow learners struggle. The best awards are reserved for the few in a very competitive atmosphere.

Figure 1. Nonmastery Instruction.

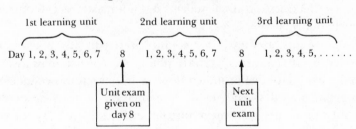

In a mastery process, instructional units follow instructional units as students demonstrate readiness for each subsequent instructional unit. Under such a format virtually all students have an opportunity to excel because each student is provided the time needed to master each learning unit and thus is ready to master the next learning unit. The best awards are reserved for all who demonstrate mastery but in a very cooperative atmosphere.

Implementing the Process in Regular Instruction. The process as thus described is readily implemented in that teachers continue to use their generally effective large-group methodologies but now have the opportunity of integrating a *time adequacy* component into the instruction. Using the corrective procedures, any student who needs more time gets it. In this manner, large-group instruction is blended with needed individualization without creating the undue complexities that are usually associated with individualization. Certainly the components of ML can be utilized within a sophisticated process providing individualized, continuous-progress instruction, but to overly emphasize continuous progress processes is to lose the support of many secondary school teachers who already are constantly struggling with severe classroom pressures. These same teachers are convinced that they

Figure 2. Mastery Instruction.

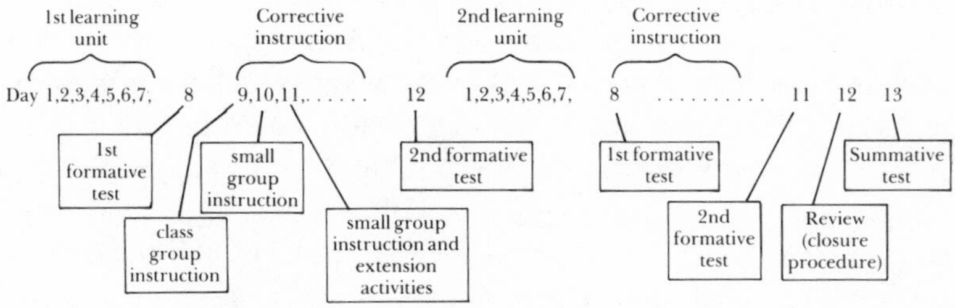

must use large-group instructional methodologies due to the large number of students they meet each day. The mastery-learning process, as described above, provides secondary teachers with a system to teach large numbers of students on a large-group basis while still addressing individual needs. (There are many students whose learning styles are commensurate with large-group instruction anyway.) Further, the format is a microcosm of what should be happening on a daily basis. Succinctly stated, teachers must design instruction so as to attain constant feedback from students to be sure that what is taught is learned.

Comprehensive Summative Testing. After one or two learning units, students should be given a summative test that also must be closely aligned with the learning objectives. To prepare students for summative testing, the formative tests in each learning unit should include items from earlier units so that students are assisted in retaining the mastery achieved over the broad scope of a subject. Constructing formative tests in this manner better prepares students for the more comprehensive summative testing, because earlier items that are missed again can be retaught during the corrective processes. Such carefully designed and systematized instruction insures the success of students on the more comprehensive tests. As indicated in Figure 2, the teacher should plan for a review period just before summative testing in order not to lose sight of the broad concepts and scope of a course. This emphasis on closure is another necessary ingredient of the ML testing process because retentive processes must also be cultivated and taught. Teachers will find that as the higher-level cognitive processes in individual disciplines are mastered, retention, which is on a lower cognitive level, will increase. When all these steps are taken, the onerous task of marking papers is lessened because teachers will be seeing more and more correct answers. A paper earning 100 percent takes half the time to score as a paper earning 50 percent. Teachers use the scores attained on summative testing for grading purposes.

Mastery and Grading

Expediting the Grading Process. In most school systems, a marking period grade is generally a combination of test grades and class work. Typically, classwork counts for about two thirds of the grade while tests count for the remaining one third. Teachers believe that this system gives students a fighting chance of passing (not to be confused with mastery) because so many students have a tendency to perform poorly on unit or comprehensive examinations. Under mastery conditions, however, students tend to perform very well on the more comprehensive summative examinations, lessening the teacher's need to have to score and record countless class assignments, some of which exist solely to protect students from the perceived tyranny of the more comprehensive examinations. Under mastery, students not only pass both formative and summative examinations, they also demonstrate mastery of the learning tasks.

The Impact of Mastery on Motivation. In addition, as students demonstrate more and more mastery on both formative and summative testing, they acquire that sense of adequacy that intrinsically motivates them to pursue the learning objectives of any curriculum area in which they experience such success. I believe that this sense of meaningful achievement on the part of students should reduce teachers' fears that students will not prepare for formative or summative examinations unless they know they are to be confronted with the unexpected. It is my experience that students will study because they want to.

Aligning Objectives and Tests

Test What You Teach. Teachers should also be aware of the importance of aligning test items with learning objectives. In an ML system, students are measured against the learning objectives of the curriculum area, not against each other. Therefore, the design of these objectives is critical. During the instructional process, teachers must be certain that the learning objectives are scrupulously explained and clarified. The merit of doing this is strongly supported in the research of Joan L. Hyman and S. Alan Cohen (1979). They found, after reviewing hundreds of research studies in which objectives were carefully constructed, clearly taught, and assessed with precision, that the achievement levels of students routinely exceeded expectations of their performance by a ratio of four to one. These research findings should also help alleviate teacher anxieties about not including surprise elements in testing

procedures to keep students on their toes, because effective alignment ultimately assures that students will attain so much more
success and so much more learning.

Aligning Objectives and Testing Facilitates Manageability.
In a word, what is taught and learned should be tested. If this
alignment does not take place, the level of student achievement
generally will not equal teacher expectations, let alone exceed them.
Alignment between objectives taught and retaught and objectives
tested and retested expedites the manageability of the mastery
learning retesting program because students are so much better
prepared to undergo both formative and summative testing. Not
only is paperwork lessened but time needed for correctives is
reduced. Student motivation is heightened and teachers experience
the exhiliration of seeing many more happy learners. Remember
that what is important in a curriculum, what is taught, and what
is tested are intrinsically interwoven.

Sacredness of Bell-Shaped Curve. Teachers, by incorporating
the components of the mastery process into their instruction, will
find that virtually all their students will learn. There may be a few
students a teacher may not be able to reach because they are
experiencing conflicts of one sort or another outside the classroom,
but so many students will achieve mastery that teachers must
prepare themselves to no longer expect a "normal" curve. Teachers
must realize that they will not be referees of the competition but
rather dynamic catalysts for mastery because most students will be
excited as long as they realize they can succeed. When students
achieve in the manner described, their academic learning time also
increases because they are more motivated to learn any subject in
which they are experiencing mastery.

ML Implementation at Young Junior High

Qualitative Data. An improved learning climate is developing in our junior high school as evidenced by the comments of
teachers who are implementing components of the mastery process
into their instructional arsenals. Foreign language teacher Gina
Bennett, after devising a retesting program, stated that "I implemented this system at the beginning of the fourth marking period
during this past school year, and found that many students did take

quizzes and tests over and their fourth marking period averages were better than those of the previous three marking periods."

Math teacher Gary Weeks, upon realizing that math teachers "were practicing their own form of mastery learning well before the term was introduced to us," proceeded to say in regard to objectives: "It was clearly laid out in the 'practice' tests exactly what the students would be asked and required to know (on the summative tests)." Then, he enthusiastically stated, "The results that the math department were able to achieve on the Regents [N.Y. State testing program] have been terrific. Most students agree that the Regents they take for a grade is easy, mainly because of this effort by teachers and students."

English teacher Ken Courtney briefly described his writing program: "After each composition is written, a conference is held with me to assess the quality of the student's work. Rewrites are allowed when necessary. When a mutually satisfactory level of achievement is reached, the student proceeds to the next unit." Courtney concludes, "The most satisfying aspect of this program is totally unexpected. Contrary to my expectations, my students continually request additional sessions of writing! They ask, beg, and even plead to be allowed to write more often than my planning allows. Although I have not finished the first year of the program, I have seen moderate to drastic improvement in much of the writing, particularly that of the weaker students."

Foreign language teacher Charles Watts commented, "There seems to be one thing that gets the attention of the worst underachiever: 'I'll give you another chance.' "

Resource room teacher Lorraine Martin remarked: "Most significantly for students with diagnosed learning disabilities, it is crucial that our tests reflect the specifics of what has been taught—even to the use of tests with similar formats. For example, if a sentence completion test is employed for vocabulary quizzes, then it is important to repeatedly use this type of test, rather than one in which students match a column of words with a column of definitions." Martin concluded, "As our children witness their own success, not only in the resource room, but also in their content area subjects, that achievement compels them to work hard and maintain an improved standard of performance."

Social studies teacher, George Cameron, after incorporating the elements of mastery learning into his instructional repertoire, tried to look at the process through the eyes of four of his students who had been struggling. He came to the conclusion that these students have benefited both academically and attitudinally. Not only have these four students gone from the F/D + range to the B +/ A- range but they also have finally developed a sense of pride that will motivate them intrinsically for many years to come.

As the teachers in our school continued to implement the components of the mastery process into their instructional procedures, outcomes other than better student achievement also have come to the fore. Because the process is so effective, teachers are experiencing a rejuvenation. In spite of relentless efforts to improve achievement, many teachers had encountered just as relentless a frustration because so many of their students had not experienced success. Mastery learning procedures are an antidote to this malaise. I find that teachers who implement the mastery process develop an immunity to burnout or exhaustion because their efforts become so much more productive. The excitement of learning is contagious. The fact that some of these outcomes may be more intangible than student achievement scores does not diminish the reality of the exhiliration teachers now experience as more and more of their students succeed. This contagion is particularly significant because our staff, similar to many others on Long Island, averages fifteen or more years in the classroom. Now it is no longer a question of doing the same futile things over and over again, but a question of what else we can do more effectively to reach an even greater number of our students.

Quantitative Data. In 1981, 31 percent of our sixth grade students fell below the New York State minimum reference point on the recently developed Degrees of Reading Power (DRP) test. According to state regulations, we had to design remedial programs for 31 percent of our sixth grade students, a totally unacceptable number in view of the largely middle-class composition of our school district. After this debacle, we provided in-service workshops on the mastery learning process, usually in the form of faculty meetings and departmental meetings so as not to impose on teachers' preparation time. I also ran a series of workshops for any teachers who wanted to come. These workshops were well attended. Then we redesigned our sixth grade reading program. As Figure 3 shows, 11 percent of our students fell below the reference point in 1982, while in 1983 only 6 percent of our students fell below it. This improvement brought our school from a median position to the top five percent on the state profile for Suffolk County. There appeared to be no statistically significant difference in the socioeconomic composition of these various classes, certainly not to the point that would explain these changes. The improvements followed our implementation of several components of the mastery process.

Figure 3. Sixth Grade Students Below State Minimum Reference Point on Degrees of Reading Power Test.

Percentage	1979-80 (110)	1980-81 (106)	1981-82 (107)	1982-83 (109)
35				
30				
25				
20				
15				
10				
5				
0				

Figure 4. Sixth Grade Students in the Superior Range on Degrees of Reading Power Test.

Percentage	1980-81	1981-82	1982-83
90			
80			
70			
50			

We have also witnessed a significant increase in the numbers of students who scored in the superior range on the DRP Test (raw score 58 or above). As shown in Figure 4, 85 percent of sixth grade students scored in the superior range on the Degrees of Reading Power Test in 1983, as compared with 52 percent in 1981.

Several other statistical phenomena indicate that the process described earlier is cultivating considerably higher achievement levels.

- In 1982, 13.7 percent of our seventh and eighth grade students earned an honor roll certificate (90 average or better) for the 1981-82 school year.
- In 1983, 13.9% of our seventh and eighth grade students earned an honor roll certificate for the 1982-83 school year.
- In June of 1984, 24.6% of our seventh and eighth grade students earned an honor roll certificate for the 1983-84 school year.

On the sixth grade level, we also note a steady growth in the achievement levels of our students: In 1981, 31 percent earned an honor roll certificate; in 1982, 35 percent; in 1983, 41 percent; and in 1984, 51 percent.

During 1983-84, we also admitted seventy students to the Junior National Honor Society. Prior to 1983-84, thirty-six students represented the highest number ever admitted to the Society.

It is evident that more of our teachers are not only using the mastery learning process but are now using it more effectively. We must conclude that these instructional changes and adjustments, while not the only components responsible for this growth, are certainly key components generating these improvements.

Although I have researched, studied, and designed curriculum within the ML format for the past six or seven years, we only introduced it to our junior high school staff approximately one and a half years ago. It is very evident that we are only at the early stages of implementing the process. For example, our students still demonstrate difficulty with comprehensive testing, such as final examinations. In 1981, 20 percent of written examinations earned a failing grade. In 1982, we reduced that to 12 percent, only to see the number return to 20 percent in 1983. In analyzing the situation, we concluded that there is insufficent alignment between what is taught, mastered, and tested. Even more fundamentally, we have concluded that we must more thoroughly define our objectives so we know what we want students to learn. In those areas where we already have done this most carefully, we made considerable progress, as indicated by the DRP scores described earlier.

Young Junior High School has a favorable ambience due to parental support and cooperation. Above all, we have a school in which the staff is commited, competent, and caring, whether the mastery learning process is used or not. All these factors contribute to the momentum and successes we are now experiencing. Yet, many of our teachers are receptive to the underpinning of the ML process because the process reflects in a more organized fashion some of the instructional methodologies that have been in place for a long time. We are convinced that by implementing the components of the mastery process—teaching, reteaching, testing, retesting—we are becoming better organized and more thoroughly systematized in the delivery of instruction, thus enabling more and more students to succeed at a high level.

Further, the teachers recognize that the retesting components of the ML process are adaptable to countless teaching situations. Many teachers who are commited to a systematized process of instruction have adapted this testing framework to their own curriculum and teaching needs. They have devised innumerable techniques to allow students time to master the necessary prerequisites before moving to the next learning task. A good testing procedure can be a faithful ally in helping students master each learning task. I believe that the components of the mastery learning process as described above provide substantive and viable solutions to some of the concerns cited in the final report of the National Commission on Excellence in Education and other recent reports that point to major learning problems in our public schools.

References

Hyman, J. L., and Cohen, S. A. "Learning for Mastery: Ten Conclusions After 15 Years and 3,000 Schools." *Educational Leadership,* 1979, *37* (2), 104–109.

National Commission on Excellence in Education. *A Nation at Risk.* Washington, D.C.: U.S. Government Printing Office, 1983.

12

❦

Strategies for Implementing Successful Mastery Learning Programs: Case Studies

Donald W. Robb

Mastery learning as an educational philosophy has become well established in the nation's schools. A number of school systems have adopted a staff development approach to mastery learning and have invested in programs to train teachers in the application of mastery learning principles.

To speed up and simplify the process of implementing mastery learning, other school systems have increasingly taken an instructional materials approach and have instituted programs that utilize textbooks organized on a mastery learning model. One such set of instructional materials, Chicago Mastery Learning Reading (CMLR), is currently in use in several thousand classrooms across the country.

Because of the widespread acceptance of mastery learning philosophy, and specifically the continued expansion in the use of mastery learning instructional materials, it seems useful to examine not only the impact but more importantly the implementation of mastery learning. Evidence already exists to support the premise that mastery learning can produce gains in achievement scores, increased learning rates, and improved student attitude and self-image. In short, the evidence is clear and forceful: Mastery learning can have a profound impact. Many educators are now concerned not with the question of *whether* to implement mastery learning but rather *how* to implement it most expeditiously.

What is needed now is information on successful strategies for implementing mastery learning: how decisions are made, how staff is trained, how time is allocated, how monitoring is accomplished. Among the major questions to be addressed are the following:

- What are the significant constants that seem to be present in successful mastery learning implementations? How are these constants handled in a variety of successful implementations?
- What conclusions can be drawn from examining specific successful implementations that might be useful to other schools that desire to adopt mastery learning materials?

This chapter will describe three specific mastery learning implementations, examining each in some detail and discussing the similarities and differences among them. Finally, on the basis of these three case studies, some preliminary conclusions will be drawn.

The three schools chosen for this analysis are Ernie Pyle Elementary School in Bellflower, California; Kent Intermediate School in Columbus, Ohio; and Border Star Elementary School in Kansas City, Missouri. These three schools were chosen because they are all examples of an effective *building-level implementation* of mastery learning. It is therefore possible to examine each one in fairly close detail, without having to rely on the kind of generalizations and qualifications that are almost impossible to avoid when dealing with a whole school district.

These three schools were chosen, too, because they are successful. That is, in a variety of ways, each has achieved some degree and some combination of desired results. Among the standards by which these schools have measured success are gains in test scores, improved school climate, increased expectations, more efficient use of time, positive teacher and student attitudes, and general effect on the curriculum.

One constant among the three schools, which differ greatly by geography, school organization, size, pupil population, and community characteristics, was the fact that each of them implemented mastery learning by adopting the Chicago Mastery Learning Reading program as an integral part of its language arts instruction. CMLR was developed by the Chicago Board of Education in order to systematize mastery learning as the instructional approach to reading throughout that city's schools. CMLR is a kindergarten through eighth grade program that consists of student workbooks, tests, and teacher manuals dealing with word attack, study skills, and comprehension concepts. The materials are intended to be used in close conjunction with a variety of materials for extended reading—stories in basal readers, library books, children's literature, magazines, and other available sources.

CMLR is organized on a mastery learning model. Specific objectives and standards for mastery are stated for each unit. The instructional units follow the four-phase cycle of mastery learning: initial instruction, a formative test to assess mastery, and (for those students who require it) corrective instruction followed by a retest to demonstrate mastery. Students who demonstrate mastery on the formative test choose from a variety of extension options.

Additionally, CMLR incorporates within the initial instruction in each unit a sequencing model that introduces and reiterates essential prerequisites in logical increments. This sequence allows for the establishment of overt cognitive links between elements of the instruction and enables students to proceed together through the unit in spite of differences in prior experience.

Also embedded within CMLR units is overt instruction in learning strategies and cognitive processes that are characteristic of high achieving students. This instruction models effective thinking patterns, guides students in linking new information to already-known concepts, and provides practice in techniques for organizing, processing, and retrieving information presented in a range of text types.

CMLR emphasizes whole-group instruction but encourages small-group and even individualized activities when appropriate.

The program provides a simple monitoring system and thorough directions for teachers.

In the three schools under examination, the CMLR materials formed the basis of a mastery learning approach to reading instruction. In each case, it was the combination of the mastery learning model, the sequencing, the learning strategies, and the whole-class instruction that served as the organizational foundation for mastery learning implementation.

With CMLR materials as a constant in every case, it is necessary to look at each of the three schools separately to assess other constants as well as to explore the variables that distinguish one successful implementation from another.

Ernie Pyle School, Bellflower, California

Bellflower is a working-class Los Angeles suburb of approximately 55,000. Ernie Pyle Elementary School, one of six in the community, serves a population of about 700 students, grades kindergarten through six. The student body is 14 percent Korean, 12 percent black, and 2 percent Mexican-American; the remaining 72 percent are non-Hispanic white. Some 10 to 15 percent of the students come from AFDC families; about half, from single-parent homes.

The mastery learning philosophy was introduced to Bellflower by Superintendent Leonard Burns, long an active member of the Network for Outcome-Based Schools. Burns presented the mastery learning concept at a meeting of his principals, and asked them to submit to him an application for a pilot with the Chicago Mastery Learning Reading program.

At Ernie Pyle, Principal Jean Keleman in turn introduced the mastery learning idea to her staff. She viewed the proposed pilot as advantageous in two ways: first, for the chance of success it would offer to students, and second, for the impact it might make on teacher renewal. Nine teachers out of a staff of twenty-two indicated. that they would like to be a part of the pilot; the rest, though not hostile, preferred to "see it work" before making a commitment.

With the support of her staff, Keleman applied for the pilot opportunity, stressing to Burns that "this school wants to succeed."

Three of the six Bellflower schools petitioned for the pilot; Ernie Pyle was the selected site. At Ernie Pyle, it was decided to concentrate the pilot in the three classrooms of grade six. (Later a fifth grade class was added.)

To place students in the CMLR program, Keleman and her staff took the entire group—all the sixth-graders and those fifth-graders who were to participate—and regrouped them on the basis of their reading scores, particularly the California Test of Basic Skills (CTBS) and teacher judgment. To facilitate placement, the four teachers all scheduled their reading period at the same time so that it would be easy to move a student quickly to an appropriate instructional level. Because reading levels at Ernie Pyle are generally below average, it was decided to organize two classes in fourth grade materials, one in fifth, and one in sixth. All four classes contained both fifth and sixth grade students.

Reading instruction at Ernie Pyle was alloted one hour per day. Over the course of a week or so, about 60 percent of this time was devoted to CMLR instruction. Basal readers were used about 30 percent of the reading time, and selected library books filled the remainder. The Ginn reading series is the adopted basal text in Bellflower. When CMLR was introduced, the use of the basal changed significantly. None of the skills material was used, and stories were selected to serve as applications of the CMLR skills and concepts. The skill sequence of CMLR became the basis of the curriculum, with stories from the Ginn series providing regular reinforcement, practice, and extension. In addition to Keleman's initial presentation on mastery learning, the staff also received direct in-service on the CMLR program, including advice on placement and pacing. Because the staff approached the mastery learning project as a joint effort, there was a great deal of cooperative planning and discussion. Keleman frequently visited classes and met regularly with the four teachers. Periodic meetings were also held with Burns to update him on progress in the classrooms.

All four classrooms used the CMLR wall charts to monitor student progress. Although the pilot did not begin until November, all classes finished the level to which they were assigned. The pacing, therefore, was challenging, especially considering that many of the students were seriously below level at the outset.

Nevertheless, the staff reported almost immediate positive response from the students. The mastery learning approach allowed many of them to achieve unaccustomed success. Though they viewed the materials as difficult, they were willing to persevere because the attainment of mastery seemed within their grasp. In fact, students themselves began to demand to know, in other subject areas, what the mastery level was.

One element in making it possible for teachers and students to maintain the demanding pace of instruction, and the generally high level of time on task, was the fact that the reading period was not subject to interruptions—no students were pulled out for special help or for extra-curricular activities. In return for a staff commitment to explore the mastery learning approach, Keleman had made the commitment to provide them uninterrupted time in which to accomplish the task.

Student enthusiasm for the mastery learning approach was extremely high. Visitors to the classroom were struck by the high degree of student participation and the absence of distracting behavior or inattention. The four teachers reported noticeable changes in student performance during the entire school day. Not only did attitudes toward school improve, there was also an improvement in work habits and in achievement in other subject areas.

At Ernie Pyle, the staff adhered closely to the mastery learning model of CMLR. Whole-class instruction was the norm, with every student expected to participate. Formative tests determined which students went into an extension cycle and which received corrective instruction. As a general rule, by the time the retest was given, most students were attaining the mastery level.

Students were graded in reading on the basis of their success with CMLR. However, no student working below grade level could receive a grade higher than C +. In spite of this grading restriction, students on the whole felt very positive about their experiences with CMLR.

The students had all taken the CTBS in the fall of 1982. In April 1983 they took the spring CTBS. Every one of the 135 students in the pilot made gains in the six-month period from November to April. Not one student gained less than six months; many gained more than a year, and thirty students topped out on the test in April where only eight had done so in November. Eight special education students gained better than a year and a half. The average gain in CTBS study skills was more than one full year. Given that many of the students were low achievers and that the survey period covered only six months, Keleman feels that the gains represent a major accomplishment for the pilot.

During the 1983-84 school year, Ernie Pyle expanded the use of the CMLR materials and the mastery learning approach. A new principal, Ralph Kerr, has overseen an expansion of CMLR into every classroom in the building. Keleman, meanwhile, has transferred to another school in the district and is implementing CMLR with the staff there.

In expanding to the entire building, Kerr and the staff regrouped all students, as had been done with fifth and sixth graders the year before, to determine appropriate CMLR placement levels. Kerr feels that in the future this procedure will still be necessary in the upper grades, but may not be essential for primary classrooms.

Building-wide, teacher acceptance has been generally enthusiastic. The four pilot teachers remain strong and vocal supporters of the program and comment that mastery learning has changed their attitudes and their style of teaching. The rest of the staff agreed readily to the expansion; one or two somewhat reluctant teachers seemed, by mid-year, to be supportive of the change.

At the upper grades, beginning the mastery learning program in September rather than November has allowed for a more reasonable pace and a bit more time for other reading activities. In some classrooms, plans are being made to increase the use of outside reading materials to give greater variety of application than the basal reader alone can offer.

Kent Intermediate School, Columbus, Ohio

Because of a desegregation plan, Columbus schools are organized on a primary, intermediate, and middle school basis. Kent School, one of about forty in the system, contains grades four and five, with about 60 percent of the students bused in from other areas of the city. It also houses a neighborhood kindergarten, and has a total enrollment of about 400 children, including special education classrooms.

Despite the busing, Kent has a relatively homogeneous student body, since the areas from which it draws are generally lower socioeconomic status, with a high minority proportion. Typically, students arrive at Kent at least a year or more below level in standardized reading scores.

On the basis of city-wide testing in the spring of 1982, Kent School ranked close to the bottom among the forty elementary schools in Columbus. More than 72 percent of its fourth graders were below grade level in comprehension, while 66 percent of fifth graders failed to meet grade level standards.

In most classrooms, students were working one to two levels below expectations in their basal readers. To meet the needs of so many who were struggling with reading, children were frequently grouped and regrouped or pulled out of the classroom for extra instructional help. Needless to say, staff morale was low, as was pupil self-image. The constant regrouping resulted in a chaotic scene with students carrying chairs in and out of classrooms or working in hallways.

In the fall of 1982, Kent School was assigned to Area Director Evelyn Jones. (In Columbus, responsibility for elementary supervision is the function of four Area Directors of Elementary Education who report to Assistant Superintendent Dr. Evelyn Luckey.) A new principal, Kenneth Pendleton, was transferred from another school to replace the retiring principal. In the reading department, Kent was assigned to Reading Resource Teacher Edwina Bradley, one of several who service the city's elementary schools.

Jones had become aware of the Chicago Mastery Learning Reading program through a desegregation project sponsored by Kent State University. Some of the CMLR materials were actually in use at Kent School, though no systematic effort had been made to implement mastery learning in the school.

Together Jones, Pendleton, and Bradley determined to make a positive impact on reading achievement in the building and agreed to use CMLR as the vehicle for their efforts. It was decided that all students—kindergarten as well as fourth and fifth grade— would have CMLR as part of their reading instruction. They further decided that CMLR would be used in close conjunction with the school's adopted basal reader, which at the time was the Houghton-Mifflin series.

Teacher reaction to this decision was initially positive, though not strongly enthusiastic. Moreover, teacher expectations of their students were extremely low. In deciding where to place students in CMLR, for example, most teachers in the building requested books that were two or three grades below level. Most also felt that they needed two or more levels within each classroom to accommodate the range of students. (One classroom at the time had seven reading groups.) Consultant Walter Thompson, a former reading specialist in the Chicago schools, spent several days at Kent, teaching demonstration classes and meeting with the staff.

Thompson insisted that in most classrooms, only one level should be used and that most students receive instruction at grade level. The staff were frankly reluctant to follow his advice, but Thompson convinced them to give his recommendations a chance, promising to make adjustments if they proved necessary.

The result was that one classroom was organized for the fifteen or so fourth graders who were farthest behind; second and third grade materials were selected. One fourth grade class was organized to work in third grade books; one fifth grade class was accommodated in fourth grade books. The remaining nine classrooms were assigned grade-level materials: fourth grade books for fourth graders; fifth grade for fifth graders, with all students in each classroom using the same level. In one of the lowest achieving schools in the city, this was a dramatic change, and the teachers were skeptical. Nevertheless, they agreed to go ahead with the project.

Initial in-service for the staff consisted of an introduction to mastery learning philosophy and principles, an overview of the CMLR materials, and the demonstration classes taught by Thompson. Follow-up visits were made several times during the school year by other mastery learning consultants, so that teachers had ample opportunity to ask questions and receive feedback. Bradley, as the school's reading resource teacher (although she also provided support service to several other schools) spent considerable time at Kent and was a regular source of on-site advice and suggestions.

Because of the need to reorganize classes, it was not until late fall that teachers began to use the CMLR materials on a full-time basis. By early January, however, CMLR had been implemented in every classroom. At Kent, this implementation was consistent across classrooms. That is, each classroom used the mastery learning materials in much the same way, with of course the normal variations in teacher style and personality.

In each classroom, instructional time for reading was set at ninety minutes per day. Approximately half this time, or an average of forty-five minutes per day, was devoted to CMLR and a like amount to basal readers. Time allotment naturally varied somewhat from day to day but on the average was divided fairly evenly between CMLR and the basals. (Basal instruction involved the stories in the anthologies, along with their associated vocabulary and comprehension activities; basal skill lessons—in the texts, workbooks, or supplementary materials—were replaced by the CMLR materials.)

Whole group instruction, which had not been common practice at Kent, at least in the teaching of reading, became the norm. Though teachers were at first unsure that they would be comfortable with whole class instruction, they followed the CMLR teacher manuals, incorporating the direct instruction modeled there, and began to observe noticeably increased student participation. As early as January, even outside observers were struck by the change in the atmosphere of the school. In place of the frenzied shuffling of students seen in September, classrooms were devoting far more time to actual instruction, and students seemed eager to participate.

Teachers followed closely the mastery learning model, using the formative tests to determine which students received the corrective instruction. To the surprise of most teachers, their students were more successful than they had anticipated. Most were, in fact, reaching the mastery level by the end of the unit. Many needed the corrective instruction, but what the staff saw was classroom after classroom of "low achievers" who were regularly mastering the units and, for the first time, meeting with success.

By early spring, staff attitude and expectations had changed radically. Teachers who had started off wanting their fifth graders in third grade materials saw that those same fifth graders could, with a mastery learning approach, function on level.

Even more impressive is the fact that at Kent, the normal year of instruction with CMLR had to be condensed into the period from December through June. Pacing was therefore very demanding and intensive, yet teachers were able to complete each grade level. This pacing was monitored by Bradley, who also helped to keep the balance between CMLR instruction and basal story reading, and by Pendleton, who kept track of progress in each classroom on a master chart in his office.

Students themselves in some of the classrooms began to take a sense of pride in monitoring their own progress. They were eager to report to Pendleton when the class had mastered another unit and especially proud when they could report that every student had reached mastery.

Though CMLR had been implemented at grade level in all but a couple of classrooms, students were still working in a variety of levels in their basal readers. A number of teachers found, however, that after a few months with CMLR, their students were making faster than normal progress in the readers. In fact, by late spring, most teachers had moved their classes on level in the basal, something which had seldom happened before.

One problem did arise in implementing mastery learning, however. Columbus district policy required that students reading below level in the basal receive a grade no higher than C in reading. At Kent, initially, many students were making excellent progress in the mastery learning program, and were reading more effectively. Yet because they were still below level in their basal, they were limited to a grade of D or at best C. The grading system became a disincentive to students. Jones and Luckey were instrumental in making it possible for Kent School to adjust the grading so as to reflect two different reports—one on progress in the basal and one in the mastery learning program.

In the spring of 1983, Columbus students were again tested, as they had been in 1982, using the CTBS. Results, naturally enough, were eagerly awaited at Kent. In comprehension, the percentage of Kent students scoring at or above grade level was as follows:

	1982	1983
Grade 4	27.8%	43.3%
Grade 5	34.0%	38.7%

Several items regarding these test scores are worthy of note. First, Kent students as a whole were scoring much closer to the city average. After the 1983 testing, Kent was no longer at the bottom. In fact, it moved into the middle third of all Columbus schools. It is by no means the top achieving school in the city, but it is now nowhere near the bottom. Second, the gains shown on this test in fourth grade scores indicate a real possibility of bringing those students up above city averages in another year. Finally, comparing 1982's fourth graders to 1983's fifth graders—essentially the same group of children—it is clear that many more of them are now at or above level.

There are other indicators of success at Kent. In the 1983-84 school year, for example, only twelve students in the school (and several of them are in special education classes) are in third grade materials. One class of fifth graders is using, successfully, the sixth grade CMLR materials. Suspensions have been cut by 50 percent over the last year. Where once it was almost impossible to develop any kind of parent or community involvement, the school now has an active parents' organization and a ready supply of parent volunteers. Most of all, the impact of mastery learning at Kent School has been an attitudinal one. The school has adopted the motto "Kent Can"—and, perhaps for the first time, Kent's students believe it's true.

Border Star Elementary School, Kansas City, Missouri

The elementary schools of Kansas City began their experience with mastery learning with five classrooms in the spring of 1981. By the 1983-84 school year, mastery learning—in the form of Chicago Mastery Learning Reading materials—had expanded to include some twenty-seven elementary schools and three junior highs.

One of the original schools, Border Star, has used CMLR school-wide since September of 1981. Border Star, a kindergarten through sixth grade building of about 350 students, is in a middle-class section of Kansas City and in some ways has an almost suburban appearance. Most of its students, for example, are now reading at or above grade level. Nevertheless, Border Star's population is 60 percent minority, consisting of Black, Vietnamese, and Mexican-American children. In addition, Border Star houses classes for visually impaired and deaf/hard of hearing students, who also participate in the mastery learning program, as well as gifted and talented students (one classroom each at grades four, five, and six).

Border Star was not always in this position. A few years ago, before the introduction of mastery learning, the average Border Star student was reading below grade level. Reading skills were being approached in an isolated, hit-or-miss fashion. Though reading instruction was allocated two hours a day, Principal Jessie Kirksey observes that "it wasn't quality time, and it wasn't meeting the needs of the children."

The introduction of mastery learning in 1981 coincided with an effort at Border Star to increase the effectiveness of both math and reading instruction. Language arts time was increased from two to three hours daily. In the morning, students receive about seventy minutes of instruction in their basal reader. (The Houghton Mifflin series is used.) They also spend about half an hour daily in English or spelling. In the afternoon, anywhere from an hour to an hour and a quarter is allocated to CMLR instruction and free reading time.

Without doubt, this dramatic increase in the time spent on reading has been a major contributing factor in the increased achievement levels noted over the last three years. Important, too, in Kirksey's opinion, is the mastery learning nature of the CMLR program, which has made it possible for more and more students to benefit from that additional time. The quality of instruction has enabled a greater number of students to develop the full range of reading skills. Gains in reading during the first full year of CMLR implementation are apparent in the following 1982 and 1983 median scores on the Iowa Test of Basic Skills:

Median Scores: ITBS

	Spring, 1982	Spring 1983
Grade 3	3.9	4.3
Grade 4	6.4	6.7
Grade 5	7.2	8.0
Grade 6	7.5	8.2

Like some other schools in Kansas City, Border Star closely follows the mastery learning model, providing corrective instruction for students who do not master immediately. Guidelines for implementing CMLR in Kansas City schools have been developed by a district-wide steering committee. The guidelines deal with time allotments and adherence to the mastery learning format.

In Kansas City, in-service on CMLR is provided to teachers and principals by the Learning Exchange, a nonprofit educational consulting group in the city. This in-service, combined with the city-wide guidelines, provides a certain consistency of implementation from school to school.

Mastery learning in Kansas City has the support of the district administration. Funds for implementing CMLR are provided by the district to any school when 75 percent of the staff has voted to go into the mastery learning program. Each school also has the services of an instructional assistant—a staff development person who works with the staff to ensure maximum benefit from the instruction. Thus, the implementation at Border Star included systematic installation, initial in-service, continuing staff support, and ongoing monitoring.

Students at Border Star are routinely placed in CMLR on the basis of their progress in the basal reading program. For most students, this means on-level placement. In gifted and talented classrooms, students are working from one to two years above level.

After three years with mastery learning, Border Star has clearly moved beyond the implementation phase; the whole philosophy of mastery learning is essentially institutionalized within the school's curriculum. Over the three year period, student achievement has improved to the point where most students are now at or above, rather than below, grade level expectations. Many fewer students are falling behind than had been true previously.

Because of the heavy emphasis on improvement in math and reading, for a time other curriculum areas received less attention. Yet Kirksey reports that skills and concepts mastered in the reading program are helping students in other subjects as well. She notes also an increased interest in learning on the part of students, citing, for example, the large and increasing number of students who willingly participate in the school's annual science fair.

At Border Star, the mastery learning program has reached the point where the plan now is to reduce the total amount of time devoted to language arts. The feeling is that with most students working at grade level, it is time to concentrate on the transfer of skills to the content areas.

Conclusion

From an examination of Ernie Pyle, Kent, and Border Star schools, several salient points emerge. There are enough similarities to point to specific conclusions regarding mastery learning in these schools:

1. Mastery learning in general, and the CMLR materials in particular, provide a model of instruction that is effective for a wide range of students. Essentially the same system of instruction has resulted in rapid gains for underachievers at Kent and has provided a means for allowing gifted and talented students to move through two levels of instruction in a year at Border Star.

2. Mastery learning has reduced the spread, in all three schools, between the lowest achiever and the highest—without slowing down the fastest students.

3. The skills and concepts taught in the CMLR materials—and presented in a mastery learning format—have been internalized by students so that they are transferred to other curriculum areas. Kent's experience in moving students to more appropriate levels in their literature series, Ernie Pyle's students who ask for mastery levels in science or spelling, and Border Star's increase in students participating in science fairs are indicative of the way in which mastery learning can impact the curriculum.

4. It is clear from observations in these three schools that along with the achievement gains typical of mastery learning, there is also a remarkable impact on student attitude and self-image. This change in attitude is reflected not only in decreased behavior problems but in the pride students take in themselves and their school. "Kent Can" is more than a slogan—it is an expression of a fundamental attitude. This same self-respect and high set of expectations are also evident at Border Star and at Ernie Pyle.

Beyond the similarities of results observed in the three schools, there are also some striking similarities of implementation that should be of interest to other schools contemplating a mastery learning program of their own.

Some of those factors relate to the way in which teachers and principals are introduced to, and prepared for, a mastery learning program:

• In all three cases the principals voluntarily entered into a mastery learning project. In each case, significantly, the principal had the support of the district administration, but in none of these cases was mastery learning imposed.

• Teachers in all three schools had at least some say in the decision to implement mastery learning. It is not always common practice to allow teachers a part in the decision-making process, but the success of mastery learning in these three cases would seem to indicate that if change is to occur in the classrooms, teachers must surely be involved. Clearly some degree of volunteerism is critical to developing staff commitment.

• Staff training—in both the underlying philosophy of mastery learning and the specific procedures applicable to CMLR— was a significant factor at all three schools. Intensive in-service was employed in both Kansas City and Columbus, while Bellflower established a support-group concept. In all three schools, teachers were not expected to function without guidance or direction. Rather, in each case care was taken to see that teachers were informed, prepared, and supported.

Other similarities among the three schools are evident in the kind of decisions that were made regarding instruction:

- Placement of students at a demand level—where the work is challenging but the expectation is realistic—seems to have been of critical importance in all three schools. Especially at Kent, students who were typically low achievers were placed at a level that required real effort and resulted in more rapid learning rates.

- Grouping of students so that whole class instruction could take place at the most appropriate level was a factor at both Ernie Pyle and Kent, where large numbers of students were seriously below level. At Border Star, where most students were fairly close to level and where large amounts of additional individual assistance were provided for low achievers, grouping was not as large an issue. But when some students need major amounts of remediation, it seems useful to do whatever regrouping will result in students operating at their maximum potential.

- Staff at all three schools realized that students working below level, if they are to make major gains, need as rapid a pace as faster students. In these schools, students were generally placed no more than one level below grade, and were expected to progress rapidly enough to make more than a year's gain for a year's instruction.

- Instructional time in all three schools was both specified and variable. Specific time allotments were made in each school for mastery learning instruction. Student-engaged time varied according to needs, with nonmastery students spending part of their time in corrective instruction. The mastery learning model was adhered to in all three schools. That is, CMLR provided the basis for instruction and was not used on a supplementary or pull-out basis.

Finally, there is one other element inherent in the success of mastery learning at Ernie Pyle, Kent, and Border Star: the role of the principal. It will come as no surprise to those who have studied the school effectiveness research to note that in each of these cases, the principal took the role of instructional leader. Instructional leadership, in these cases of mastery learning implementation, involved a thorough understanding of mastery learning principles, a commitment to preparing and supporting the staff, a constant awareness—through classroom visits and staff conferences—of what was happening in classrooms, and a system for setting and monitoring, jointly with the staff, the goals, directions, and results of the program.

The conditions cited in the case of Ernie Pyle, Kent, and Border Star have resulted in successful implementations of mastery learning. Concrete results have been observed in the areas of reading score gains, transfer of skills, improved attitudes, and increased expectations. It is interesting to note that in all three cases, mastery learning was implemented by plan rather than by chance. Perhaps the most meaningful constant among all the three schools is that notion of plan. The process of planning involved several steps:

1. Developing an understanding of mastery learning principles.
2. Building a staff commitment to those principles.
3. Selecting materials (in these cases, CMLR) that would organize instruction in conformity with those principles.
4. Making the appropriate instructional decisions regarding placement and pacing.
5. Monitoring student progress and teacher attitudes so that results were consistent with these underlying principles.

The success of these three schools—and the significant number of children who now view themselves as successful learners—suggests that this five-step process for implementing mastery learning could be instrumental in helping other schools attain the excellence that is increasingly demanded of them.

13

❦

Key Considerations
for Achieving Success
in Mastery Learning Programs

Daniel U. Levine

One overall theme of this chapter is that mastery learning (ML) must be made manageable and feasible for teachers or it will not work. Of course, this generalization can be made regarding most or all instructional innovations, but it may be relatively easy to ignore for mastery learning because the fundamental ideas behind ML (that is, teaching, testing, reteaching) are so simple and logical.

A second theme, closely related in some ways to manageability, is that implementation must avoid or overcome the specific flaws and pitfalls that sometimes lead to failure of ML programs.

A third major theme is that implementation should recognize and reflect other fundamental understandings of research on school improvement, instructional delivery, and organizational development. Again, such understandings are important for all innovations but deserve specific analysis from an ML perspective.

The chapter concludes with a discussion of two of the most general considerations bearing on successful implementation of mastery learning—time for instruction and grouping.

Manageability

No major instructional innovation will succeed on a widespread basis unless it is manageable or is made manageable for the average classroom teacher in the target school population. For many decades now, educational philosophers and reformers have described the ineffectiveness of schools in which teachers proceed page-by-page through textbooks that are either too easy or too difficult for many students, who sit passively and do meaningless seatwork much of the day. Reformers plead for instruction that is adapted to individual student needs and enables them to proceed at their own rate in mastering important skills and understandings. Yet, as John Goodlad has pointed out still another time in *A Place Called School* (1984), the "regularities" of schooling are such that traditional unproductive patterns are still the norm in most elementary and secondary classrooms.

One of the main reasons why innovations either have failed or have not even been tried is that they make such heavy demands on teachers' time and energy. This is particularly true with respect to the reformers' calls for individualized, continuous progress instruction, which cannot be implemented effectively without vast amounts of planning and staff development, materials, record-keeping, and other resources. One observer, for example, has described individualized instruction as an "exhausting endeavor and a major physical and psychological drain" (Sealey, 1976, p. 619). Even in the "normal" classroom with little or no individualization, most teachers appear to be unable to follow publishers' recommendations for using basal readers effectively, because they have too little time and energy to follow the major guidelines (Durkin, 1983). No wonder that individualization has been described by Michael Scriven (1975) and other observers as requiring "stupendous and continuing" costs to implement effectively.

Mastery learning as a mode of instruction is not necessarily as demanding of teachers and administrators as is individualized instruction, which probably is one of ML's principal virtues. When implemented in a small-group and individualized framework as described in Chapter Nine, it requires years of preparation and development, but mastery learning that emphasizes whole-class instruction for the first teaching phase (see Chapters Two, Ten, and Eleven) can be made manageable for teachers and implemented with some success within one or two years.

This does *not* mean, of course, that whole-class mastery learning can ignore teacher manageability issues. Because ML in any form requires, among other demands, substantial planning of the instructional sequence, selection and preparation of suitable materials, and recordkeeping (see Chapters Three and Six), considerable effort is required to make it manageable for teachers. Experience and some research (for example, Levine and Stark, 1982; Chapter Ten, here) indicate that the following supportive actions and policies may be particularly important:

1. Provision of staff and program development time as part of the regular school day. Some of the emphasis in using this time should be on grade-level meetings or other collegial arrangements that encourage and require teachers to work together in improving instruction.
2. Provision of staff developers and other instructional support personnel at the school building level.
3. Introduction of techniques to minimize record-keeping burdens. At some ML schools this has been done through reducing the number of skills for which records must be maintained, avoiding seductive computerized schemes that promise to reduce recordkeeping but instead increase it, utilization of whole-class progress charts rather than a proliferation of individual profiles, and provision of personnel (such as a staff developer) to help collect and maintain data.

A good rule-of-thumb for determining the amount of time that should be set aside for teacher planning and staff development is the following: observe and talk with teachers who presently are implementing ML and make a liberal estimate of the amount of time required; then double your estimate.

The preceding list might well be viewed as implementation *prerequisites* that help ensure that ML is manageable for teachers. That the three prerequisites are important in implementing other types of innovations (Chapter Seven) makes them no less critical in installing mastery learning.

Beyond these prerequisites, successful implementation of ML programs requires continuing, explicit attention to teachers' classroom manageability problems. For example, the Johnson City approach described in this book requires that teachers utilize more than one instructional mode as part of the larger teaching sequence, and that corrective instruction try to address students' learning style differences by using a different mode than initial instruction. Given sufficient time for planning and staff development, this simple guideline has proven to be manageable for teachers, whereas some other approaches that require attention to twenty or thirty learning-style dimensions for twenty-five or thirty students are beyond the capacity of most teachers in real schools no matter how much training and support are provided for them.

Pitfalls in Mastery Learning

Like any other instructional approach, ML is particularly susceptible to misimplementation of its central concepts and practices. Misimplementation may result from its deceptively simple instructional framework, which allows plenty of room for utilizing the form but not the substance. Thus ML frequently is implemented as a skeletal program in which both the flesh and the spirit have been stripped away leaving only a shadow of the original. In other words, a phantom program. I will refer to these tendencies to misimplement as *pitfalls*, and will begin by citing the following five "flaws" that Anderson and Jones (1981, pp. 122–123) identified as being characteristic of "less than successful" ML programs:

1. Failure to establish priorities among instructional objectives . . . . Given the realities of subject matter (and classroom instruction), some instructional objectives are (and must be seen as) more important than others. . . .
2. Failure to organize objectives into instructional units and to order/sequence the units based on rational or empirical considerations. . . .
3. Failure to properly orient students . . . ; failure to specify in advance the duration of the units or the tentative date of the formative test and the amount of time to be devoted to corrective instruction/learning (both in-class and out-of-class). . . .

4. Failure to make rational, justifiable decisions about performance standards. Rather, 'quick and dirty' figures of 80 percent are used. . . . .Performance standards should be set based on answers to the question, 'What evidence will I (we) accept that learning has occurred?' . . . standards should be set *after* careful examination of the objectives and the appropriate [test] items . . . and may differ from objective to objective . . .
5. Tendency to over-test [with formal testing]. . . .

It should be noted that two of the flaws cited by Anderson and Jones are closely related to manageability of ML for teachers. If there is not careful selection of objectives, and if there is over-testing, teachers likely will be teaching too many skills and doing too much recordkeeping. Not only do these pitfalls subvert the concept of mastery learning, they also make ML unimplementable in many classrooms. In addition, failure to establish priorities among objectives eliminates a potentially great advantage of ML: If objectives are carefully prioritized, from some points of view the job of the teacher is *more* rather than less manageable. For reasons such as these, Chapters Three and Six stress the overriding importance of preactive and proactive components in the role of administrators and supervisors responsible for implementing an ML program.

To the flaws cited by Anderson and Jones, I will add the following pitfalls: neglect of higher order skills; neglect of students' interest and enjoyment in learning; failure to coordinate mastery learning instruction with other instructional approaches; and slow pacing of instruction.

Regarding higher order skills and understandings, the major reason that teachers tend to neglect these goals of instruction is because they are more difficult to teach and test than are lower order skills such as simple computation in math, decoding in reading, and recall of chronological dates in social studies. (Actually, some teachers may be incapable of teaching or even testing higher order skills). One reason why ML programs are particularly prone to this pitfall is because they provide the appearance of productive instruction even when they neglect the most important higher order skills in a subject; administrators and teachers who do this can defend their instructional approach by pointing to a large number of low order skills that have been taught, retaught, and "mastered," using sophisticated and imposing record systems that may resemble education.

Bloom (1984) recently has offered evidence indicating that ML can be as effective in dealing with "higher mental processes" as it is in teaching lower order skills. Several chapters in this book stress the importance of focusing ML instruction on the development of higher order comprehension skills. In practice, unfortunately, it is tempting to institute a mastery learning framework as a substitute for attention to higher order skills and understandings. Teachers and administrators who either seize on ML for this purpose or neglect higher order skills as part of a sincere improvement effort are doing much to discredit it.

Regarding neglect of students' interest and enjoyment in learning, again ML not only is susceptible to this pitfall because teachers may become consumed with formal aspects of planning, delivering, and recording the results of mastery lessons, but in some cases teachers actively seize on ML in part to avoid dealing with the need to make learning interesting and active. This is a great tragedy because as James Block points out in Chapter Four, ML has the potential to improve the "flow" of instruction and make learning more "playlike" for students. Through ensuring student success, it can vastly improve students' interest in learning. There is no inherent reason why ML must leave students bored and passive, and in managing the myriad demands teachers face in any classroom, one must resist the temptation to use an ML framework as an excuse for not dealing with fundamental instructional issues such as student motivation.

Regarding failure to coordinate mastery learning instruction with other instructional approaches, this is currently an important pitfall in ML because mastery lessons typically address only part of the content in a given subject. Leaving aside the question of whether ML should eventually constitute the only instructional approach for a given subject area, effective ML lessons take time to plan and deliver, and most teachers using ML are not now in a position to do so for their entire curriculum, particularly with reference to higher-order skills and understandings. In this context, it is tempting to use ML mainly to duplicate instruction already delivered earlier or elsewhere. This spares teachers much hard work involved in planning both mastery learning instruction and other lessons, and in coordinating within and across subject areas. And who can object in the face of complicated charts showing that 80 percent of students are proceeding on schedule in mastering and remastering 80 percent of (trivial, lower order) skills?

Regarding slow pacing of instruction, pitfalls take a variety of forms which include the following: initial placement of students at a lower level in an instructional sequence than they can handle with good instruction; overly stringent policies and criteria for mastery such that individual students or groups of students are held back until everyone can be checked off on a mastery profile; detours through material that may be interesting but is not vital to the development of skills required for subsequent learning; and lack of sufficient planning time for teachers to prepare themselves for an accelerated schedule.

Pacing ML instruction too slow may be due to failure to deal adequately with manageability issues (for example, too large a number of slow learners), lack of understanding of the concepts underlying mastery learning, low expectations for a group of students, or other causes. In Chapter Twelve, Don Robb emphasizes the importance of insisting on high initial placement and accelerated pacing at three exemplary ML schools. But as Mary Kennedy points out in discussing teacher testing, teachers can destroy the intent of ML by doing just exactly what you ask them. This is true of many aspects of ML but particularly its pacing aspects, which require difficult and sophisticated decisions involving needs to "overlearn" some key skills but de-emphasize others, to avoid too many detours in instruction without killing students' or teachers' interest in learning, to stress but not overstress initial entry skills, and to reach these decisions with a view to individual student's characteristics, the nature of subject matter within an instructional sequence, and selection of appropriate assessment measures. I suppose this is just another way of stating the obvious: Mastery learning is in no way self-implementable, and ML teachers must receive substantial, continuing support from staff development personnel at the school-building level.

I hope it is evident that the various flaws and pitfalls of ML described above are intimately connected with manageability issues described in the preceding section. To the extent that ML is not made manageable for the average teacher in the typical school, to that extent ML implementation efforts will fall prey to the tendency and the temptation to neglect critical components required for its success in improving students' performance in the schools.

School and Organizational Development

There are many generalizations from the school and organizational development literature that warrant attention in implementing mastery learning, but two that stand out involve the importance of *shared goals* among faculty and of *organic adaptation and monitoring* of proposed innovations.

Shared goals, sometimes referred to under alternate headings such as *common culture, goal consensus,* and *agreed values,* are particularly important because ML requires changes in so many of the familiar arrangements in a school, especially those involving the allocation of time and students. To implement ML successfully may require such changes as: assigning a higher percentage of slower students to experienced teachers who previously have worked only with fast students; reduction or elimination of textbooks that teachers have used for ten or fifteen years; switching of teachers' rooms to facilitate better placement of students; especially at inner city schools, reduction of time allocated from science or social studies or some subject a teacher enjoys to a subject such as math the teacher detests; renunciation of strongly held ideologies involving placement and assessment of students on a normal curve; accelerated pacing of instruction beyond an experienced teacher's initial comfort level; intensive and frequent meetings focusing on instructional concerns with colleagues and others who previously did not know what a teacher was doing in the classroom; reduction in the amount of convenient (for the teacher) seatwork in favor of emphasis on higher order skills instruction; and so on. These kinds of difficult changes are unlikely to happen unless all or most of a faculty truly agree that improved achievement takes precedence over business as usual.

The extent to which shared culture is a central problem in installing ML varies a good deal from school to school. I have seen schools in which faculty generally were dedicated to improving instruction through ML and were fundamentally ready to change existing practices, but achievement did not improve because teachers did not know, for example, how to assess performance in a mastery format or to deliver corrective instruction. In this case, the main implementation issue is technical: What must teachers know to implement the program successfully?

In other schools where lip-service is given to the need for improvement but teachers are unwilling to change existing practices and arrangements, the problem is lack of shared goals within the organization. In schools where this is true, large doses of technical knowledge and analysis are unlikely to result in improved student performance; instead, one must work on building readiness and willingness to change. Clearly, schools in which shared culture is the major problem require initial interventions focusing on development of a consensus strong enough to allow for effective change in organizational and instructional arrangements. I will not digress here to discuss this very difficult challenge that may well be insurmountable in some schools, given existing leadership and staffing, but will merely point out that a large and growing literature on organizational development and the school improvement process is available to guide efforts that frequently will be required to build or enhance shared values among members of a faculty (for example, Argyris, 1980; Crandall and others, 1982; Fullan, 1982; Schmuck, 1977).

Regarding organic adaptation and monitoring, I am using this term as a contrast to bureaucratic implementation and monitoring. In essence, instructional innovations are implemented bureaucratically when they are mandated in detail by administrators in a school or school district, each step in delivering instruction is specified in advance and must be followed exactly, and compliance is monitored primarily through formal check-off mechanisms reflecting elaborate schedules and minute enumeration of activities and completion points. Recent writings in organizational theory stress that formal organizations seldom succeed in attaining their goals through the traditional bureaucratic paradigm. Instead, analysts are developing a different, ostensibly less rational paradigm that emphasizes adaptation of technical approaches to unique circumstances, tolerance of deviation from a grand plan, assessing success and working out adjustments through personal observation and familiarity with grass roots problems in the organization, and needs to couple units or sub-units in an organization through means other than the traditional bureaucratic ones (Schwartz and Ogilvy, 1979; Weick, 1979).

Schools provide no counter-examples to emerging theories stressing the importance of organic adaptation and monitoring, and mastery learning constitutes no exception within the realm of instructional innovation. As mentioned above, ML may be particularly susceptible to misuse in the hands of administrators who perceive it largely as a bureaucratic means for holding teachers accountable for students' mastery of skills specified in a district's list of instructional objectives or of teachers who perceive it largely as a protection (by checking off skills mastered) against administrators' questioning of their effectiveness. The ML landscape is already strewn with failed programs that, for whatever reason, conceived implementation as mostly a bureaucratic exercise prescribing and describing students' and teachers' progress through the curriculum. Unless adaptation and monitoring are both organic, future ML programs will have much the same result.

At the risk of repeating some conclusions offered in different language in the preceding pages, I would like to give some examples of organic adaptation and monitoring.

Adaptation is organic when teachers not only depart from but are encouraged and assisted to depart from guidelines when necessary to achieve the overall purposes of the instructional program. This can happen, for example, when teachers have good reason to adjust (up or down) general criteria for mastery of a skill, to provide more or less corrective instruction than is generally recommended, or to take time from one subject when it is needed for another. Adaptation is organic when some teachers have smaller groups of students than other teachers because they have a concentration of slow learners and when materials recommended for instruction can be and are replaced because the teacher discovered better materials for teaching a particular skill to a given group of students.

Monitoring is organic when forms and check-off sheets are reduced to a minimum, in favor of collegial teacher planning and decision-making with close and personal support from administrators and supervisors. In District 19 in New York, for example, one staff development person was placed in each of twenty-seven schools and six central-office reading specialists were available to help teachers implement mastery learning in reading. Although some appropriate use was made of progress charts, questionnaires, and other relatively bureaucratic monitoring devices, these latter mechanisms were used sparingly and were not meant or allowed to substitute for supervisors' personal knowledge of progress and problems derived through classroom- and school-level contact. In Johnson City, New York elementary schools, instructional monitoring is organic because effective team arrangements are used wherein teachers monitor each others' work informally in the course of meeting with teammates and with administrators to plan the delivery of their instruction.

The Time Issue in Mastery Learning

Recently, issues involving the use of instructional time in mastery learning have been raised prominently in a paper by Marshall Arlin (1984). In line with analysis presented by Herbert Walberg in Chapter One of this volume, Arlin's basic argument is that there tends to be a time-achievement dilemma in designing and implementing a mastery learning program. By this he means that individualized mastery learning may help all students learn more, with the faster students proceeding at their own rate and attaining higher levels of achievement than slower students. In group-based mastery learning, as Arlin reads the limited research now available, slower students learn more because greater attention is given to their needs for prerequisite skills instruction and corrective instruction, but faster students tend to be slowed down because they are likely "to be held back while waiting for slower students to catch up" (p. 78).

Arlin acknowledges that "mastery strategists have provided overwhelming evidence that it is possible to raise achievement of 'poorer' students to levels that many would have considered unattainable" (p. 80), but he concludes that mastery learning poses a fundamental dilemma between equality of achievement (attained in group-based ML by slowing down faster students) and equality of learning time (attained in individualized ML at the cost of unequal achievement outcomes).

Space is not available here to analyze or evaluate all of the points raised in Arlin's research review, but I do want to call attention to several that bear on implementation of mastery learning. First, Arlin's conclusions depend in part on the assertion that enrichment activities provided for formative mastery students during corrective instruction in group-based mastery learning do not enable them to learn as much as they would in teacher-paced instruction geared more directly to their status within the instructional sequence. This generalization may well be true of many or even most contemporary group-based programs. However, we should keep in mind that few schools have had extensive longitudinal experience implementing mastery learning, and systematic development work in the future may result in much more effective enrichment and acceleration assignments for students who master the formative test. In this regard, much more research is needed on the topic of effective enrichment in mastery learning, as indeed is also true regarding the delivery of corrective instruction.

Second, part of Arlin's argument is based on the generalizations that within a "relatively fixed time framework educators can make [only] minor adjustments, such as providing extra time for slower learners in remedial instruction" (p. 82), and this remedial time takes away from faster learners. But in implementing mastery learning, educators should *not* view the instructional time framework as fixed to this degree. There are other alternatives than extending corrective instruction in a group-based program to the extent that faster learners, or most learners, are waiting to proceed on mastery by the slowest learners. Without necessarily turning to elaborate and complicated modular learning schedules—which have their own serious implementation problems—mastery learning planners can implement such alternatives as the following:

- provide additional learning time for slower students before and after school

- develop and coordinate homework policies so that slower students gain more from homework than most do now
- at the intermediate and secondary levels, reduce or eliminate electives for slow learners, substituting more time on fundamental skills
- institute some (limited) degree of homogeneous grouping. I will discuss this topic more fully in the next section.

Granted that the types and mixture of alternatives for increasing time for slower students without detracting from faster students will differ from school to school—depending on a variety of considerations involving (among other things) the staff, the students, and curriculum—this only means that effective implementation of mastery learning depends on organic adaptation in accordance with the unique situation at each school. The point is that effective ML *must* reflect the fact that some students need more time to learn than others, at least during the initial phases of an ML program, and time can be made available for this imperative in a variety of ways without greatly detracting from the achievement of faster learners.

Although they are not exclusively addressed to the issue of how to provide additional time for implementing mastery learning, several additional observations are in order before concluding this section. First, there are many inner city schools all over this land in which instruction is so ineffective that teachers and students alike have become totally frustrated, and even faster students currently are making little progress after the primary grades. In this situation, there is no way that an effective group-based ML program will "slow up" faster learners; instead the latter group will learn much more because it is part of a more productive educational environment.

Second, instructional time considerations appear central in accounting for the relative ease with which mixed-social-class schools (frequently desegregated) can use ML to improve the achievement of poverty students. Compared to predominantly poverty schools (frequently segregated minority), mixed-class schools have a much more manageable task in making instructional time and other resources available to ensure mastery by students who initially are slow learners. The obvious reason is because they have a much smaller percentage of students who need this special assistance. A good example is the Border Star elementary school in Kansas City described by Don Robb in Chapter Twelve, where a number of approaches, including assistance from instructional resource specialists, are used to provide more learning time for slower learners.

Grouping

In Chapter Nine, Albert Mamary and Lawrence Rowe describe ML arrangements in Johnson City that emphasize small-group learning and minimize homogeneous grouping. The eloquent introduction to this chapter points out that homogeneous grouping has tended to reflect industrial-age conditions that sorted out—and today still sort out—more than one third of students for a career characterized by low academic achievement and, eventually, low attainment in the schools and the economy.

As described by Mamary and Rowe, Johnson City students are placed in small groups homogeneous as to needs for specific skills instruction and, as much as possible, assignment to a homogeneous group defined in this way is limited, with group composition within and across subjects constantly changing. The achievement gains from this approach have been spectacular (see Chapter Nine, Table 1).

Much as I sympathize with and advocate the goals and value of Johnson City's grouping approach, I believe it is important to recognize that some other successful ML programs depend much more on homogeneous grouping than does Johnson City. For example, the elementary schools in New York District 19 (Chapter Ten) generally have a considerable amount of homogeneous grouping within grade-levels, and nearly all of them place the student lowest in reading achievement in small, parallel classes taught by trained reading teachers. The three successful elementary schools described by Donald W. Robb in Chapter Twelve use some degree of homogeneous grouping within or across grades in providing whole-group instruction using the Chicago Mastery Learning Reading materials. Young Junior High School in Bayport, New York

(Chapter Eleven), also uses homogeneous grouping in English/ language arts and math.

Differences in grouping practices at successful ML schools raise many questions involving theory, research, and practice regarding the homogeneous/heterogeneous grouping issue. Large amounts of research and even more voluminous advocacy-type analysis have been published on the grouping issue, so I will limit the remaining discussion in this section to a few general comments.

1. Grouping practices clearly raise issues that are *par excellence* involved in determining whether ML or any other instructional approach is manageable and feasible for teachers. If there is a large number of subgroups in a class (usually more than two or three) or if there is considerable spread within the subgroups, most teachers will be unable to deliver instruction effectively unless they have much more training and many more resources than most have now. As pointed out earlier in this chapter, such a degree of individualization/small-group organization is very difficult and expensive. One alternative is to utilize more whole-class instruction with some degree of homogeneous grouping (Jones, 1982).

2. Research indicates that a key variable in determining whether grouping practices within a classroom are likely to be effective is the number of low achieving students in the classroom. Recent research by Barr and Dreeben (1983), for example, shows that regarding teachers' decisions about organizing and delivering instruction, "it is not the size of the class per se that is important . . . but the size of the low aptitude contingent of children" (p. 159). This finding is neither surprising nor a mystery. Teachers with a relatively large number of low achieving students are likely to have a much more difficult task, compared to other teachers, in providing sufficient time for mastery of prerequisite skills, in assigning productive seatwork and independent learning assignments, in providing corrective instruction, and in implementing other instructional activities.

Problems in delivering effective instruction for low achieving students are soluble, particularly through a mastery-learning approach, if the teacher is not overwhelmed by too many such students. For various reasons, many schools with unusually effective instruction have chosen to group students homogeneously for much of the school day, but this approach seems to work best when the lowest achieving classes are kept small and other special steps are taken to make it effective. Examples include inner city junior high schools described by Levine, Levine, and Eubanks (1984), Young Junior High School in Bayport, New York, and District 19 elementary schools, in which low achieving classes not only are the smallest in the school, but many other actions (for example, assignment of outstanding teachers to slow classes, continuous staff development, reduction of nonessential electives for low achievers) are taken to ensure the success of homogeneous grouping.

3. The preceding generalizations would seem to question the conclusions of much research that has stressed negative effects of homogeneous grouping on the performance of low achieving students. For example, Slavin and Karweit (1984) recently reviewed the research on ability grouping and concluded that between-class ability grouping (that is, tracking) generally has negative effects and within-class ability grouping frequently has negative effects, in part due to relatively slow pacing of instruction as well as related problems (for example, student behavior, low morale) in low ability groups or classes. Good and Marshall (1984) also reviewed much of the research and concluded that negative "peer influences in low ability groups tend to be unavoidable and strong enough to overwhelm the potential instructional advantages of grouping" (p. 22). Hallinan (1984) reached the general conclusion that "tracking and ability grouping are deterrents to learning for students assigned to low groups" (p. 232).

On the other hand, recent research also is beginning to clarify why homogeneous grouping frequently has had negative outcomes and, more important, what can be done to avoid them. For example, Leinhardt and Pallay (1982) studied the research on "restrictive settings" (that is, placement in separate groups, usually in special education or compensatory education) for children in the lowest achievement quartile, and concluded that "setting itself is not the primary variable affecting performance" (p. 572); rather, what counts most is what is done to improve performance and overcome the problems in restrictive or nonrestrictive settings. Key variables that Leinhardt and Pallay identified in this regard include the following: small classes permitting one-to-one instruction by a qualified teacher, efficient use of student and teacher time, regular monitoring of progress, increased time in cognitive activities, a formal management system encouraging high task orientation, positive teacher affect, and positive student self-concept. Mastery learning can be valuable in attaining several of these goals with low achieving students.

Other recent studies that have shed light on the homogeneous/heterogeneous grouping controversy have been conducted by Gamoran (1984) and by Barnett and Filby (1984). Based on data collected at several points during the school year in twelve first-grade classrooms, Gamoran found that within-class ability grouping had greatly different achievement effects from one classroom to another, depending on whether the teacher used "elitist" or "egalitarian" practices that emphasized or de-emphasized the distinctions between reading groups. Gamoran concluded that egalitarian practices that de-emphasize distinctions (for example, neutral naming of groups, minimization of ability differences between groups, provisions for cross-group contact, intergroup mobility), together with appropriate attention to pacing, quantity, and quality of instruction, can result in positive outcomes for students in low achieving groups. Barnett and Filby studied the reading performance of students in three first-grade classes, and found that students in low reading groups can perform as well as those in high groups, provided that a fast pace is maintained and slow students are provided adequate opportunity for practice and re-exposure. These latter provisions are, of course, key components of an ML approach.

4. If research and theory say (or are interpreted as saying) that homogeneous grouping cannot help low achievers, and if experience and other data indicate that homogeneous grouping sometimes does help low achievers, there is something wrong with the research and the theory (or one's interpretation of them). I am somewhat reluctant to offer the generalization that homogeneous grouping, either within or between classes, can be useful in implementing an ML program, partly because readers who *know* that homogeneous grouping can't possibly work will immediately tune out, but mostly because many teachers and administrators who turn to homogeneous grouping are likely to use it to further limit opportunities for low achievers. To reduce that possibility, ML

implementers should follow a set of guidelines such as the following:

a. Make sure that conditions specified by Leinhardt and Pallay are adequately attended to in planning and implementing arrangements for low achievers.
b. Minimize homogeneous grouping so that low achievers are isolated as little as possible in the classroom or the school.

5. Homogeneous grouping may work better in some situations and schools than others. For example, ability grouping may be less stigmatizing for low achievers in poverty schools with a high percentage of initally low achievers than in mixed-class schools with a wide range of achievement. And, as I have argued elsewhere (Hare and Levine, 1984), grouping is more questionable (and possibly illegal) in a desegregated school with high achieving nonminority students and low achieving minority students than in a segregated school or a desegregated school in which minority and nonminority students are nearly the same in achievement.

6. If students assigned to a slow group are so low in achievement that they are not yet able to function well in seatwork or in group activities, the group must be small enough so that the teacher or other persons (for example, aides, older tutors) can provide extensive individual attention and assistance. Many experts in reading education believe that one of the most frequent problems encountered in working with slow groups is that their members tend to function poorly in independent learning and are unable to provide each other with productive assistance; if so, such assistance must be provided by others.

7. Efforts to minimize homogeneous grouping at some point take one across a fuzzy line at which emphasis shifts to individualized/small-group methods if instruction is to be delivered effectively for heterogeneous classes or groups. (Of course, there also are many opportunities for a productive mixture of heterogeneous and homogeneous approaches in designing the instructional program). In considering what is known about instruction emphasizing whole-group teaching with homogeneous groups compared with individualized instruction for heterogeneous groups, a colleague

and I (Levine and Eubanks, 1983) have concluded that successful improvement efforts in the latter situation tend to constitute *fundamental reform* of instruction, while successful efforts emphasizing whole-class, homogeneous grouping arrangements represent *incremental reform*. (As James Block points out in Chapter Four, "group-based/teacher paced" ML can be implemented "without major structural changes in classroom organization.") Individualizing instruction so as to attain continuous-progress learning requires years of effort and very large resources to change and improve all the underlying arrangements in the school, whereas improvements in whole-class or whole-group instruction for homogeneous groups that presently exist in most schools require merely large resources and can begin to yield significant achievement gains the first year. (We also believe that instructional change emphasizing integrated teaching across subjects tends to involve fundamental reform). There is reason to believe, however, that gains associated with incremental reform tend to plateau after two or three years, thus making it necessary to further review and revise instructional arrangements, generally in order to improve instruction dealing with higher order skills.

Conclusion

Some of the fundamental messages of this chapter are relatively simple. Mastery learning is a potentially potent approach for generating very large gains in student achievement, but it will not work unless implementation is manageable for the teacher. Considerable staff development time and help from resource personnel must be provided as part of the regular school day. Most teachers cannot implement ML effectively if they start with too large a number of low achievers. Pitfalls such as poor selection and sequencing of objectives, slow pacing of instruction, and neglect of affective goals in education must be assiduously avoided. Teachers should not succumb, or be allowed to succumb, to the temptation to overemphasize lower order skills, which are most easily taught and tested. Successful implementation must address a whole litany of considerations, such as involvement of staff in the change process, development of shared goals among all faculty, and development of organic rather than bureaucratic monitoring procedures, which are stressed in research literature on the school improvement process, organizational development, and school effectiveness.

Although I am a little embarrassed to be stating, and sometimes restating, such obvious truisms, it is scarcely possible to overstate their importance. Several decades of attempts to introduce educational innovations have shown that schools have an almost inexhaustible capacity to misimplement good ideas, in part because they neglect the kinds of considerations discussed in this chapter. (For additional reasons, see Kennedy, Chapter Seven.) As long as key implementation issues are treated as afterthoughts in planning and delivering mastery learning (or other promising educational innovations), efforts to reform the schools will be more notable for their failures than for improvements made in classroom practice.

References

Anderson, L. W., and Jones B. F. "Designing Instructional Strategies Which Facilitate Learning for Mastery." *Educational Psychologist*, 1981, *16* (3), 121–137.

Argyris, C. "Making the Undiscussable and Its Undiscussability Discussable." *Public Administration Review*, 1980, *40* (3), 205–213.

Arlin, M. "Time, Equality, and Mastery Learning." *Review of Educational Research*, 1984, *54* (1), 65–86.

Barnett, B. G., and Filby, N. N. "Effects of the Presentation of Reading Materials and Instructional Pacing on First Graders' Reading Fluency." Paper presented at the annual meeting of the American Educational Research Association, New Orleans, April 25, 1984.

Barr, R., and Dreeben, R. *How Schools Work.* Chicago: University of Chicago Press, 1983.

Bloom, B. S. "The Search for Methods of Group Instruction as Effective as One-to-One Tutoring." *Educational Leadership*, 1984, *41* (8), 4–17.

Crandall, D. P., and others. *People, Policies, and Practices: Examining the Chain of School Improvement.* (Ten volumes.) Andover, Mass.: The Network, 1982.

Durkin, D. "Is There a Match Between What Elementary Teachers

Do and What Basal Readers Recommend?" Reading Education
Report No. 44. University of Illinois at Urbana-Champaign:
Center for the Study of Reading, 1983.

Fullan, M. *The Meaning of Educational Change.* New York:
Teachers College Press, 1982.

Gamoran, A. "Egalitarian Versus Elitist Use of Ability Grouping."
Paper presented at the annual meeting of the American Educational Research Association, New Orleans, April 24, 1984 (draft).

Good, T. L., and Marshall, S. "Do Students Learn More in
Heterogeneous or Homogeneous Groups?" In P. L. Peterson, L.
C. Wilkinson, and M. Hallinan (Eds.), *The Social Context of
Instruction.* Orlando, Fla.: Academic Press, 1984.

Goodlad, J. I. *A Place Called School.* New York: McGraw-Hill,
1984.

Hallinan, M. "Summary and Implications." In P. L. Peterson, L.
C. Wilkinson, and M. Hallinan (Eds.), *The Social Context of
Instruction.* Orlando, Fla.: Academic Press, 1984.

Hare, B. R., and Levine, D. U. *A Critical Overview of Issues
Involving Effective Desegregated Schools.* Washington, D.C.:
National Institute of Education, 1984.

Jones, B. F. "Key Management Decisions for Implementing Mastery
Learning." *The School Administrator,* 1982, *39* (3), 45–48.

Leinhardt, G., and Pallay, A. "Restrictive Educational Settings:
Exile or Haven?" *Review of Educational Research,* 1982, *52* (4),
557–578.

Levine, D. U., and Eubanks, E. E. "Instructional and Organizational Arrangements at an Unusually Effective Inner-City Elementary School in Chicago." Paper presented at the annual
meeting of the American Educational Research Association,
Montreal, April 14, 1983.

Levine, D. U., Levine, R. F., and Eubanks, E. E. "Characteristics
of Effective Inner-City Intermediate Schools." *Phi Delta Kappan,*
1984, *65* (10), 707–711.

Levine, D. U., and Stark, J. "Instructional and Organizational
Arrangements that Improve Achievement in Inner-City
Schools." *Educational Leadership,* 1982, *40* (3), 41–46.

Schmuck, R. A., and others. *The Second Handbook of Organizational Development in Schools.* Palo Alto, Calif.: Mayfield, 1977.

Schwartz, P., and Ogilvy, J. *The Emergent Paradigm*. Menlo Park, Calif.: SRI International, 1979.

Scriven, M. "Problems and Prospects for Individualization." In H. Talmage (Ed.), *Systems of Individualized Education*. Berkeley, Calif.: McCutchan, 1975.

Sealey, L. "Open Education: Fact or Fiction?" *Teachers College Record*, 1976, 77, 617–623.

Slavin, R. E., and Karweit, N. L. *Mathematics Achievement Effects of Three Levels of Individualization: Whole Class, Ability Grouped, and Individualized Instruction*. Center for Social Organization of Schools Report No. 349. Baltimore: Johns Hopkins University, January 1984.

Weick, K. *The Social Psychology of Organizing*. Reading, Mass.: Addison-Wesley, 1979.

Index

A

Abrams, J. D., 28, 40, 95, 147
Accountability, test use for, 173-183
Ackerson, G., 16, 42
Adaptation, organic, 281-282
Administrators: and Management Plans, 166-167; preactive and proactive supervision by, 45-67; role of, 63-64; and teaching quality, 181-182; test options of, 180-182. *See also* Principals
American School (Beirut), mastery learning at, 24, 28, 29-31, 35-37
Ames, W., 16, 42
Amiran, M. R., 29, 41-42, 75, 90, 100, 143, 147, 150
Anania, F., 13-14, 40
Anderson, L. W., 52, 56, 59, 64-65, 69n, 76, 88, 93, 98, 101, 104, 106, 107, 114, 119, 125, 126-127, 147, 226, 239, 276-277, 292
Anderson, R. C., 100, 114, 147
Anderson, T. H., 17, 41, 100, 114, 147
Angoff, W. H., 187, 191, 201
Answer keys, as teaching step, 123

Anticipatory set, for enhanced mastery learning, 36
Aptitude, and mastery learning, 5-6
Argyris, C., 281, 292
Aristotle, 1, 5
Arlin, M., 283-284, 292
Armbruster, B. B., 17, 41, 100, 147
Arricale, F. C., II, 224-226, 228-230
Atkinson's theory, 72

B

Bacon, F., 1
Bailey, G. W., 95, 147
Bandura, A., 72
Barber, C., 95, 147
Barker, R. G., 54, 65
Barnett, B. G., 69n, 289, 292
Barr, R., 287, 292
Barrett, R., 205, 221
Bayport, New York, testing and retesting in, 241, 248-253, 286-287, 288
Bean, T., 120, 152
Beez, W. V., 205, 221
Bell-shaped curve, and mastery, 248

Bellflower, California, reading program in, 256-261, 269-272
Bennert, G., 248-249
Berman, P., 223, 239
Berry's theory, 72
Bettelheim, B., 70, 88
Biddle, B., 74, 89
Block, J. H., xii, xiv, 56, 59, 64, 65, 69-90, 93, 95, 98, 101, 147, 226, 239, 278, 291
Bloom, B. S., xi, 2, 4, 10, 11-17, 18, 36, 41, 76, 88, 93, 97, 99, 100, 101, 104, 105, 106, 110, 112, 114, 117-118, 126, 130, 148, 155, 167, 171, 205, 206n, 221, 226, 227, 239, 278, 292
Bluth, G. S., 114, 151
Board of education, reporting to, 169-170
Board of Education of the City of Chicago, 39, 41, 62, 110, 117n, 148, 229, 257
Bolster, A. S., Jr., 179, 183
Border Star Elementary School, reading program in, 256-257, 266-272, 286
Bradley, E., 262, 263, 265
Brandon, R. K., 32, 41, 104, 148
Brandt, A., 24, 41
Brandt, D. M., 114, 151
Brooklyn. *See* Community School District 19
Brophy, J., 205, 221
Brown, A. L., 104, 114, 148
Bruce, B., 100, 148
Bryan, M., 204, 221
Burns, L., 258
Burns, R. B., 52, 55, 56, 57, 58, 59, 65, 76, 88, 95, 147, 148

C

California: reading program in, 256-261, 269-272; textbooks in, 156
California Achievement Test, 19-20
California Test of Basic Skills (CTBS), 259, 260-261, 265-266
Cameron, G., 250

Campione, J. C., 104, 114, 148
Càponigri, R., 95, 148
Carroll, J. B., 2, 4, 10, 80, 88-89, 93, 97, 148, 226
Casteel, J., 194, 195, 201
Cavert, C. E., 102, 149
Center School, enhanced mastery learning at, 21-22, 24, 25-27, 28, 34-35, 37, 39, 75
Chabotar, K. J., 223, 239
Challenge, in flow activities, 82-83
Champlin, J. R., 34-35, 95, 149
Change, top-down, bottom-up model of, 223-239
Cheska, A., 72-73, 89
Chicago: continuous progress/master learning (CP/ML) in, 101-104; enhanced mastery learning in, 32, 38, 39, 92n; mastery-based instruction in, 62, 75; reading collaboration in, 111. *See also* Board of Education of the City of Chicago
Chicago Mastery Learning Reading (CMLR): and enhanced mastery learning, 29, 31, 36-37 39, 92n, 101, 102-103, 110, 113; implementation of, 227-239, 255, 257-272, 286; and Management Plan, 158
Clark, C. M., 179, 183
Clarke, W. E., 205, 221
Classroom progress charts, for recordkeeping, 133-134
Cognitive entry characteristics: concept of, 12; equalizing, 13
Cohen, D. K., 223, 240
Cohen, D. L., 225, 226, 239-240
Cohen, E. G., 63, 65
Cohen, S. A., 95, 149, 247, 253
Coleman, J., 70, 89
Collaboration to Improve Reading in the Content Area (CIRCA), 92n, 111, 115, 120-121
College Board, 131
Colorado, mastery learning in, 75
Columbus, Ohio, reading program in, 256-257, 261-266, 269-272
Community, reporting to, 170
Community School District 19

(Brooklyn): grouping in, 286; organic monitoring in, 283; reading program in, 224–239

Comprehension: in enriched mastery learning, 91–153; instruction and assessment for, 100

Connecticut, enhanced mastery learning in, 21–22, 24, 25–27, 28, 34–35, 37, 39, 75

Constant-sum constraint, and passing scores, 194

Content courses, horizontal sequencing for, 111–112, 113

Continuous progress, and mastery learning, 97, 98, 99, 101–104

Cooper, E. J., 131, 149

Coordination, of flow activities, 83–84

Correction of errors, as teaching step, 123

Course, as structural unit, 54

Courter, R. L., 63, 65

Courtney, K., 249

Covington's theory, 72

Cox, B. E., xii, 91–153

Crandall, D. P., 281, 292

Crosby, P. B., 155, 171

Csikszentmihalyi, M., 69n, 72–73, 74, 75, 85, 86, 88, 89, 90

D

Dalfen, S., 205, 221

Dallas, Texas, outcome-based instruction in, 62

Darling-Hammond, L., 183

Darwezeh, A., 110, 152

Datta, L., 223, 240

Day, J. D., 104, 114, 148

Deal, T. E., 45, 66

Decisions, preactive and interactive, 52

Degrees of Reading Power (DRP), 131–132, 250–253

Deighan, W. P., 158, 171

Denham, C., 226–227, 240

Denver, mastery learning in, 75

DeSanctis, J. E., 223, 240

DeVries, D. L., 41

Dewey, J., 70, 89

Dollard, J., 1, 2, 10

Donlan, D., 114, 152

Donmoyer, R., 70, 89

Dornbusch, S. M., 49, 65, 66

Dreeben, R., 52, 65, 287, 292

Duckett, W., 226, 240

Dunkin, M., 74, 89

Durkin, D., 100, 125, 149, 274, 292–293

E

Eash, M. J., 60, 67

Ebel, R. L., 187, 201

Ecological tasks, of teachers, 55

Edmonds, R., 226, 240

Educational Records Bureau, 170

Ellis, J. A., 106–107, 108n, 149

Enhanced or enriched mastery learning: analysis of, 11–43, 93–104; checklist for, 135–141; continuous progress/flexible delivery models of, 24–28, 31–33, 35; development and implementation problems in, 97–104; examples of strategy variations in, 142; and existing texts, 97–98, 99–100, 102; factors in success of, 31–37; guidelines for, 91–153; for large city systems, 37–39; learning unit organization and delivery in, 117–124; maximal conditions for, 15–16, 33–35; and objectives, 105–117; one-sigma results from, 12–13; programs of, 18–31; recordkeeping in, 132–135; simultaneous or sequential development of, 136–137; and skills instruction, 99; standard of excellence for, 11–18; testing and curriculum alignment in, 124–132; whole group/self-contained models of, 28–31, 35–37, 39

Entry information, in organization and delivery, 118–119

Episodes, as structural unit, 54

Equality of Educational Opportunity survey, 3

Ernie Pyle Elementary School, read-
ing program in, 256-261, 269-272
Eubanks, E. E., 288, 291, 293
Evaluation. *See* Testing
Examples and nonexamples, as teach-
ing step, 121-122
Excellence, standard of, 11-18, 155
Exemplary Center for Reading In-
struction, 158, 163, 168
Explanation, as teaching step, 122
Extend, as teaching step, 123

F

Far West Regional Educational Laboratory, xiv
Farrar, E., 223, 240
Feedback, in flow activities, 84-86
Filby, N. N., 289, 292
Findley, W., 204, 221
Fisher, C. W., 24, 41
Flow: activities, and mastery learning, 81-86; challenge in, 82-83;
concept of, 73; conclusion on,
86-88; coordination for, 83-84;
implications of, 87; and mastery
learning, 74-75; as model for
learning activities, 72-73
Forest Hills School District, Management Plan in, 158
Formative tests: and correctives,
242-243; diagrams of process for,
244-245; for feedback, 84-85; first,
242; implementing process for,
245-246; second, 243-244; strategy
for, 241-246; in testing and curriculum alignment, 124, 146
Frames, in instructional input, 121
Frederick, W., 3, 5, 7, 10
Fredericks, P. S., 106-107, 108n, 149
Friedman, L. B., xii, 91-153
Fullan, M., 281, 293
Functional equivalency, of teacher
behaviors, 58

G

Gallagher, M. C., 112, 151
Gamoran, A., 289, 293

Geoffrey, W., 58, 67
Glassner, B., 70, 89
Glickman, C., 70, 89
Glidwell, J. C., 205, 221
Glossary: example of, 146; as teach-
ing step, 124
Goals, shared, 280-281
Good, T. L., 205, 221, 288, 293
Goodlad, J. I., 203, 221, 274, 293
Grading, and mastery, 246-247, 265
Grannis, J., 69, 89
Griffin, G. A., 45, 65
Gronlund, N., 87, 89
Grouping: advantages and disad-
vantages of, 212-213, 215-216,
219-221; issue of, 286-291; and
manageability, 287; studies of,
288-289
Grove, A. S., 156, 171
Guest, H., 95, 147
Guided practice, as teaching step,
122
Gump, P., 54, 65
Guskey, T., 76, 89

H

Haertel, G. D., 2, 4, 10
Hallinan, M., 288, 293
Hambleton, R. K., 87, 89
Hare, B. R., 290, 293
Hargreaves, D. H., 179, 183
Hartwig, M., 69n
Hastings, J. T., 126, 148, 205, 221
Havighurst, R. J., xvii
Herber, H. L., 25, 41, 104, 106, 114,
119, 120, 126, 149
Hickcox, E. S., 46, 50, 59, 67
Howey, K. R., 61, 65
Hsia, J., xiv
Huitt, W. G., 156, 172
Hunter, M., 36, 41, 119, 149
Huynh, H., xiii, 185-201
Hyman, J., 95, 149, 247, 253

I

Illinois. *See* Chicago
Illinois at Urbana, University of,

Center for the Study of Reading at, 92n, 111, 148

Independent practice, as teaching step, 122-123

Individually Guided Education (IGE), 98, 101, 102

Instruction: arrangements of, 203-221; background on, 203-206; fragmentation of, 111-113; group formation and management for, 209, 211, 213, 215, 217; grouping advantages and disadvantages for, 212-213, 215-216, 219-221; guidelines for, 91-153; in higher mental processes, 17-18, 277-278; improved materials for, 16-17; improved student processing of, 15-16; interdisciplinary teaming for, 213-216; intradisciplinary teaming for, 216-221; and learning principles, 211-212, 215, 217; management of, 45-67; mastery-based, and mastery learning, 96-97; and mastery learning, 5-8; in multi-age performance groups, 208-213; organization and delivery of, 119-123; pacing of, 279; and postinstruction, 208; and preinstruction, 206-207; in reading program, 226-227; quality and time balanced in, 9; quality of, 12, 178-179, 181-182; quality of variables in, 17; quantity of, and tests, 178; sequencing objectives and, 109-117, 146; stages of, 115-117, 146; and standardization, 204-205; steps in, 119-123, 207-208; teacher responsibilities for, 208-209, 213, 216; teaming and grouping models for, 208-221; timing of, and tests, 177; traditional, and mastery learning, 95-96

Instructional input, as teaching step, 121

Instructional management: analysis of, 45-67; background on, 45-47; current process orientation of, 47-51; direction or delegation in, 49-51; implications for, 58-61; problems in, 100-104; for reading program, 228-231; teacher preactive tasks and, 51-61; team approach to, 61-64; training for, 47-48, 64

Instructional support and development tasks, of teachers, 55-56

Instructional Systems Design (ISD), 32, 102, 104, 105

InterAmerica Research Associates, 92n

International Association for the Evaluation of Educational Achievement (IEA), Classroom Environment Study of, 52

Iowa Test of Basic Skills (ITBS), 267-268

J

Jackson, P. W., 52, 66, 69, 89

Jacobson, L., 204-205, 221

Japan, mastery and time in, 4, 6

Jenkins, J., 98, 149

Johnson, D. D., 104, 126, 151

Johnson City, New York: enhanced mastery learning in, 19-20, 23, 24-25, 28, 34-35, 36, 37, 39, 75; instructional arrangements in, 205-221, 286; and manageability, 276; organic monitoring in, 283

Jones, B. F., xi, xii, 11-43, 56, 59, 62, 63, 65, 66, 75, 90, 91-153, 276-277, 287, 292, 293

Jones, E., 262, 265

K

Kansas City, Missouri, reading program in, 256-257, 266-272, 286

Kaplan, C., 223, 240

Karweit, N. L, 288, 294

Kaskowitz's work, 227

Katims, M., 29, 41-42, 59, 62, 63, 66, 75, 90, 95, 100, 150

Kean, M., xiv

Keel, D. S., 223, 239

Keleman, J., 258, 259, 260, 261
Keller, F., 76, 90, 155
Kennedy, M. M., xii, 173–183, 279, 292
Kent Intermediate School, reading program in, 256–257, 261–266, 269–272
Kent State University, and reading program, 262
Kern, R. P., 102, 150
Kerr, R., 261
King, N., 69n, 70, 86, 90
Kirksey, J., 267, 269
Klare, G., 131, 150
Klausmeier, H. J., 98, 100, 150

L

Larson, R., 73, 75, 89, 90
Learning: activities, as task- or ego-involving, 71–72; cues, as teaching step, 122; determinants of, 60; Management Plans for, 162–167; phases in, 114; playlike activities for, 69–90; requirements, in Management Plan, 156–157; strategy, explicit instruction for, 122
Learning Exchange, 268
Learning unit organization and delivery: analysis of, 117–124; checklist for, 139–140; in enhanced mastery learning, 94; phases in, 117–118, 146; as structural unit, 54
Leavey, M., 27, 43
Lebanon Model of Mastery Learning, 24, 28, 29–31, 35–37
Leinhardt, G., 288, 290, 293
Lesson segments, as structural unit, 54
Lessons, as structural unit, 54
Levin, J. R., 17–18, 114, 150–151
Levine, D. U., ix–xiv, 29, 42, 46, 59, 62–63, 64, 66, 95, 151, 227, 240, 273–294
Levine, R. F., 288, 293
Leyton, F. S., 15–16, 42
Lieberman, A., 226–227, 240

Linn, R. L., 199, 201
Livingston, S. A., 187, 201
Locke, J., 1
Lockland School District, Management Plan of, 159–162
Lortie, D. C., 179, 183
Luckey, E., 262, 265
Luiten, J., 16, 42
Lysakowski, R. S., 2, 9, 10

M

McCombs, B., 75, 90
McLaughlin, M. W., 223, 239
Madaus, G. F., 126, 148, 205, 221
Madden, N. A., 27, 43
Maehr's theory, 72
Mager, R. F., 106, 151
Mamary, A., xiii, 95, 149, 203–221, 286
Manageability: and grouping, 287; of mastery learning, 273–276
Management by objectives (MBO): and recordkeeping, 132, 134–135; and test use, 174
Management by units of instructions (MBU), and recordkeeping, 133, 134–135
Management Plan: analysis of, 155–172; defined, 156; developing, 158–162; foundations of, 156–158; goals in, 159–160; materials and equipment in, 170; procedures in, 161–162; and reporting learning results, 169–170; standards in, 155, 160–161; and student learning, 162–167; teaching techniques in, 158; tests in, 157, 163; treatment systems in, 157–158, 167–168
Management tasks, of teachers, 56–57
Mann, D., 229, 240
March, J. G., 225, 226, 239–240
Markle, S. M., 104, 151
Marshall, S., 288, 293
Martin, L., 249
Marx, G., 11, 43
Mastery: concept of, 1; and grading,

246-247, 265; issues of, 8-9; levels of, 130
Mastery learning (ML): achieving success in, 273-294; analysis of, 1-10, 93-104; and aptitude, 5-6; background on implementing, 255-258; comparisons with, 95-97; concepts and techniques of, 77; conclusions on, 291-292; and continuous progress, 97, 98, 99, 101-104; coordinated with other methods, 278-279; defined, ix, 12, 75-76; effects of, 2-8, 95; elements of, 12; enhanced or enriched, 11-43, 91-153; and flow activities, 74-75, 81-86; group-based form of, 76-78; grouping issue in, 286-291; and higher order learning, 17-18, 277-278; implementation case studies for, 255-272; and instruction, 5-8; instructional arrangements for, 203-221; and instructional support and development tasks, 56; and learning effects, 5-8; and manageability, 273-276, 287; Management Plans for, 155-172; and mastery-based programs, 96-97; as mastery of learning approach, 80-81; and Matthew effects, 3; phases in, 117-118, 146; philosophy and principles of, 93-94; pitfalls in, 276-280; practice of, 75-81; and preactive teaching tasks, 60-61; as proactive approach, 78-79; and productivity effects, 4-5; psychological components of, 2; for reading achievement, 223-240, 255-272; and school and organizational development, 280-283; supervision of, 45-67; supplementary factors in, 8; as systematic approach, 76-78; and test use, 173-183; testing and retesting in, 241-253; testing programs for, 185-201; theory of, 1-2; and time, 3-4, 6-8, 9, 283-286; and traditional instruction, 95-96
Matthew effects, concept of, 3

Mayer, R. E., 104, 153
Measurement. See Testing
Menahem, M., xiii, 223-240
Merrill, M. D., 106, 107, 110, 152
Metropolitan Achievement Test (MAT), 21-23
Mevarech, A. R., 17-18, 42
Meyer, B.J.F., 114, 151
Meyer, J. W., 45, 66
Miller, D. P., 63, 66
Miller, N. E., 1, 2, 10
Miller, R. H., 63, 65
Minimax procedure, for passing scores, 195-197
Minimum competency, testing for, 185-186
Missouri, reading program in, 256-257, 266-272, 286
Monitoring: for enhanced mastery learning, 34; organic, 282-283; and recordkeeping, 132-135; as teaching step, 122
Montague, W. E., 114, 147
Motivation, and mastery, 71-72, 247

N

National Commission on Excellence in Education, 11, 42, 45, 67, 253
National Science Foundation, 5
Natriello, G., 49, 66
Nedelsky, L., 187, 201
Nelson, J., 25
Network for Outcome-Based Schools, xiv, 18, 62, 258
New Canaan, Connecticut, enhanced mastery learning in, 21-22, 24, 25-27, 28, 34-35, 37, 39, 75
New Jersey, enhanced mastery learning in, 22-23, 24, 28-29, 31, 35-37
New York City: enhanced mastery learning in, 38; reading program in, 224-239, 283, 286
New York City Reading Test, 233-235
New York state. See Bayport; Johnson City; New York City

Nicholls, J., 71–72, 75, 90
Nicholson, S., 69n

O

Objectives: analysis of, 105–117; checklist for, 138–139; classification of, 108; comparative, 107; components of, 105–106; and content type, 106–109; in enriched mastery learning, 93; examples of, 117; hierarchical sequencing of, 109–110, 146; horizontal sequencing of, 110–114, 146; and sequencing instruction, 109–117, 146; and test use, 176; tests related to, 125–127, 247–248; vertical sequencing of, 114–117, 146
Ogilvy, J., 282, 294
Ohio, reading program in, 256–257, 261–266, 269–272
Olsen, J. P., 225, 226, 239–240
O'Neil, H. F., 104, 151
Ontario, supervision in, 48
Organizational development, 280–283
Ornstein, A. C., xvii
Osborn, J., 17, 42, 100, 125, 129, 147, 151
Outcomes: attention to, 45–46; means and variances balanced in, 9
Overview, as teaching step, 119–120

P

Pallay, A., 288, 290, 293
Pany, D., 98, 149
Parents, reporting to, 169
Passing scores: adjusting, 192; content-based linked with data-based, 191–192; contrasting-group procedure for, 188–189, 190; equal-percent-failing procedure for, 189–190; minimax procedure for, 195–197; Rasch model for, 194–199; setting, 186–191; on subtests and overall test, 193–194;

undecided-group procedure for, 189–191
Pauley, E. W., 223, 239
Pearson, P. D., 104, 112, 114, 126, 151, 153
Pease, S. R., 183
Pendleton, K., 262, 265
Pennsylvania, cooperative learning in, 75
Phi Delta Kappa, 63, 66
Philadelphia, cooperative learning in, 75
Piaget, J., 5
Playlike learning activities: analysis of, 69–90; challenge, coordination, and feedback in, 81–86; conclusion on, 86–88; and flow, 72–75; methods for, 72–81; reasons for, 70–72
Pohland, P. A., 50, 67
Polgar, S., 70, 90
Potter, E., 69n
Price, G. G., 60, 63, 66
Principals: and Management Plans, 164–166; and reading program, 231–232, 234, 270, 271–272. See also Administrators
Pringle, P. R., xii, xiv, 155–172
Project Talent, 13

Q

Quality: defined, 12, 155; of instruction, 9, 17, 178–179, 181–182

R

Raphael, T., 126, 151
Rasch model, 132, 194–199
Readiness, as teaching step, 120–121
Reading program: basal readers in, 259, 263, 264, 265, 267; case studies of, 223–240, 255–272; conclusions on, 237–239, 269–272; instruction in, 226–227; instructional context for, 227–228; local commitment to, 224–226; management of, 228–231; and princi-

pals, 231–232, 234, 270, 271–272; and student achievement, 233–237; teacher trainer for, 230–231; and teachers, 233

Recordkeeping: checklist for, 141; in enriched mastery learning, 94; in Management Plans, 164–165; unit by unit, 132–135

Red Bank, New Jersey, enhanced mastery learning in, 22–23, 24, 28–29, 31, 35–37

Reed, F. H., 24, 28, 29–30, 42, 95, 151–152

Reid, E. R., 155, 168, 172

Reid, F., 95, 152

Reigeluth, C. M., 106, 107, 110, 152

Reinforcement: effects of, 5–7; as teaching step, 123

Reporting: forms of data for, 193–199; of learning results, 169–170

Reteach, as teaching step, 123

Retest: defined, 241: as teaching step, 123; in testing and curriculum alignment, 124, 146. *See also* Testing and retesting

Robb, D. W., xiv, 255–272, 279, 286

Rohwer, W. D., Jr., 114, 152

Romberg, T. A., 60, 63, 66

Roney, G., 63, 66

Rosenshine, B. B., 35, 42–43, 87, 90, 100, 104, 152

Rosenthal, R., 204–205, 221

Rossmiller, R. A., 98, 150

Rothbart, M., 205, 221

Rowe, L. A., xiii, 203–221, 286

Rubin, S. E., 25–26, 35, 43, 95, 152

Ryan, D. W., xi, xiv, 45–67

S

Saily, M., 98, 150

Salmon-Cox, L., 179, 183

Sarason, S. B., 63, 67

Saunders, J. C., 201

Schmidt, M., 59, 60, 67

Schmuck, R. A., 281, 293

Schools: organizational development in, 280–283; progress charts of, for recordkeeping, 134; progress tracking, over several years, 200

Schwartz, P., 282, 294

Schwartzman, H., 70, 90

Scott, W. R., 45, 49, 65, 66

Scriven, M., 274, 294

Sealey, L., 274, 294

Segars, J. K., 156, 172

Seligman's theory, 72

Sherman, J., 76, 90

Singer, H., 114, 120, 152

Size, for enhanced mastery learning, 34

Skills instruction: and enriched mastery learning, 99; horizontal sequencing for, 112–113

Skinner, B. F., 1

Slavin, R. E., 23, 27, 41, 43, 288, 294

Slinde, J. A., 199, 201

Smith, L., 58, 67

Smith, W. J., xiii, xiv, 241–253

Sosniak, L. A., 13, 41

South Carolina, Basic Skills Assessment Program (BSAP) of, 186–198

Spady, W. G., xi, 11–43, 46, 67, 95, 96, 104, 152

Spiraling, as objectives sequencing, 109

Spiro, R. J., 114, 147

Squires, D. A., 28, 40, 156, 172

Stability, for enhanced mastery learning, 34–35

Staff development: for enhanced mastery learning, 24–25, 36, 38–39; proactive, 61–62

Stallings' work, 227

Stamm, G., 160, 161, 162, 172

Stark, J., 29, 42, 46, 59, 62–63, 64, 66, 95, 151, 227, 240, 275, 293

Stauffer, R. G., 114, 120, 152

Stein, M., 17, 42, 100, 129, 151

Sternberg, R. J., 114, 152

Stevens, G., 223, 240

Stipek, D., 69*n*

Stoll, L. J., 112, 152

Stone, M. H., 132, 153, 194, 201

Stringer, L. A., 205, 221

Students: achievement of, and horizontal sequencing, 113–114; attitudes of, in reading programs, 260, 265, 270; grouping models for, 208–221, 271; and learning activities, 71–72; low achieving, 287–288, 290; and Management Plans, 159–160, 167–168, 169; neglect of attitudes of, 278; reading achievement of, 233–237; and test scores over several grades, 199–200

Summative tests: for feedback, 85–86; in test and retest program, 246; in testing and curriculum alignment, 124, 129–130, 146

Supervision. *See* Instructional management

Syracuse University, training by, 25

T

Talmage, H., 60, 67

Task analysis: for sequencing instruction, 110; of teaching tasks, 52–58

Taylor, L., 69*n*

Teachers: attitudes of, in reading programs, 263, 264–265, 270; conceptualizing work of, 52–58; expectations of, 204–295; implications of tasks of, 58–61; and manageability, 273–276; and Management Plans, 159–160, 162–164; preactive tasks of, 51–61; proactive stages for, 78–79; quality of, 178–179, 181–182; and reading program, 230–231, 233; responsibilities of, 208–209, 213, 216; shared goals among, 280–281; staff development for, 24–25, 36, 38–39, 61–62; structural units for, 54–55; test options of, 175–179; and test use, 173–183; timing of decisions by, 52; types of tasks for, 55–58, 80

Teaching. *See* Instruction

Team Assisted Individualization (TAI), for enhanced mastery learning, 23–24, 27–28, 34

Tenenbaum, G., 17, 43

Testing: administration of, 176–177; administrator options for, 180–182; content-based programs of, 185–201; corruptibility reduction for, 180–181; criterion-referenced, 127–128; curriculum alignment and, 94, 124–132, 140–141; for feedback, 83–86; issue of, 9; items for, 175–176; in Management Plan, 157, 163; objectives related to, 125–127, 247–248; parallel structure in, 128–129, 143–145; and passing scores, 186–197; population for, 177; and program evaluation, 131–132; purpose of, 185–186; reactions to use of, 173–183; and reporting data as percent, 197–199; and reporting objective-referenced data, 193–197; teacher options for, 175–179; as teaching step, 123; and tracking scores over several years, 199–200; validation in, 130–131. *See also* Formative tests; Summative tests

Testing and retesting: analysis of, 241–253; formative strategy for, 241–246; and grading, 246–247; implementation of, 248–253; qualitative data on, 248–250; quantitative data on, 250–253

Texas: outcome-based instruction in, 62; textbooks in, 156

Texts: basal reading, 259, 263, 264, 265, 267; considerate and inconsiderate, 17; existing, 97–98, 99–100, 102

Thompson, W., 263

Thorndike, L., 1

Tiemann, P. W., 104, 151

Tierney, R. J., 100, 104, 114, 147, 153

Time: engaged, 226–227; and grouping, 211–212, 215, 217; issue of, 3–4, 6–8, 9, 283–286; in reading programs, 260, 264, 267, 271; and school types, 285–286

Tinzmann, M., xii, 91–153
Toffler, A., 203, 221
Treatment systems, in Management Plan, 157–158, 167–168
Tsai, S.-L., 3, 10
Tuckman, B. W., 157, 172
Turney, C., 60, 67
Tutorial model, and instructional quality, 13–14
Two-sigma results: problem of, 14–15; programs with, 19–24; solutions for, 15–18; as standard of excellence, 11–18; and tutorial model, 13–14

U

United Federation of Teachers (UFT), 228
U.S. Army, 32, 102, 107; Extended Task Analysis Procedure (ETAP) of, 110; Research Institute for the Behavioral and Social Sciences of, $91n$–$92n$
U.S. Commission on Excellence in Education. *See* National Commission on Excellence in Education
Units: concept of, 1; learning, 54, 117–124

V

Validation, for tests, 130–131
Vaughan, J. C., 61, 65
Vocabulary, instruction in, 120–121

W

Walberg, H. J., xi, 1–10, 15, 43, 283
Ward, B. A., 63, 65
Watts, C., 249
Weeks, G., 249
Weick, K. E., 225, 240, 282, 294
Weiner's theory, 72
Weinstein, C. E., 104, 153
Weinstein, T., 2, 4, 10
Weisman, L., xiii, 223–240
White, R. W., 74, 90
Whole-group model, problems of, 101
Wise, A. E., 183
Wisconsin Design, 98, 101, 102
Wittrock, M. C., 104, 114, 153
Wood, C. J, 50, 67
Wright, B., 132, 153, 194, 201
Wulfeck, W. H., 106–107, $108n$, 149

Y

Yinger, R. J., 179, 183
Young Junior High School: grouping in, 286–287, 288; testing and retesting at, 241, 248–253

Z

Ziesky, M. J., 187, 201